The Jew in the Court of the Foreign King

Ancient Jewish Court Legends

Harvard Dissertations in Religion

Editors

Margaret R. Miles
and
Bernadette J. Brooten

Number 26

The Jew in the Court
of the Foreign King
Ancient Jewish Court Legends

Lawrence M. Wills

The Jew in the Court
of the Foreign King
Ancient Jewish Court Legends

Lawrence M. Wills

Fortress Press   Minneapolis

THE JEW IN THE COURT OF THE FOREIGN KING
ANCIENT JEWISH COURT LEGENDS

Copyright © 1990

The President and Fellows of Harvard College

Write to: Permissions, Augsburg Fortress, 426 S. Fifth St., Box 1209, Minneapolis, MN 55440.

Internal design: Chiron, Inc.

Library of Congress Cataloging-in-Publication Data

Wills, Lawrence M. (Lawrence Mitchell), 1954-
    The Jew in the court of the foreign king : ancient Jewish court
legends / Lawrence M. Wills.
        p.   cm.—(Harvard dissertations in religion : no. 26)
    Includes bibliographical references.
    ISBN 0-8006-7080-9
    1. Bible. O.T. Daniel—Criticism, interpretation, etc.
    2. Bible. O.T. Esther—Criticism, interpretation, etc.   3. Courts
and courtiers in literature.   4. Middle Eastern literature—History
and criticism.   I. Title.   II. Series.
BS1555.2.W55   1990
809′93352.3924—dc20   90-31690
                                                                      CIP

The paper used in this publication meets the minimum requirements of American National Standard for Information Sciences—Permanence of Paper for Printed Library Materials, ANSI Z329.48-1984. ∞™

Manufactured in the U.S.A.   AF 1-7080

94   93   92   91   90   1   2   3   4   5   6   7   8   9   10

Harvard Dissertations in Religion

Recent Titles in the Series:

Contents

Preface

Looking back on the evolution of this book, I am struck by the debt that I owe to so many people who have influenced its progress. First of all, my thesis advisor, John Strugnell, deserves special mention. It was his interest in Jewish court narratives which originally inspired me to attempt a comprehensive description of the genre. His support was unflagging, and his far-reaching suggestions pushed me to move into many fruitful new directions. Helmut Koester, Frank Moore Cross, and James Kugel also served on my thesis committee, and the direction I received from all of them was invaluable in bringing my research to completion.

Other professors have also been important to the development of this project. Dieter Georgi raised many questions that will always continue to motivate me to further inquiry. Although Amos Wilder had already retired from Harvard by the time I arrived, he was nevertheless always available to discuss my project. I have been very strongly influenced by his methodological premise that literary analysis is the ally, and not the enemy, of historical reconstruction. George MacRae also saw this thesis halfway completed, but to the great impoverishment of Biblical studies, died suddenly in 1985.

Others have been very generous with their time and advice, some from afar, and I have valued their responses to my work: Dennis MacDonald, Adela Yarbro Collins, John Collins, and Susan Niditch. My fellow graduate students in the doctoral program at Harvard were perhaps the most demanding and the most rewarding interlocutors I shall ever have. The editors of the Harvard Dissertations in Religion series, Margaret Miles and Bernadette Brooten, have been very helpful, and Joe Snowden and Pamela Chance have given very valuable editorial assistance.

Finally, above all, I would like to thank my wife, Shelley, and my children, Jessica and Daniel, for allowing my obsession to become their obsession.

Short Titles

Information appears here for frequently used works which are cited by short title. A few short titles do not appear in this list, but in each instance full bibliography is given on the page(s) preceding such references. Abbreviations used in this volume for sources and literature from antiquity are the same as those used in *HTR* 80:2 (1987) 243–60. Some abbreviations are adapted from that list and can be easily indentified.

Berg, *Esther*
> Sandra Beth Berg, *The Book of Esther: Motifs, Themes, and Structures* (Chico: Scholars Press, 1979).

Blenkinsopp, *Wisdom*
> Joseph Blenkinsopp, *Wisdom and Law in the Old Testament: The Ordering of Life in Israel and Early Judaism* (Oxford: Oxford University Press, 1983).

Charles, *Book of Daniel*
> R. H. Charles, *A Critical and Exegetical Commentary on the Book of Daniel* (Oxford: Clarendon, 1929).

Clines, *Esther*
> David J. A. Clines, *The Esther Scroll: The Story of the Story* (JSOT Supp 30; Sheffield: JSOT, 1984).

Collins, *Vision*
> John J. Collins, *The Apocalyptic Vision of the Book of Daniel* (HSM 16; Missoula: Scholars Press, 1977).

Cross, *Canaanite*
> Frank Moore Cross, *Canaanite Myth and Hebrew Epic* (Cambridge: Harvard University Press, 1978).

Collins, "Court-Tales"
> _____, "The Court-Tales in Daniel and the Development of Apocalyptic," *JBL* 94 (1975) 218–34.

Haag, *Errettung*
 Ernst Haag, *Die Errettung Daniels aus der Löwengrube* (Stuttgarter
 Bibelstudien 10; Stuttgart: Katholisches Bibelwerk, 1983).

Hartman and DiLella, *Daniel*
 Louis F. Hartman and DiLella, A. A., *The Book of Daniel* (AB; Garden
 City: Doubleday Anchor, 1978).

Heaton, *Solomon's New Men*
 E. W. Heaton, *Solomon's New Men: The Emergence of Ancient Israel as a
 National State* (New York: Pica, 1974).

Hengel, *Judaism and Hellenism*
 Martin Hengel, *Judaism and Hellenism: Studies in their Encounter in
 Palestine during the Early Hellenistic Period* (2 vols.; Philadelphia:
 Fortress, 1974).

Jahn, *Buch Daniel*
 G. Jahn, *Das Buch Daniel nach der Septuaginta hergestellt* (Leipzig:
 Pfeiffer, 1904).

Krappe, "Ahikar the Wise"
 Alexander H. Krappe, "Is the Story of Ahikar the Wise of Indian
 Origin?" *JAOS* 61 (1941) 280–84.

Lebram, *Buch Daniel*
 Jürgen Christian Lebram, *Das Buch Daniel* (Zürcher Bibelkommentare
 AT 23; Zürich: Theologischer, 1984).

Lebram, "Purimfest"
 _____, "Purimfest und Esterbuch," *VT* 22 (1972) 208–22.

Lindenberger, "Ahiqar"
 James Lindenberger, "The Gods of Ahiqar," *UF* 14 (1982) 105–17.

McKane, *Proverbs*
 William McKane, *Proverbs: A New Approach* (London: SCM, 1970).

Montgomery, *Daniel*
 James A. Montgomery, *The Book of Daniel* (ICC; New York: Scribners,
 1927).

Moore, *Studies*
 Carey A. Moore, ed., *Studies in the Book of Esther* (New York: KTAV,
 1982).

Müller, "Die weisheitliche Lehrerzählung"
 Hans-Peter Müller, "Die weisheitliche Lehrerzählung im Alten
 Testament und in seiner Umwelt," *WO* 9 (1977) 77–98.

Nickelsburg, "Genre"
 George W. E. Nickelsburg, "The Genre and Function of the Markan
 Passion Narrative," *HTR* 73 (1980) 153–84.

Nickelsburg, *Jewish Literature*
_____, *Jewish Literature Between the Bible and the Mishnah* (Philadelphia: Fortress, 1981).

Nickelsburg, *Resurrection*
_____, *Resurrection, Immortality, and Eternal Life in Intertestamental Judaism* (HTS 26; Cambridge: Harvard University Press, 1972).

von Rad, "Joseph"
Gerhard von Rad, "The Joseph Narrative and Ancient Wisdom," in idem, *The Problem of the Hexateuch and Other Essays* (New York: McGraw-Hill, 1966) 292–300.

von Rad, *Wisdom*
_____, *Wisdom in Israel* (Nashville: Abingdon, 1972).

Satran, "Fourth Chapter"
David Satran, "Early Jewish and Christian Interpretation of the Fourth Chapter of the Book of Daniel" (Ph.D. dissertation, Hebrew University, 1985).

Talmon, "Esther"
Shemaryahu Talmon, " 'Wisdom' in the Book of Esther," *VT* 13 (1963) 419–55.

Thompson, *Folktale*
Stith Thompson, *The Folktale* (Berkeley/Los Angeles/London: University of California Press, 1977).

The Jew in the Court
of the Foreign King

Ancient Jewish Court Legends

1

Methodology in the Study of Jewish Court Legends

A number of Jewish narrative writings from the ancient period are set in the court of a foreign king, telling the dramatic story of a wise and righteous Jewish courtier who undergoes various adventures while serving in the king's court. The fact that Genesis 37 – 50, Esther, Daniel 1 – 6, Bel and the Dragon and 1 Esdras 3 – 4 all share these characteristics has led some scholars to speak of an ancient literary genre of "court narrative." This has opened up a significant new approach to this literature, which is to consider these stories and others like them as examples of a literary tradition which presented ideals of popular wisdom in a narrative form. Not only has this approach proved helpful in the investigation of the social background of the Jewish stories, but it has also placed them in the context of an international literary genre, since it can be shown that other national literatures contained such legends. This genre, however, has not been sufficiently defined or understood, and the application of it as a means of analyzing Jewish texts has been strongly criticized, especially in regard to the purported wisdom content.

There have been important contributions to the analysis of motifs and formal structures of the court legends, but the seemingly simple step of grouping similar ancient texts and searching for social and historical connections behind them was slow to develop. Ludwig Rosenthal in 1895 noted the structural similarites between the Joseph story in Genesis 37 – 50, Esther, and Daniel 1 – 6, but he simply attributed these similarities to direct literary dependence of the latter two on Genesis, and not to the influence of an ongoing, popular literary genre.[1] Similarly, G. A. Barton posited a literary dependence of Daniel 3 and 6 on *Ahikar*.[2] Max Haller and James Montgomery, in commentaries on Esther and Daniel respectively, each noted the common literary traditions out of which the books they were studying arose.[3] Their short statements about genre were quite suggestive; both also brought *Ahikar* into the study, and Montgomery labeled the various court stories "Wisdom stories." Neither, however, went beyond this observation to any kind of systematic treatment of the origins or development of court legends, or of the presuppositions and tendencies that the genre might exhibit. Several commentaries on Daniel noted that the stories of chapters 1–6 were "court tales," but there was little comparative discussion,[4] and it was not until the 1950's and '60's that court legends were given protracted treatment by scholars.

First, Gerhard von Rad and Shemaryahu Talmon analyzed Genesis 37–50 and Esther respectively, focusing on the wisdom values reflected in the works and the paradigmatic role of the protagonist as embodying those values.[5] They both concluded that in the narratives under study the ideals of Hebrew proverbial wisdom were embodied by the protagonists, and that the stories served to dramatize the proper role for a wise Jew in the world. Talmon combined this approach, however, with a more formal one, wherein he compared the genre of what he called the "historicized wisdom-tale" with parallels in Ancient Near Eastern literature.[6]

A decade later W. Lee Humphreys and John J. Collins carried the study a significant step forward by inquiring into the social situation reflected in

---

[1] Rosenthal, "Die Josephgeschichte, mit den Büchern Ester und Daniel verglichen," *ZAW* 15 (1895) 278–84. See also P. Riessler, "Zu Rosenthals Aufsatz, Bd. XV, S. 278ff," *ZAW* 16 (1896) 182; Rosenthal, "Nochmals der Vergleich Ester, Joseph, Daniel," *ZAW* 17 (1897) 125–28; and Moshe Gan, "The Book of Esther in Light of the Story of Joseph in Egypt," *Tarbiz* 31 (1961–62) 144–49 (Hebrew).

[2] Barton, "The Story of Ahikar and the Book of Daniel," *AJSL* 16 (1899/1900) 242–47.

[3] Haller, *Das Judentum* in *Die Schriften des Alten Testaments* (Göttingen: Vandenhoeck & Ruprecht, 1914) Bd. 2/3, 277; and Montgomery, *The Book of Daniel* (ICC; Edinburgh: Clark, 1959) 100–101.

[4] E.g., Walter Baumgartner, *Das Buch Daniel* (Giessen: Töpelmann, 1926) 6–10; idem, "Ein Vierteljahrhundert Danielforschung," *Theologische Rundschau* n.s. 11 (1939) 131; H. Louis Ginsberg, *Studies in Daniel* (New York: Jewish Theological Seminary, 1948) 27; E.W. Heaton, *The Book of Daniel* (London: SCM, 1956) 32–47; Arthur Jeffery, "The Book of Daniel," *IB* 6.359–60; and Georg Fohrer, *Introduction to the Old Testament* (Nashville: Abingdon, 1968) 474.

[5] Von Rad, "The Joseph Narrative and Ancient Wisdom," in idem, *The Problem of the Pentateuch and Other Essays* (New York: McGraw-Hill, 1966) 292–300; and Talmon, "Wisdom in the Book of Esther," *VT* 13 (1963) 419–55.

[6] Talmon, "Wisdom in the Book of Esther," 426–30.

Esther and Daniel 1 – 6, and began in earnest the sociological analysis of the genre.[7] It was Humphreys who introduced the distinction between court "contests" and "conflicts," a distinction carried on by Collins and others, and which will be used in this thesis. The "contest" refers to those court legends in which a wise person of undistinguished status (but from within the court), against all expectations makes wise judgments, solves a problem, or interprets a dream or omen which none of the other courtiers are able to do, and as a result is elevated to high position in the court. In the more dramatic "conflict," the wise courtier begins in a respected position, but is persecuted or conspired against, usually by the other courtiers, suffers a fall, and is finally vindicated before the king.

George W. E. Nickelsburg, though conversant in the method of Humphreys and Collins, approached the material differently.[8] Although he analyzed in depth the theological content of the court conflict stories, he shifted the focus of his study from the literary genre as a whole to one of its principal motifs, that of the persecuted and vindicated righteous person. He follows this motif beyond the court legends proper into other works with various settings and plot structures, such as Wisdom of Solomon 2 – 5 and 2 Maccabees 7. Although he says that the passages he analyzes constitute a "genre," he evidently uses that term to mean a set of writings that have a common group of elements in the same or nearly the same order. This ignores, however, the vastly different settings of, for example, Genesis 39, Susanna, Wisdom 2 – 5, and 2 Maccabees 7. Despite his many fruitful observations about the tradition history of this motif, it is clear that his study goes beyond the court legend proper, and in this thesis the term "genre" will refer to more than just a set of similar motifs; a common setting and certain conventions of plot, theme, character, intention, and audience will also be considered.[9]

In addition to the studies of the literary genre of the court legend, there have been several attempts to analyze the court legends in terms of folk

---

[7] Humphreys, "A Life-Style for Diaspora: A Study of the Tales of Esther and Daniel," *JBL* 92 (1973) 211 – 23; and Collins, "The Court-Tales in Daniel and the Development of Apocalyptic," *JBL* 94 (1975) 218 – 34; see also Hengel, *Judaism and Hellenism*, 1. 30 – 31.

[8] Nickelsburg, *Resurrection, Immortality, and Eternal Life in Intertestamental Judaism* (HTS 26; Cambridge: Harvard University/London: Oxford University, 1972) 49 – 57; idem, "The Genre and Function of the Markan Passion Narrative," *HTR* 73 (1980) 153 – 84; and idem, *Jewish Literature Between the Bible and the Mishnah* (Philadelphia: Fortress, 1981) 19 – 28.

[9] The documents which he groups together reflect a mutual relatedness of theme "the rescue and vindication of a persecuted innocent person"—but a common theme does not constitute a genre. His focus on the motif in several genres, however, does provide insights into the theological uses of this popular tradition. See also below on genre, and a possible defence of Nickelsburg's method.

motifs. Alexander Krappe in 1941 produced a convincing array of parallels in various folk literatures to the conflict in *Ahikar*.[10] Despite the fact that he sees a direct literary connection between an Indian story and *Ahikar*, his evidence would suggest a wider oral transmission, against his stated conclusions. Also, Susan Niditch and Robert Doran cite tale type 922 from the Aarne-Thompson index of tale types as the paradigm for the court scene in Daniel 2, Genesis 41, and *Ahikar* 5–7.[11] They succeed in arriving at a more precise description of the common structure of these court narratives, and their study and Krappe's indicate that a fruitful area of investigation is the oral background of the legends.

Several issues raised by Niditch and Doran are relevant for this study. First, they advocate, in contrast to Nickelsburg and Humphreys, a "morphological" analysis, which insists that the mere accumulation of parallel motifs is not the central criterion for relatedness between narratives, but rather, one must demonstrate that the set of motifs are in the same or a similar order and, most important, that there is a similar relationship between them. This concern of folklorists for a morphological analysis arose from the impetus of Vladimir Propp.[12] In his study of Russian fairytales, Propp pointed out that beneath the apparent variety of individual characters and motifs in the stories, there was actually a small, finite number of kinds of actions that occurred, such as interdiction, followed by violation of interdiction, and that these "functions" could be easily catalogued and applied to the analysis of any Russian fairytale, and presumably to all others as well.

This approach has become common in folklore studies, although different terminology is sometimes used. It is, for example, sometimes called a "synchronic," as opposed to "diachronic," approach, since the inner structure of tales is analyzed rather than their historical and geographical distribution. The individual characters and events of a tale are also known as the "etic" units, while the relationships between the motifs which structure the plot as a whole are called "emic," terms which are taken, on the analogy of linguis-

[10] Krappe, "Is the Story of Ahikar the Wise of Indian Origin?" *JAOS* 61 (1941) 280–84.

[11] Niditch and Doran, "The Success Story of the Wise Courtier," *JBL* 96 (1977) 179–93. The reference to tale type numbers is to Antti Aarne and Stith Thompson, *The Types of the Folk-Tale* (Folklore Fellows Communications 74; Helsinki: Suomalainen tiedeakatemia, 1928). Susan Niditch's excellent new study, *Underdogs and Tricksters: A Prelude to Biblical Folklore* (San Francisco: Harper and Row, 1987), was published after my thesis was completed, and I have unfortunately been unable to incorporate her work into this project.

[12] *Morphology of the Folktale* (2d ed.; Austin: University of Texas, 1968). By way of introduction, note the essay in this edition by Alan Dundes. Pamela J. Milne's Proppian analysis of Daniel 1–6 (*Vladimir Propp and the Study of Structure in Hebrew Biblical Literature* [Sheffield: Almond, 1988]) became available to me too late for use here.

tics, from "phonetic" and "phonemic." The structural interrelationships in this "syntagmatic" approach are, further, delineated in a particular order from beginning to end, unlike the binary oppositions in Claude Levi-Strauss's "paradigmatic" approach, which can be seen in any order and even repeated.

This new trend in folklore studies has many implications for the present thesis. The morphological approach has been taken up successfully by some of the main scholars of oral tradition, including Alan Dundes and Dan Ben-Amos.[13] The issue of "genre" has figured prominently in their discussions, as they have tried to dismantle the previous dependency on the definition of genre as a conglomerate of motifs, that is, a definition based on "thematic similarity." Dundes, for example, finds that a broad sampling of North American Indian tales can be reduced to a small set of structural patterns, regardless of how different the individual motifs and *dramatis personae*. For instance, the dramatic problem of many of the tales is a broadly experienced lack of some sort, which is liquidated through the adventurous actions of the protagonist, often aided by a helper. Thus "lack" and "lack liquidated" describe one of the simplest structural patterns of the tales, no matter what the particular lack is, how it is liquidated, or by whom.

What is even more challenging from the point of view of definition of genre, is that in some cases the same pattern, for example, Warning/Violation/Result/Resolution, was discerned both in tales and in superstitions, very dissimilar forms of discourse. Far from defining a genre in terms of setting, motifs, plot, characters, and themes, this approach makes sweeping structural comparisons which cut across conventional separations of genres.[14] This challenges the usual literary categories which have been applied to court legends and similar Jewish and ancient Near Eastern literature, and necessitates a careful discussion of "genre" before our particular genre can be mapped out.

Structuralist folklorists have focused on the underlying structural patterns

[13] See esp. Alan Dundes, "On the Psychology of Legend," in Wayland D. Hand, ed., *American Folk Legend: A Symposium* (Berkeley/Los Angeles/London: University of California, 1971) 21–36; idem, "Structural Typology in North American Indian Folktales," *Southwestern Journal of Anthropology* 19 (1963) 121–30; the last two reprinted in Dundes, *Analytical Essays in Folklore* (The Hague/Paris: Mouton, 1975); Ben-Amos, "The Concept of Genre in Folklore," *Studia Fennica* 20 (1976) 30–43; "Analytic Categories and Ethnic Genres," *Genre* 2 (1969) 275–301; both reprinted in Ben-Amos, *Folklore in Context: Essays* (New Delhi/Madras: South Asian Publishers, n.d.).

[14] This finding of Dundes ("Structural Typology") would perhaps be the starting point for a reevaluation of Nickelsburg's "mixing" of genres concerning the persecution/vindication pattern, if there can be discerned an underlying morphological structure in the various attestations of this pattern.

in the folk traditions of a culture as the key category which will allow them to compare traditions. It is not that the older thematic analyses which underlie the type and motif indexes of Aarne and Thompson are now irrelevant, but that that approach gave rise to imprecision in the identification of genres. The structuralist method has given these folklorists a controllable method for identifying "essential" similarities. Similarities which lie outside this structural delineation are construed as particular nuances, while those that are part of it now become constitutive of the genre. This is no trivial controversy being waged, since nothing less is at stake than the "proper" understanding of the traditions at hand; however, certain considerations must be given in regard to applying this method to the kinds of traditions being studied here:

1) It is not always clear whether the legends studied here originated in oral or written form, and thus they may not even come under the realm of folklore studies. Structuralist analyses have also been carried out on written works, but the oral/written distinction will be important at certain points.[15]

2) The main difficulty which Dundes and Ben-Amos saw in the thematic approach was the difficulty in making cross-cultural comparisons. For folklorists, of course, who seek universal principles of all folklore, this was critical. Within a given culture in one time period, however, the thematic approach to genres may be quite valid, as these two folklorists concede.[16]

3) The structuralist theory originating with Propp was developed and expanded mainly in respect to tales, where a small number of patterns might be isolated. Legends, however, which are under study here, must be distinguished from tales. The situation of legends is quite different, in that the variety of structural patterns, both within one culture and cross-culturally, is much greater, as Dundes himself has stated.[17] Thus the reduction of legends to structural patterns may not be as workable for cross-cultural comparison.

The article of Niditch and Doran is an excellent example of a structuralist approach to Jewish legends about the court. They emphasize the morphological relationship of the story elements in Daniel 2, Genesis 37–50, and *Ahikar* 5–7. Their analysis of these narratives reveals the following elements, in this order:[18]

---

[15] Ben-Amos, "Concept of Genre," 30–32 (66–67 in reprint).

[16] Ben-Amos, "Analytic Categories," 279 (42 in reprint); Dundes, "Structural Typology," 76–77.

[17] Dundes, "Psychology," 24 (165 in reprint).

[18] Niditch and Doran, "Success Story," 180.

1) person of lower status is called before a person of higher status to answer difficult questions or to solve a problem requiring insight;
2) person of high status poses the problem which no one seems capable of solving;
3) person of lower status does solve the problem; and
4) person of lower staus is rewarded for answering.

In keeping with the structuralist method, they criticize previous studies, particularly Humphreys and Nickelsburg, for defining genres strictly in terms of thematic similarity. For practical reasons they still refer to the Aarne-Thompson index of tale "types" (as do other structuralist folklorists), but here several problems arise as to the appropriate designation of the tale type and the comparison of it to other tales and legends. The tale type numbers which they adduce from the Aarne-Thompson index to designate their pattern, 922 and 922A, do not correspond exactly to the narratives they analyze. On the one hand, they use a more narrowly defined description than the "contest" designation which Humphreys uses (and which is used in this thesis), while on the other hand the type numbers of Aarne-Thompson are too broad. For type 922 the latter give the designation, "The shepherd substituting for the priest (or other official) answers the king's questions," and for 922A, "Falsely accused minister reinstates himself by his cleverness," with *Ahikar* listed as an example. Type 922A is perhaps not intended by Aarne and Thompson to describe *Ahikar* as a whole, and Niditch and Doran, in invoking it, focus on a single subplot of the story, that is, the contest episode of chapters 5–7. This contest episode is, however, better categorized under the motif (not type) number H561.5, "King and clever minister."[19] *Ahikar* is long enough and complex enough to require comparisons with several tale types and motifs for a complete analysis, which Niditch and Doran recognize.[20] The conflict story line of the narrative, chapters 1–4 and 8, does fit appropriately under 922A, "Falsely accused minister reinstates himself by his cleverness."

But once they have isolated this narrative type in Genesis 37–50, Daniel

---

[19] Antti Aarne and Stith Thompson, *Motif-Index of Folk-Literature* (6 vols.; Bloomington: Indiana University, 1932–36).

[20] "Success Story," 180. One might also consider, e.g., type number 981 (= motif J151.1), "Wisdom of hidden old man saves kingdom," and motif P111, "Banished minister found indispensable and recalled." The artificiality of category numbers is not the point, however, and this difficulty should not detract from the many positive aspects of Niditch's and Doran's study. Other folklore studies of type 922 and 922A include Walter Anderson, *Kaiser und Abt* (Folklore Fellows Communications 42; Helsinki: Suomalainen tiedeakatemia, 1923); Jan De Vries, *Die Märchen von klugen Rätsellösern* (FFC 73; 1928); and Stith Thompson, *The Folktale* (Berkeley/Los Angeles/London: University of California, 1977) 161.

2, and *Ahikar* 5 – 7—correctly and successfully, I believe, if the question of
its location in the folklore indexes is set aside—there remain other issues as
to how to compare it with other similar narratives. For instance, they compare their type to Jewish and other tales listed in Aarne-Thompson under
types 922, which are actually very different in some crucial respects. Briefly,
in the ideal type isolated from Daniel 2, Genesis 37 – 50, and *Ahikar* 5 – 7
(and in court contests generally), a *courtier* of undistinguished status proves
himself worthy of elevation to high status, while in the parallel tales which
they analyze, the low-born protagonist from outside the court agrees to sub-
stitute for a bungling priest or petty official in the presence of a higher
official, and thereby solves the difficult questions. This narrrative type to
some extent satirizes the priest or petty official, while the court contests generally allow the other courtiers to retain their dignity, in order to emphasize
even more strongly the superiority of the protagonist's wisdom. This second
group of tales which they analyze does correspond with the Aarne-Thompson
designation for type 922, "The shepherd substituting for the priest answers
the king's questions," but the difference between 922 and 922A is precisely
the issue, and is probably underemphasized in the Aarne-Thompson index.

Niditch and Doran note this motif of the substitution of the protagonist for
the official as a variant within their ideal type,[21] but the two groups of stories
should be considered separate types on morphological grounds, since a different set of interrelated actions occur, as well as on the grounds that they
have different settings. The ancient stories with which they begin their
analysis are all *court* legends, set in a royal court, in which the dramatic focal
point of the narrative becomes the moment of accomplishment of the wise
and righteous hero in the court of highest authority. The second group of
narratives with which they compare their isolated structural pattern are tales,
not legends,[22] set in local or minor courts or in church governance settings,
which have a more complex dramatic focus: the satirical and ironic interchange where the official and shepherd agree to change places, and also the
moment when the disguised shepherd answers every test of wisdom. From
the morphological point of view, it is the relationship of these two scenes
which defines this group of humorous and even satirical tales, while the
simpler court legends retain only one focus. The humorous tales also operate
on the premise of a character throughly foreign to the court or official milieu

---

[21] Niditch and Doran, "Success Story," 180.

[22] They do not impose the distinction between "legends" and "tales," which will be discussed below. Likewise, a distinction between a clever protagonist and a wise one is also necessary, and it should also be noted that court legends almost always take noble males as their protagonists, while the other tales *generally* have establishment outsiders as the protagonists:
shepherds, peasants, and women.

being thrust into this capacity.[23] One has to admire the greater artistry of the humorous tales, but this thesis will resign itself to the study of the dreary court legends.

Although Niditch and Doran essentially downplay the court aspect of the narratives as an incidental detail of the legends, and maintain that the morphological pattern of the court narratives and of the other tales is the same, the court setting in Daniel 2, Genesis 37–50, and *Ahikar* 5–7 is of utmost importance, and is constitutive for the generic definition. It corresponds to the broader difference in morphological structure noted just above. Despite some variations, such as Susanna, the *high* court setting communicates the universal, empire-wide consequences of the action of the stories. The structural varieties which exist within the designation "wisdom court legend" must not restrict us from applying the term to the larger, yet still meaningful, genre category. Niditch and Doran, for instance, are exactly correct in positing a single morphological sub-genre which includes Genesis 37–50, Daniel 2, and *Ahikar* 5–7, and their study is an important contribution to the study of these legends. Yet, if one followed their reasoning that this is the *exclusively* correct approach to the genre classification, one must conclude that Daniel 1–6 consists of five separate genres (2 and 5 together and four others), even though these chapters have in common wise courtiers of an ethnic minority, who experience dramatic adventures in the potentially hostile atmosphere of the greatest court in the world, where their claim to wisdom is tested and finally upheld and acclaimed. At the very least, one wonders why the redactor placed these six legends together.

It is true, to be sure, that in addition to Niditch and Doran, other scholars have suggested genre descriptions which include Esther and Daniel 1–6, and yet have nothing to do with the court. The results have often been interesting analyses which impose upon the writings different definitions of the genre from that of the present study, but which are nevertheless not necessarily in contradiction. Where different criteria are invoked, we must contend with overlapping genre categories. Arndt Meinhold approaches the Joseph story and Esther as written documents and introduces the term *Diasporanovelle* as the key descriptive term of the genre.[24] Humphreys and Edward F. Campbell, Jr. also introduce the literary categories of novella and short story respectively.[25] The *literary* tradition, as opposed to the oral tradition, should be

---

[23] Cf. Thompson, *Folktale*, 159 on type 875, "Clever girl called to court," which he likens to type 922. The Egyptian *Eloquent Peasant* will be discussed in Chapter 2 as a somewhat similar example.

[24] Meinhold, "Die Gattung der Josephsgeschichte und des Estherbuches: Diasporanovelle, I, II," *ZAW* 87 (1975) 306–24; 88 (1976) 79–93.

[25] Humphreys, "Novella," and "The Story of Esther and Mordecai: An Early Jewish Novella," both in George W. Coats, ed., *Saga, Legend, Tale, Novella, Fable: Narrative Forms in*

emphasized with those works such as Esther which betray a heavy literary reworking of older, possibly oral, sources. In contrast to these authors, however, literary analyses in this thesis will emphasize literary genres and developments which can be postulated for the ancient world. Modern literary criticism, as interesting as it may be, generally does not address the question of the social and historical setting of ancient works, and often exaggerates esthetic qualities. The terms novella and short story, for example, were introduced by Humphreys and Campbell purely in regard to twentieth century distinctions of novel/novella/short story, and at times obscure the social functions of ancient literature.

The most interesting and thoroughgoing of the studies which propose new genre categories, however, is that of Hans-Peter Müller. He takes his point of departure from the suggestions of Gerhard von Rad concerning "didactic narrative" (*Lehrerzählung*), and includes in this category the Joseph story, the prose frame of Job, Genesis 37 – 50, Daniel 1 – 6, Tobit, Esther, and *Ahikar*.[26] Müller's study is indebted to the structural approach of Propp, and thus has much in common with Niditch and Doran, in that he is foremost interested in a morphological-synchronic analysis of the stories, rather than a diachronic or thematic. As a result, he does not focus on the court as the setting of the narratives, but proposes the following morphological structure (examples which Müller gives are in parentheses):

Introduction:

1a) Protagonist described in respect to his or her virtue (e.g., description of Job, Joseph's dream).

1b) Symbolic deed which arises from the virtue, and confirmation of its worth (e.g., Job's offering, Joseph loved by father, resented by brothers).

1c) Antagonists introduced, with their intermediaries (e.g., Job's wife, interlocutors, Joseph's brothers as antagonists, and king in court legends as intermediary).

Body:

2a) Conflict arises, instigated by virtue (e.g., Job's arguments, Joseph's brothers' conspiracy, Joseph's restraint re: Potiphar's wife).

2b) Testing and proving of the virtue (e.g., Job's despair, Joseph's sojourn in Egypt).

Old Testament Literature (JSOT Supp 35; Sheffield: JSOT, 1985) 82 – 96 and 97 – 113, respectively; Campbell, "The Hebrew Short Story: A Study of Ruth," in H. N. Bream, R. D. Heim, and C. A. Moore, eds., *A Light Unto My Path* (Philadelphia: Temple University, 1974) 83 – 101.

[26] Müller, "Die weisheitliche Lehrerzählung in Alten Testament und seiner Umwelt," *WO* 9 (1977) 77 – 98. Von Rad's comments can be found in *Wisdom in Israel* (Nashville: Abingdon, 1972) 46 – 47.

Conclusion:

3a) Confirmation of virtue of protagonist through punishment of antagonists (e.g., God's answers in Job, Joseph's superior position over brothers).

3b) Confirmation of virtue through rewarding of protagonist e.g., Job upheld, Joseph benefactor of family).

3c) Confirmation of virtue sometimes through miraculous demonstrations (e.g., Job summons God, Joseph interprets dreams).

Müller is not attempting here to explain the peculiar role of the court setting in some of these narratives, but at certain points it can be argued that he bends some aspects of the court legends to fit the "didactic narrative" genre, for instance, the king in Esther and *Ahikar* as an intermediary for the antagonist.[27] The king in the court legends, as I shall try to show, is viewed from many different perspectives, sometimes changing within a narrative, and essentially has the role of sitting over the court with absolute power. He is usually equally disposed to all courtiers, except when one courtier is rightly or wrongly viewed as opposed to the king and his welfare. To see the king as an intermediary in those stories mentioned is perhaps forced. However, I do find that his overall classification is instructive, and at times it illuminates certain aspects of the narratives, such as the polar opposition of the protagonist and antagonist in terms of their attributes. The conflict of the court conflict legends can, in fact, be seen as the meeting of the virtue of the protagonist and the mirror-image vice of the antagonist.

What Müller has shown is that there is good reason to postulate an ancient genre of "didactic narrative," although his postulated framework may comprise only one of the structures of didactic narrative that existed. The court conflict legend also fits into this structure with minor modifications; the conflict may be considered a subset of this didactic narrative structure which is strongly influenced by its court setting, although contests and short court legends which are neither contests nor conflicts may lie outside of Müller's model. The result, then, is than within the very broad category which we may style "sapiential narrative," two overlapping groupings of narratives emerge, "didactic narrative" and "wisdom court legend." Conflicts constitute the intersection of these two groups, and the fact that they can be considered in either "genre" does not reflect a weakness of the categories as much as it does the necessary untidiness of the objects of study. The court setting of the conflict brings with it certain constitutive attributes which make it a distinct subset within the category didactic narrative, and these attributes

[27] Müller, "Die weisheitliche Lehrerzählung," 84.

are also observable in court legends, short and long, which do not fall in Müller's sampling.

The definition of genres, then, can proceed along different lines; different sets of criteria give rise to different groupings of exempla of the genre, which can be conceived, for instance, in overlapping circles. It was asserted above that the court conflict was a subset of Müller's "didactic narrative," in that the structural analysis of the two was quite close, the main difference being the specific nuances of the court setting in the conflict legends. The court contests, however, do not have this same structural pattern, yet they do have the court setting and many other similarities with the court conflicts, and so a circle could be drawn around the contests and the conflicts as belonging to the same genre so-defined. The structuralists would reject this last judgment (as indeed Niditch and Doran do), but defining genre purely in terms of structural pattern stretches the limits of that word. For instance, if Dundes finds the same structural pattern in a group of tales and in the statement of a superstition, we would do damage to the word if we placed both of these in the same "genre." They still, however, exhibit the same "structure." Ben-Amos recognizes this when he critiques Propp and Dundes, and insists that the structural pattern alone is not sufficient to delineate a genre. He promulgates a "holistic" approach which utilizes different criteria operating on different levels, including the structural pattern, but also such things as the performance situation.[28]

In this thesis, "genre" will be defined on the basis of several criteria which operate on different levels. The structural pattern of contests and the structural pattern of conflicts (defined broadly) will both be found within the genre, but other narrative patterns will also be found which reflect other underlying structures. The main criteria will arise from the following discussion.

Definition of Legend

It can indeed be shown that there did exist such a genre as the "wisdom court legend," and that investigating certain narratives using this genre category bears important implications for the study of post-exilic Judaism. This thesis does not deny the positive conclusions of Niditch and Doran or of Müller, but proposes to provide a comprehensive description of a differently defined genre which will complement those studies. This would properly begin with a careful definition of terms. The exact species of writing that is being

---

[28] Ben-Amos, "Concept of Genre," 39–40 (78–79 in reprint).

isolated and addressed here is the "wisdom court legend," or the legend of the wise hero or heroine in the court of the king. For the sake of brevity, however, throughout this thesis this genre will simply be referred to as "court legend." The three parts of this genre designation will be defined in inverse order, from the broadest aspect to the most specific.

"Legend" here is not used in exactly the same way as it has in the German form-critical school of Hermann Gunkel and his followers. Gunkel himself began with a definition of legend that was only slightly differentiated from "saga," which must be explained first. Saga for Gunkel is essentially an oral telling of history.[29] In the attempt to distinguish saga and history, he arrived first at a definition of the former: saga treats major events in terms of the actions of individuals, is not bound by rational and scientific explanations, and most important, is "poetic" rather than "prosaic," in that it is intended to entertain and inspire, not merely inform.[30] Legend, for Gunkel, was very similar to saga, but following the use of the former term in medieval Christian tradition, he limited it to reverential narratives of religious figures, such as prophets, priests and saints, as well as cult sites. Legends are intended to edify and teach, focusing on the protagonist's acts of faith and virtue.[31] Followers of Gunkel kept to this definition of legend as edifying saga concerning a "religious" person or site.[32] According to this definition, the narrative quality of legends is definitely devalued in relation to oral sagas, "stories," and literary novellas, such as the Joseph story. Gunkel provocatively said that sagas celebrate the hero, while legends celebrate God alone,[33]

---

[29] Unfortunately, much confusion arises from the translation of German *Sage* as both "saga" and "legend." This is true for the English title of Gunkel's main work on the subject, *The Legends of Genesis: The Biblical Saga and History* (New York: Schocken, 1964). See pp. 3–4 of that work and Jay Wilcoxen, "Narrative," in John H. Hayes, ed., *Old Testament Form Criticism* (San Antonio: Trinity, 1974) 57–98.

[30] Gunkel, *Legends*, 3–12; and Wilcoxen, "Narrative," 60.

[31] Gunkel, *RGG* (1st ed.) 5.194–6; Wilcoxen, "Narrative," 69, 78; and Ronald M. Hals, "Legends: A Case Study in OT Form-Critical Terminology," *CBQ* 34 (1972) 167–68.

[32] Hugo Gressmann, *RGG* (1st ed.) 5.178–79; Otto Eissfeldt, *The Old Testament: An Introduction* (New York: Harper and Row, 1965) 32; Sigmund Mowinckel, "Legend," *IDB* 3.108–9; and Fohrer, *Introduction*, 90–93. In the new *Form Criticism of the Old Testament* series, the edifying aspect seems to be retained, but the insistence that the protagonist must be a "religious" figure has been dropped: George W. Coats, *Genesis* (FOTL 1; Grand Rapids: Eerdmans, 1981) 318; Burke O. Long, *One Kings* (FOTL 9, 1984) 252; and Roland E. Murphy, *Wisdom Literature* (FOTL 13, 1981) 177. In New Testament form criticism, Martin Dibelius (*From Tradition to Gospel* [New York: Scribner's, n.d.] 104) used a similar definition.

[33] Gunkel, *RGG*, loc. cit. This devaluation of the narrative art of legends when compared with saga, story, or novella was echoed in the scholars of the FOTL series mentioned in the previous note.

and the interest in the human response to divine initiatives is replaced by a static focus on miracles.

This definition has dominated biblical studies where a separation of saga and legend was thought to be necessary, and where the influence of the medieval use of the term *legendum* as "saint's legend" was felt. An alternative approach would be to consider the definitions adopted in recent folklore studies. Although it is not always clear whether the legends we shall be investigating were originally oral or written, the possibility that they derived from oral folk traditions is a very real one and, as we shall see, contributions from the discipline of folklore studies will be of interest either way. The folklorist William Bascom, for example, gives a simpler and broader definition which is still influential in the field of folklore studies today, despite many criticisms. He divides prose narratives into myth, legend, and tale, and defines a legend as a reverential narrative about a figure from the more recent past, which is presumed to be true by those who transmit it.[34] This definition is asserted by him to apply in all cultures, and in both "religious" and "secular" contexts. Legend is here equivalent to German *Sage*, and thus includes both "saga" and "legend" in Gunkel's usage. Although myth and legend are both presumed to be true by the people who transmit them, legend differs from myth in that the latter is set in primordial time only and gives free reign to the actions of gods as main characters. Legends are concerned with human characters from a less distant past. Tales (or *Märchen*), though often similar to legends, veer off into fantasy and are not presumed to be true by those who transmit them.

Other folklorists have explored more extensively than Bascom the nuances of the definition of legend, sometimes introducing important modifications of his categories. Max Lüthi, working before Bascom, explored in greater detail the more realistic and exemplary nature of the protagonist of legends, as opposed to the protagonist of tales.[35] He notes, for instance, that the world of the legend can be somewhat oppressive, as compared with the tale. The world in the legend is close, real, and disordered, while in the tale is distant, unreal, ideal, and ordered. Whereas the tale

[34] Bascom, "The Forms of Folklore: Prose Narratives," *Journal of American Folklore* 78 (1965) 3–20; and idem, "Folklore," in David L. Sills, ed., *International Encyclopedia of the Social Sciences* (17 vols.; New York: Macmillan, 1968) 5.497. For an excellent survey of folklore studies on legends and other prose narratives, see Linda Dégh, "Folk Narrative," in Richard M. Dorson, ed., *Folklore and Folklife: An Introduction* (Chicago/London: University of Chicago, 1972) 53–83.

[35] Lüthi, "Aspects of the *Märchen* and the Legend," in Dan Ben-Amos, ed., *Folklore Genres* (Austin/London: University of Texas, 1976) 17–34; and Lüthi, *Volksmärchen und Volkssage: Zwei Grundformen erzählender Dichtung* (Bern/Munich: Franke, 1961), esp. 51–52.

generally focuses on family relations, the legend focuses on the relation of the individual to society. Linda Dégh modifies Bascom's neat categorization of legends by noting that the reverential aspect is sometimes downplayed, for instance, in ghost stories, leaving the main criterion that of the belief of the transmitter or hearer.[36] It is also true that the bearer of a legend may doubt its veracity, or even be determined to disprove it, but the *issue* remains one of belief. The bearer and hearer of a legend may agree that it truly happened, as in the recounting of saints' legends, or the bearer may attempt to engage the hearer in a reconsideration of the legend, as, for example, when unusual events of legends are explained "scientifically."[37] Further nuancing of Bascom's definition was carried on by Alan Dundes, who, for example, stressed that the difference in temporal perspective between myth and legend is not necessarily remote versus recent past, but a time frame with definite endpoints versus one with indefinite.[38] Myth takes place at the beginning of time, but legend within the real time frame that we all experience. This leads to a very important conclusion for our study of the use and impact of these legends:

> What this means in part is that individuals may well feel closer to the action of legend than to the action of myth that happened long, long ago, and closer to the action of legend than to the action of folktale that never really happened.[39]

This immediacy of time in legends is paralleled by the immediacy in the dimension of space. The unknown, distant or fantasy space of myth and tale is not found in legend, but instead the action generally occurs in familiar and definite places. Although folklorists have generally lumped legend with saga, the biblicist may be permitted to make finer distinctions where it is useful: if legends in general have greater immediacy in time and space than myths, it should be remembered that the biblical sagas, for instance, the patriarchal narratives,[40] may lie on the "mythical" end of the continuum of legends for later readers, whereas the etiological legends contained within them would have been strictly "legends" when they circulated orally. Sagas, and epics too, can represent that end of the definite, "legend" continuum of time and space which borders on indefinite, primeval time and space.

---

[36] Dégh, "Folk Narrative," 73–77.

[37] Dégh and Andrew Vázsonyi, "Legend and Belief," in Ben-Amos, *Genres*, 93–124.

[38] Dundes, "Psychology," in idem, *Analytic Essays in Folklore* (Studies in Folklore 2; The Hague/Paris: Mouton, 1975) 164.

[39] Ibid., 165.

[40] The Joseph story of Genesis 37–50 has often been considered more of a legend than a saga, a view which I will argue for below.

Thus Dundes's distinction between myth and legend could also apply to the distinction between sagas and epics on one hand and the kind of reverential legends which will be investigated here. The fact that the protagonists in these stories live in very familiar and definite types of settings makes the dramatic turns of the narratives more real, even if they are often less artistically composed.

The social function of legends cross-culturally has also been investigated to some extent, although as Dundes suggested, perhaps comparative research in this category lags far behind that in regard to either myth or tale. Américo Paredes has reported on mestizo legends in Mexico and applies the same sort of class-affirming function that I would apply to Jewish legends in regard to ethnic identity, that is, that "legends are ego-supporting devices. They may appeal to the group or to individuals by affording them pride, dignity, and self-esteem."[41] The somewhat separate mestizo class, neither Spanish nor native Indian, presents some issues of ethnic identity not unlike that of Jews in the ancient diaspora. Further comparisons of the legends of such groups might be very illuminating.

Most of the materials dealt with in this thesis would fit into the category of "legend" in either Gunkel's or the folklorists' understanding of the word, since, as reverential stories about religious figures, transmitted as true, they count as legend by either definiton. The choice of the definition of "legend" does not so much dictate which works we look at, but how they are to be interpreted. The complexities and controversies of the folklorists' debates on genre, mentioned above, should not be ignored, however. Neither such internal criteria as typical legend content ("thematic similarity") nor such external criteria as the belief of the speaker in the veracity of a legend were considered sufficient for a universal definition. When all the elements of folklore analysis are brought to bear on the question of genre definition, it is seen that Bascom's categories do not have the universal applicability that he had hoped for. If, however, we follow Dundes and Ben-Amos in considering it possible to define legends in one cultural and historical milieu using concrete criteria, then the main difficulties of universalizability of genres, to which the folklorists are quite sensitive, disappear. Some questions still remain, to be sure, such as the reliance on structural versus thematic definitions of generic similarity, but these can be addressed within the acceptable limits of ancient Near Eastern reverential legends.

This review of literature would give the impression that folklorists have

---

[41] Paredes, "Mexican Legendry and the Rise of the Mestizo: A Survey," in Wayland D. Hand, ed., *American Folk Legend: A Symposium* (Berkeley/Los Angeles/London: University of California, 1971) 98; see also 106–7.

played a merely negative role as naysayers to the biblical scholars' overly facile definitions of legend, but the broader perspective which they have offered for the underlying presuppositions of legends is quite significant. Biblical scholars have wanted to differentiate legends from sagas and myths, but without digging too deeply into the significance of legends. The folklorists mentioned above could easily have addressed some of their words to the court legends, where the protagonist is usually a one-dimensional type, not a real character.[42] The true legend—at least those legends which depict the religious hero—have a mechanical predictability about them, which does not give the antagonists a fighting chance. At the same time that the forces arrayed against the protagonist may increase, the certain knowledge that God will providentially save the day renders the legends somewhat unengaging to the modern sensibility. Dundes puts this well in regard to the general disinterest in legends which prevailed in folklore circles a few decades ago:

> It is difficult to think of any area of folklore research which has continued to be as sterile and unrewarding as the study of legend ... folklorists have utterly failed to convince anyone, including themselves, of the significance and relevance of legend with respect to the ultimate goal of understanding the nature of man.[43]

The dramatic intervention of God in Daniel 3 or 6, for example, leaves the stories with a static, undramatic feel, despite what should be very dramatic threats to the heroes. Miraculous events which occur so readily cease to be miraculous, or at least, cease to be awesome. The awesome feeling of the presence of God in human affairs is much more real in the patriarchal sagas of, say, Jacob going to the mat with an angel (Gen 32:24–32), or Abraham's three visitors (Genesis 18). Since Gunkel, this kind of distinction between saga and legend has been noted. However, later writings as well sometimes seek out indirect means to show God at work which are less tedious than the repetitive legends. Within Acts of the Apostles, for instance, we find both kinds of narrative. In chapter 8 Philip has a successul missionary swing through Samaria, and after baptizing the Ethiopian eunuch, it is said:

> But when they came up out of the water, the spirit of the Lord seized Philip, and the eunuch did not see him anymore. . . . But Philip was found in Azotus, and as he passed through he preached the good news to all the cities, all the way to Caesarea.(vss 39–40)

---

[42] One has to be careful to distinguish the true legends from literary reworkings. The MT version of Esther, e.g., already begins to turn Esther into a romantic heroine.

[43] Dundes, ''Psychology,'' 163.

This legend, probably from a relatively unredacted source of Acts, can be contrasted with a section more typical of the redactional layer of Acts, 18:12–15:

> While Gallio was proconsul of Achaia, the Jews in one throng attacked Paul, and brought him before the tribunal, saying, "Contrary to the law, this man persuades people to worship God!" But when Paul was about to open his mouth, Gallio said to the Jews. . . . "I refuse to be a judge of these things."

Since this unintentional protection of Paul follows immediately after God's promise of safe passage (18:9–10), we are left to assume that God orchestrated these events, and will continue to do so. The indirect understatement of the miracle, the vivid depiction of action, and the humor of this boisterous mob scene—not to mention what appears to be the comic emphasis of the Jews' "Contrary to the law, this man persuades people to worship God"—all work to avoid the dreariness of legend. One must bring a great deal of credulousness *to* the legend in order to believe it—not surprising, since belief is one of the chief criteria used to distinguish legends. In the words of the romantic poets, it is a case of letting the will do the work of the imagination.

Emotions are often lacking in the hero of the true legend.[44] This is not the case in sagas, and it is even more unlike romances. The protagonist of legend is not buffeted by events, either physically or psychologically. A faith in God is usually responsible for such invulnerability. In contrast to biblical sagas, there is also an overstatement in legends which dilutes the dramatic effect. Although Daniel, for example, accomplishes great things in the highest royal courts in the world, it ultimately has no effect on Jewish history. Legends have a "typical" quality, and, although they are set in a definite time-frame in the not-too-distant past, it is interchangeable with almost every other definite time-frame. That is, the order and significance of the events of history are not altered by the achievements of the protagonist.[45] This is particularly clear in Daniel 1–6, where the stories have no interrelation in terms of the progression or alteration of events. The king does not even remember that he has been visited by God in the previous story. Contrast this with the patriarchal sagas, where, if Abraham so much as spits to the left, off goes the Hebrew people! What is altered in most of the Jewish

[44] Müller ("Märchen, Legende und Enderwartung. Zum Verständnis des Buches Daniel," *VT* 26 (1976) 339) notes this in regard to Daniel 1–6. The addition of prayers to these chapters, however, changes this a great deal.

[45] The story of the three youths in 1 Esdras 3–4 is somewhat of an exception, in that the rebuilding of the temple is sanctioned here. It is, however, not purely a court legend.

court legends is the relationships of the Jews to competing groups in the eyes of the king. Even Daniel 5, based on a condemning prophecy against the king, is altered, as we shall see, to conform to the model of a wise Jew winning the favor of a pagan king.

The possibility of substantial personal development of a character is also limited in pure legends, although as we shall see, character development is poossible in some of the literary expansions of legends, such as MT Esther and the later versions of Ahikar. Von Rad held that Joseph develops as a character, but John H. Hayes and J. Maxwell Miller[46] contend that the motif of reversal becomes the focus of the narrative, and not Joseph's character. What will be shown in this thesis is that court legends in general depict a change of status of a good and wise protagonist and an evil and foolish antagonist, and that in the post-exilic period, both in Jewish and non-Jewish contexts, the principal characters often come to stand for ethnic groups in competition for social position.

The appeal of legends, then, can be studied in a broader context than just "wisdom court legends," and such a beginning can clarify the exact nature of this type of narrative and the psychological and artistic presuppositions inherent in it.

Definition of Court

The use of the word "court" in the genre definition must also be examined carefully. The court as setting for these legends provides a colorful and dramatic stage for the action. In Asia Minor, Mesopotamia, and Israel, the power of the centralized court evidently captured the imagination of the masses in a way that is not true, for example, in ancient mainland Greece. In Egyptian literature, the court setting is used, but not for the same purpose. The practical concerns of royal chronicles, propaganda, courtly instructions, and even history writing are to be distinguished from the entertaining and edifying court legends.[47] The court in the legends is generally an elevated

---

[46] Von Rad, "Joseph"; and Hayes and Miller, *Israelite and Judaean History* (London: SCM, 1977) 178–79. Certainly character is *revealed* in the long interchange at the end between Joseph and his brothers, but it is not clear that character is *developed*. Even if this does constitute character development, it is quite possibly introduced in the later literary stages of the Joseph legend.

[47] This distinction is crucial for an analysis of the literature even though court legends are sometimes merged with other genres, such as instructions (e.g. *Ahikar* and *Onkhsheshonq*), court chronicles (1 Kings 3–11), history writing (1 Esdras), and likely other genres as well. E. W. Heaton's interesting work (*Solomon's New Men* [New York: Pica, 1974]) comparing Egyptian and Israelite literature, can be criticized for making too little distinction between various genres in these two bodies of literature.

and dramatic setting for bourgeois entertainments. The high stakes of actions in the royal court and the import of words is emphasized, even when the tone can be temporarily comical, as in 1 Esdras 3–4. The gracious gifts to be received or the terrible punishments to be inflicted were here greater than anywhere else. This is, of course, not only true of court legends, but also of tales set in the court (such as the fool who wins the hand of the princess); but in the legend the facts of the story are presumed to be true, and therefore the level of tension generated over the decisions of the king is much higher.

Indeed, despite the elevation of the courtly setting, the definite and familiar space which Dundes associates with legend is reflected in the court legends as well. The space of the king's court is presented as real and definite by the composer of legends even though he or she may never have seen it. Paradoxically, even the king's court, that sanctum forbidden to most Jews, becomes "real," definite, and familiar. Here alone does a king become merely human, or in many cases even base, petty, and contemptible. The royal court is scrutinized closely and often demythologized.

The peculiar position of the courtier as a vulnerable interloper in the authority structure of the court is also emphasized by Jürgen-Christian Lebram.[48] This type is a social climber who substitutes intellectual abilities for family connections and military power.[49] The competition with other courtiers on a similar footing is thus keenly felt, and he is dependent on the good will of the king, which is depicted as a fickle thing indeed. In the Persian context, however, when a courtier is established in a "Friend-of-the-King" status, there is an emphasis on the mutual loyalty of courtier and king.[50] The court legends which I am analyzing depict the attempt of the courtier to establish such a relationship.

The courtly aspect of the court legend, however, must be seen in a slightly broader context than the one envisioned by the scholars mentioned above. In those studies the only stories analyzed involved a *courtier* as hero, yet there are many similar legends in which the king is depicted as the wise hero, and there are still others in which a noncourtier, for example a woman, enters into the world of the court. In 1 Kings 3 and 10, Solomon's wisdom is demon-

---

[48] *Das Buch Daniel* (Zürcher Bibelkommentare AT 23; Zürich: Theologischer Verlag, 1984) 10.

[49] The protagonist, usually already a member of the circle of courtiers, is as a result almost always male, although a woman sometimes finds herself at court in a similar role, for instance, the wise woman of Tekoa in 2 Samuel 14. According to Talmon ("Esther," 450; citing Johann Fichtner), of all ancient Near Eastern literature, only the Hebrew Bible depicts women as wise, separate from the domestic role.

[50] Karl Reinhardt, "Herodots Persergeschichten," in Walter Marg, ed., *Herodot: Eine Auswahl aus der neueren Forschung* (2nd ed.; München: Beck, 1965) 328, 337–38.

strated first in his adjudication over which of two prostitutes is the true mother of a baby, and second in answering all the riddles of the Queen of Sheba.[51] Here, for instance, the court perhaps retains some of its majesty, and the same phenomenon occurs in court legends from other cultures which focus on the king as the bearer of wisdom, such as the pro-Cyrus legends in Herodotus and Xenophon's *Cyropaedia*. In 2 Samuel 14 a "wise woman" of Tekoa is enlisted to intercede for Absalom at the court of David, and carries out her mission prudently and effectively. To understand how any subset of court legends was used, it is necessary to understand how the genre as a whole functioned and what it included; legends of the wise king making pronouncements in his court and of noncourtiers who function at court must also be considered as related parts of the same genre. As will become clear below, this broader perspective of the use of the genre illuminates the particular Jewish examples which will be the focus of this study.

Despite the demythologized view of the Great King which is often found in court legends and the often antagonistic relationship of the Jewish courtier to his colleagues, there generally exists in court legends the idea that it is in the court where all moral conflicts have their just resolution. This is not, it should be emphasized, because the wisdom and virtue of the king render it so—Ahasuerus is obtuse, Cambyses is a fickle tyrant, and in *Ahikar* Asarhaddon is foolish and weak—but because the power and centrality of the court hold absolute sway over human events, and behind this temporal power is the hand of just retribution.

Although the search for a modern analog to the ancient court legend need not detain us long, it is interesting that the modern courtroom drama exhibits many interesting similarities to the court conflict, indicating that the reappearance of the "court," albeit a totally different court, is not accidental. In the courtroom drama in movies, television, and in plays, an innocent person is typically placed in jeopardy by the weight of overwhelming evidence that he or she is guilty. The machinery of the state and society, compelled by the evidence, moves inexorably against the victim. A brash, brilliant, irreverent defence attorney pleads the case before a benign but well-meaning and impartial judge, and the truth of the accused person's innocence is finally brought to light, as the guilty party is exposed.[52] Aside from the obvious

---

[51] These stories act as an envelope for the chronicles of Solomon's reign which lie in between. See Heaton, *Solomon's New Men*, 16–24.

[52] We need not restrict this scenario to the modern world; Susanna tells the same story. Robert H. Pfeiffer (*History of New Testament Times* [New York: Harper, 1949] 448) calls Susanna the first "detective story," which is really not quite accurate. It is a variation on the court legend which is set in the local "court," as Nickelsburg (Jewish Literature, 25–26) notes, and it is a "courtroom drama" more than a "detective story."

similarity of the plight of the accused person who is ultimately vindicated, there is also in common between the ancient and the modern versions the implicit faith that justice will ultimately prevail *in the court*, that is, that where life and death is held in the balance, the "wheels of justice may grind slow but exceedingly fine."[53]

The analogy of the modern courtroom drama with the ancient court legend may have a further implication for the worldview of the latter. The usual analysis of these narratives as wisdom narratives asserts that it is God's hand that providentially brings the truth to light. This is, however, not always the case, and it may be a misleading approach. One wonders if in some of the ancient legends, as in their modern counterparts, the presumption is not that God protects, but that the authority of the court is finally affirmed. Esther does not mention God, *Ahikar* does not mention any god in the vindication section, the Joseph story barely mentions God,[54] and neither *Onkhsheshonq* nor the court legends of Herodotus mention God, even though Apollo saves Croesus in a noncourt legend. To be sure, in some court legends God is explicitly brought in, especially in the Daniel cycle. There miracles are introduced which prevent the execution of the heroes. We shall find, however, that it is necessary to distinguish those narratives where the protagonists are *falsely* accused of committing a real crime, and those in which the protagonist is fairly accused of committing what is wrongly forbidden, as in Daniel. The former tend to be "secular," the latter are protomartyr stories; the former depict the protagonist exonerated, the latter protected by the hand of God. In these the authorities do not actually vindicate the protagonist, but acknowledge the protection of God.[55] Court legends, as we shall see, by

---

[53] In general the modern courtroom drama reflects a conservative faith in the court system as finally acquitting the innocent and condemning the guilty. In the hands of some directors, this expectation on the part of the audience was exploited with unexpected reversals of the genre: Billy Wilder's "Witness for the Prosecution," Alfred Hitchcock's "The Paradine Case," Orson Welles's "Touch of Evil," Nicholas Ray's "Knock on Any Door," and Otto Preminger's "Anatomy of a Murder" all intentionally blur the neat separation of good and evil and the means of revealing it in a courtroom setting.

[54] God is most conspicuous in chap. 39, which is probably to be separated from the main court legend. Note that God is mentioned an extraordinary number of times at the beginning and end of chap. 39, but only at 39:9 in the middle. Verses 20–23, usually ascribed to J, have a parallel section usually ascribed to E, 40:2–4, which does not mention God once. Elsewhere, events are attributed to God's providence at 45:5, 7, 8 and 50:20, but here too one wonders whether they might be glosses.

[55] Susanna is the only exception to this division, in that she is wrongly accused, but God enters in explicitly to inspire Daniel to uncover the truth. Note, however, that she is not miraculously protected from execution, but is instead exonerated, as we would expect in a "falsely accused" story.

focusing on the court, often leave God out of the picture. Whether God is there implicitly will remain a matter of debate, but it often appears that events are viewed from the point of view of human causality in the most powerful human realm in the world—the court. In addition to those examples mentioned above, one might also note the "background" role of God in the Succession Narrative.[56] The lack of any references to God in the Persian stories in Herodotus has also been noted by Reinhardt.[57] Can it be that the court legend naturally brings with it a focus on the drama of human events at court, to the exclusion of a reference to God's activity? Of course, this lack of a reference to God is often invoked as a "wisdom" influence,[58] as indeed it may be. The genre of the court legend in general, however, may be much more respectful and conservative in respect to the state ideology of the court than we might have thought. This brings us to our next problem of definition.

Definition of Wisdom

The wisdom content of the legends will surely be regarded as the most controversial aspect of the genre definition. This may seem surprising at first, when certain basic associations of the legends with wisdom are noted. The very notion of activity in the court in the ancient Near East to some extent presupposes "wisdom" as a prerequisite. Aside from the professional courtier-scribes of Egypt and Mesopotamia who were associated with wisdom, we find in Israel courtiers routinely referred to as "the wise" (Gen 41:8; Is 19:11, 29:14; Jer 18:18, 50:35, 51:57; Esth 1:13; Dan 2:13; cf. Pr 16:14), kings are "wise" (2 Sam 14:20; 1 Kgs 3:12), as are the leaders of the tribes in Deut 1:13. Women active in the court or in public decisions are "wise" (2 Sam 14:2, 20:16). Wisdom is an attribute very closely associated with the king's court.[59] In many of the court legends wisdom is also specifically ascribed to the protagonist. Joseph is called "discreet and wise" (נבון וחכם, Gen 41:39); Daniel and his companions are constantly compared

---

[56] Von Rad ("Joseph," 198–201) notes three places where God plays a role in events (2 Sam 11:27, 12:24, 17:14), but notes their intrusive nature. He nevertheless maintains that the role of God is crucial to the theology of the work.

[57] "Persergeschichten," 330, 337–38. According to Reinhardt, Herodotus sometimes introduces a religious element into his eastern sources. Others are skeptical of Reinhardt's conclusions, but cannot offer counterevidence; Walter Burkert (review of Reinhardt's *Vermächtnis der Antike*, in *Gymnasium* 67 [1960] 549) simply assumes that a religious view must be present; likewise Richard Harder ("Herodot 1,8,3" in Marg, ed., *Herodot* 374): "It only *appears* that the gods are lacking. . . ."

[58] Von Rad, "Joseph," 293, 296–300; and Talmon, "Esther," 429–31.

[59] S. H. Blank, "Wisdom," *IDB* 4.853–56.

to the wise men of Babylon (Dan 1:20, 4:15 MT, and 5:11 – 16), and Zerubbabel is found by King Darius to be "wiser" (σοφώτερος) than the other pages. In non-Jewish court legends, Ahikar is revered as a sage and teaches with proverbs; Aesop, the most famous figure of Greek popular wisdom, is represented as playing a role in the courts of several famous kings; and in Herodotus three Greeks who advise Croesus wisely are among the "Seven Sages" of Greek tradition. Other examples could be given, but the point is clear: there was a natural association of the court with wisdom. The two are of course not coextensive in ancient literature—there are non-wisdom court traditions and non-court wisdom traditions—but the wisdom of the courtier was a common motif in the literature of the ancient Near East. The court legends were evidently seen by the ancients to be very amenable to wisdom teachings, since in a number of cases the legends circulated with sizable collections of wisdom teachings, for example, *Ahikar*, *Life of Aesop*, *Onkhsheshonq*.

Despite this, however, it has become common in recent scholarly literature to dissociate these legends from any "wisdom" influence, which is part of a broader lament concerning the lack of precision in the definition of wisdom and "wisdom literature." The larger issues of the definition of wisdom in Israel must also be brought in to the discussion of the particular situation of these legends. Perhaps more than any other topic, wisdom has become a battleground between maximalists and minimalists, between those who would erect a thoroughgoing theoretical reconstruction of ancient Israelite and Jewish intellectual tradition and those who would resist this temptation as being too speculative. The doubts that some scholars voice about our ability to discern wisdom influences in texts outside the traditional wisdom "canon" (Proverbs, Job, Ecclesiastes, Ben Sira, Wisdom of Solomon, and, for some scholars, the wisdom psalms) are indeed justified in part, since in early Israel sages and scribes did not leave behind evidences of a clear and independent function in society, as they did, for example, in Egypt, and therefore the distinctive indicators of wisdom cannot be agreed upon. None of the wisdom literature of early Israel has the clear and explicit markings of a scribal class, except for Proverbs, and even here the bulk of the book is ascribed to a king, Solomon, and not to a sage.[60] He may be the patron saint of Jewish sages, but he does not embody the separate profession of the scribe.

---

[60] Cf. Egyptian instructions which are attributed to famous sages. In Israel priests, prophets, and courtiers sometimes have roles less differentiated than their professions might imply. There are priestly prophets (Ezekiel), cult prophets (Haggai, Zechariah, Joel, and Malachi), and courtier-prophets (Nathan).

A common difficulty in the study of wisdom is the flexibility of the term, which allows for different senses in different contexts. Most scholars of wisdom would agree that several categories of wisdom can be distinguished, based on the various social contexts where wisdom traditions might arise, such as clan wisdom, courtly wisdom, scribal wisdom, theological wisdom, mantic wisdom, and philosophical wisdom. Corresponding to the various provenances of wisdom are different conceptions of wisdom and particular literary and oral forms in which the conceptions are couched. For example, clan wisdom depends almost entirely on the transmission of wisdom through proverbs, usually expressed in indicative clauses in parallel lines, while courtly wisdom uses collections of proverbs which are addressed to the young courtier in training, utilizing imperatives and motive clauses.[61] Scribal or school wisdom, emanating from the local schools independent of the royal court, makes use of these same collections, but they are often greatly expanded, with more highly developed poetic compositions. In addition, wisdom psalms and other didactic compositions were employed in this milieu.[62] Theological wisdom more closely associates the role of wisdom with divine processes, especially in the hypostasis of wisdom as a "handmaiden" of God,[63] while in mantic wisdom, rare in Israel, God directly communicates divine intentions to the deserving adherent.[64] Last, philosophical wisdom uses dialogues and meditations to reflect on the truth of the received

---

[61] The use of collections of proverbs in royal court schools is clear in Egyptian instructions, but only apparent in some sections of Proverbs, e.g., 16:1–22:16 and 25:2–27. See W. Lee Humphreys, "The Motif of the Wise courtier in the Book of Proverbs," in John G. Gammie, et al., eds., *Israelite Wisdom: Theological and Literary Essays in Honor of Samuel Terrien* (Missoula: Scholars Press, 1978) 177–90. On the formal nature of proverbs in these different settings, see William McKane, *Proverbs: A New Approach* (London: SCM, 1970) passim.

[62] A school setting separate from the royal court schools is most obvious in Ben Sira, but on the school setting of Proverbs see Patrick W. Skehan, "Seven Columns of Wisdom's House in Proverbs 1–9," "A Single Editor of the Whole Book of Proverbs," and "Wisdom's House," all in idem, *Studies in Israelite Poetry and Wisdom* (CBQMS 1; Washington, D.C.: Catholic Bible Association, 1971) 9–14, 15–26, and 27–45, respectively. William Riehl Poehlman ("Addressed Wisdom Teaching in *The Teachings of Silvanus*: A Form-Critical Study" [Ph.D. dissertation, Harvard University, 1974]) has proposed a school *Sitz* for some of the poetic, nonproverbial passages of Proverbs, Ben Sira, and other documents.

[63] Several classic passages reflect a well developed myth of the role of the female figure of Wisdom: Pr 8:22–31, Ben Sira 24:1–12, Bar 3:3–4:1, and 1 Enoch 42. Note also the similarity of Elephantine *Ahikar* saying no. 12, which has been generally overlooked; and cf. James Lindenberger, "The Gods of Ahiqar," *UF* 15 (1982) 68–70.

[64] On mantic wisdom see esp. Hans-Peter Müller, "Magisch-mantische Weisheit und die Gestalt Daniels," *UF* 1 (1969) 79–94; idem, "Mantische Weisheit und Apokalyptik," VTSup 22 (1972) 268–93; Collins, "Court-Tales," 218–34.

tradition and the possibility of justice and divine involvement in human affairs.

The variety of meanings which the term "wisdom" may bear thus requires preliminary explanations of the particular application being used. But it is by no means clear that the possibilities of the meanings have already been exhausted; the use of the term will have to be rethought in relation to the genres being discussed in this thesis. Our problem, then, is to ask again the basic questions about wisdom genres, focusing now on "narrative wisdom" in addition to the types which have already been analyzed in the scholarly literature. Most of the conclusions about wisdom genres in Israel can be applied equally well to the other literatures of the ancient Near East. We are confronted with a well developed international intellectual tradition which is didactically transmitted, and which has fairly identifiable interests and methods. The scholarly literature on ancient Near Eastern wisdom is vast and need not be summarized, but here our problem can be proposed in three interrelated questions: How do we define the essential characteristics of wisdom in the "canon" of wisdom writings?[65] By what method does one discern these characteristics outside this canon? Last, how are these writings outside the canon related to the circles that produced the major bodies of ancient Near Eastern wisdom texts?

The first two questions are often answered together, that is, the constitutive characteristics of wisdom are arrived at in the process of arguing for their presence outside the canon. There are three ways in recent research in which this is generally carried out. The most common is the form-critical approach that identifies didactic forms in, for example, the prophetic writings. Isolated proverbs and metrical sayings can be found in Amos and Isaiah, and the extent to which this indicates a wisdom influence has been vigorously debated.[66] Second, certain words which are encountered in the

---

[65] A conservative canon of wisdom texts outside of Israel could also be arrived at, which would include in Egypt and Babylonia, the proverbs collections and instructions genre, dialogues, and philosophical reflections. W. G. Lambert's (*Babylonian Wisdom Literature* [Oxford: Clarendon, 1960] 1) oft-quoted phrase that " 'Wisdom' is strictly a misnomer as applied to Babylonian literature," should be compared to the rest of that page, and indeed to the title of the book, where he makes it perfectly clear that the "wisdom" genres of Hebrew literature are found in essentially the same form in Mesopotamia. His reservation is simply that in Babylonia the word for "wisdom" appears to refer only to a sort of wisdom which Müller and Collins would call "mantic wisdom."

[66] Hans Walter Wolf, *Amos' geistige Heimat* (WMANT 18; Neukirchen-Vluyn: Neukirchener, 1965) 24–26; Samuel Terrien, "Amos and Wisdom," in Bernhard W. Anderson and Walter Harrelson, eds., *Israel's Prophetic Heritage: Essays in Honor of James Muilenberg* (New York: Harper and Row, 1962) 108–15; W. M. W. Roth, "The Numerical Sequence x/x + 1 in the Old Testament," *VT* 12 (1962) 300–11; and idem, "Numerical Sayings in the Old Testament," (VTSup 13; Leiden: Brill, 1965); but cf. James Crenshaw's ("The Influence of the Wise Upon

known wisdom texts are used to postulate wisdom influences elsewhere. R. N. Whybray followed this method to arrive at a list of words which lay at the core of Israel's "intellectual tradition," and by means of this list determined which texts should be included in this tradition.[67] Last, the subject matter of the agreed-upon canonical wisdom texts, and the attributes of the wise person found there, are sometimes used to identify wisdom influences in other writings. Especially significant here are the studies by von Rad on the Joseph story in Genesis and by Talmon on Esther mentioned above, although many others have gained considerable attention.[68] Although in this approach terminology is also used for comparison with wisdom texts, the prime evidence of association with wisdom is taken to be the theological and anthropological point of view, along with implicit teachings of such wisdom commonplaces as the proper time for silence or wise counsel in the court of the king.

In addition to these three different ways of identifying wisdom elements, there is also the question of where wisdom traditions are to be located. Is it necessary to locate a wisdom text in a definite *Sitz-im-Leben*, or at least in a certain social milieu?[69] The wisdom forms such as collected proverbs, numerical sayings, or wisdom psalms are the most easily identified with a social milieu, that is, the scribal or court schools, and very likely with a distinct *Sitz-im-Leben*: education within the schools. Indeed, much writing on wisdom presumes that this tradition is coterminous with "sages," and that much of the literature of ancient Israel is to be ascribed to this group.[70] "Wisdom," then, would refer to the intellectual tradition of this professional class.

The association of writings with a certain wisdom tradition could probably also be based on the use of special wisdom terms, the second method above,

---

Amos," *ZAW* 79 [1967] 42–52; and "Amos and the Theophanic Tradition," *ZAW* 80 [1968] 203–15) criticism of this enterprise in regard to the prophetic writings.

[67] Whybray, *The Intellectual Tradition in the Old Testament* (BZAW; Berlin/New York: de Gruyter, 1974); and cf. Terrien, "Amos," on his analysis of *sôd*.

[68] Other notable attempts to trace wisdom influence in narrative writings outside the wisdom canon are reviewed in the negative assessment given by James Crenshaw, "Method in Determining Wisdom Influence upon 'Historical Literature,'" *JBL* 88 (1969) 129. To be added to his list are Roth, "The Wooing of Rebecca: A Tradition-Critical Study of Genesis 24," *CBQ* 34 (1972) 177–87; and Heaton, *Solomon's New Men*, 129–61. Von Rad (*Wisdom*, 46–47) is surprisingly skimpy on "didactic narrative."

[69] "Social milieu" can be a general designation of the segment of the population to which a writing belongs, such as a certain class or occupation, but the technical term *Sitz-im-Leben* is much more precise and requires a description of how and under what conditions a document or oral form was actually used.

[70] Heaton, *Solomon's New Men*, passim; and McKane, *Prophets and Wise Men* (Napierville, IL: Allenson, 1965) 15–54.

but with less certainty that it could be attributed to a special school situation or scribal class. The language of the tradition could conceivably go well beyond the precincts of the court or scribal school. In regard to wisdom theology or the attributes of a wise person found in writings outside the main wisdom canon, it is even more difficult to attach these *definitively* to a scribal class or courtly milieu, although von Rad does press for the latter on the analogy of Egyptian wisdom.[71] James Crenshaw notes these difficulties and criticizes this last method especially, rejecting the attempts to identify wisdom influence on narrative texts. His categorization of writings as "wisdom" rests on one main requirement, which he sees as unfulfilled in these studies: an adequate description of the *Sitz-im-Leben*. He limits the province of wisdom proper to those texts whose *Sitz* can be carefully delineated:

> Accordingly, one must distinguish between family/clan wisdom, the goal of which is the mastering of life, the stance hortatory and style proverbial; court wisdom, with the goal of education for a select group, the stance secular, and method didactic; and scribal wisdom, the goal being education for all, the stance dogmatico-religious, and the method dialogico-admonitory.[72]

However, various recent studies of wisdom in Israel have taken the approach that, whereas wisdom forms such as the proverb can often be associated with a particular group or even a *Sitz*, many wisdom motifs and even the special forms associated with the schools become part of the more general intellectual tradition. Roland Murphy, for example, forgoes the problem of locating every text in a particular *Sitz* by noting that wisdom provided a common language of intellectual discourse in Israelite society: "It is not a question of direct influence of the sages or of wisdom literature, but of an approach to reality that was shared by all Israelites in varying degrees."[73] Thus studies of wisdom have sometimes attempted to place writings in a certain *Sitz* or social milieu, and have at other times merely analyzed them in terms of motifs which are part of a broad and ongoing wisdom tradition. Some also take a middle path between the two extremes, such as E. W. Heaton, Joseph Blenkinsopp, and Hartmut Gese, who notes that wisdom is generally passed on in a "didactic transmission," whether in the clan, the court or the school, and whether in Israel or elsewhere in the ancient Near East.[74]

---

[71] Von Rad, "Joseph," 294, 299. Heaton (*Solomon's New Men*, 130), though uneasy with the term "wisdom," also locates the many products of the wisdom tradition in early Israel in the scribal circles of the royal court.

[72] Crenshaw, "Method," 130. Blenkinsopp (*Wisdom*, 40) leans in this direction, but perhaps not quite as strongly as Crenshaw.

[73] Murphy, *Wisdom Literature* (FOTL 13; Grand Rapids: Eerdmans, 1981) 3.

[74] Gese, "Wisdom literature in Persian period," in W. D. Davies and Louis Finkelstein, eds.,

This associates wisdom with a certain role in society—education and transmission of values—but not with any specific social milieu.

In regard to wisdom influence in narrative writings, however, the issue is not just one of locating the precise *Sitz-im-Leben*. The controversy between Crenshaw on the one hand and von Rad and Talmon on the other arose over the difficulty of establishing a clear set of parallels between the stories of Joseph or Esther and the wisdom canon. Von Rad and Talmon are required by their hypothesis to show that the principal point of the writings they are analyzing is to impart certain ideals of the wise person, that is, that themes are present which can be summed up in the proverbial instructions known from elsewhere in Israel. True, each of the proponents of a "narrative wisdom" saw other, more complex evidences of a wisdom point of view, such as "humanism," "individualism," or "psychological interest," but the stories were still seen to serve, as Talmon says, to "portray *applied* wisdom."[75] Von Rad states that Joseph "possessed the twin virtues of outspokenness and good counsel—precisely the qualities upon which the wisdom-teachers continually insist."[76] However, Joseph fails to defend himself with his brothers (37:18–28), fails to defend himself before Potiphar (39:19–20), and is only called before Pharaoh through the intervention of another (41:9–14).[77] Joseph is not depicted as the model of courtly success, the walking embodiment of proverbial wisdom, and had he been, the story would have been boring beyond endurance.[78] We have thankfully been saved from reading any ancient stories—if they existed—which portrayed a hero who spoke at the right time and was silent at the right time, who rose not too early nor retired too late, in other words, who lived by proverbial wisdom. Joseph succeeds because he *deserves* to succeed, based on his righteousness and innocence—this is, after all, a moral story. He succeeds through the supernatural powers that are bestowed upon him and the providential good fortune that more than once places him in the right place at the right time. His "secular" courtly wisdom is not emphasized. The search for a

---

Cambridge History of Judaism (Cambridge: Cambridge University, 1984) 190; and Heaton, *Solomon's New Men*, 130.

[75] Talmon, "Esther" 426–27 (italics his). Nickelsburg takes a similar position in his references to the "wisdom tale" (*Resurrection*, 54–58).

[76] Von Rad, "Joseph," 294; and cf. Heaton, *Solomon's New Men*, 136.

[77] On Joseph's failures see Crenshaw, "Method," 136–37. The sage Ahikar, another hero of a court legend, has just these same difficulties in defending himself.

[78] Heaton (*Solomon's New Men*, 136–37) states: "The author . . . avoided turning his hero into a dummy civil servant spouting proverbial wisdom. . . ." However, Heaton seems to want it both ways. In the previous paragraph he ties Joseph's reluctance to show his emotions in public to scribal training.

"proverbial correlative" as a prime consideration in wisdom narratives, while pointing us in a fruitful direction, was ultimately unsuccessful.

Others, of course, have tried to tie the wisdom orientation of the Joseph story and Esther, as well as the Succession Narrative, to the themes of the invisible but providential working of God. Whybray, Ronald Hals and R. B. Y. Scott[79] note the inexorability of these narratives as they move toward a positive conclusion, and see this as an affirmation of the central wisdom tenet of providence. Two objections can be voiced here, however. First, God is not necessarily noted as the grand artificer of the working out of the stories. Above it was noted that in court narratives of all kinds, from different cultures, there appears to be a focus on human actions within the court that simply ignores the role of God. To take one famous example, Esther never so much as mentions the name of God. Recently, however, Sandra Beth Berg and David J. A. Clines have restated the argument for an implicit theocentric theme in Esther, but I am skeptical.[80] Is any story with a happy ending to be construed as an affirmation of God's providential role in worldly affairs, and therefore as wisdom? This is not as farfetched as it sounds at first, since a correspondence between God's active involvement and one's personal fortunes could perhaps be presumed in most ancient literature, except, of course, for the literature of pessimistic wisdom. This is, however, still much too broad. It merges on one side with the notion of divinely controlled history, as in the deuteronomistic conception, and on the other with romances and all manner of narrative literature. A sense of order and justice rules the court legends which does not derive from an atheistic consciousness, but which, in some cases, simply does not emphasize God. As Müller puts it:

> The function of the didactic narrative can in general be described as two-fold: 1) By means of the depiction of the hero, it renders a virtue or a complex of virtues as paradigmatic. 2) It interprets reality according to a postulate of order, on the basis of which the virtue represented becomes meaningful. At the same time, the incongruency of such a postulate to the experienced reality is never denied; it is merely understood as a temporary condition.[81]

The statements above about the role of the court in these legends even pushes

---

[79] Whybray, *The Succession Narrative* (Napierville, IL: Allenson, 1968) 62–66; Hals, *The Theology of the Book of Ruth* (Philadelphia: Fortress, 1969) 53; and Scott, *The Way of Wisdom in the Old Testament* (New York: Macmillan, 1971) 86–92.

[80] Berg, *The Book of Esther* (SBLDS 44; Chico: Scholars Press, 1979) 173–87; and Clines, *The Esther Scroll* (JSOT Supp 30; Sheffield: JSOT, 1984) 155–58.

[81] Müller, "Die weisheitliche Lehrerzählung," 94.

us to the conclusion that the "postulate of order" here is not an implicit affirmation of the ultimate justice of God, but the ultimate justice of the court.

In addition, this view of wisdom narratives as the working out of the theme of providence does not focus enough on the moral and psychological position of the protagonist. Von Rad and Talmon are correct in maintaining this focus, as opposed to an emphasis on providence. The wisdom orientation of the court legends is, as von Rad says of the Joseph story, "humanistic" and ahistorical. However, von Rad's and Talmon's method of identifying the wisdom elements and the main point of the stories is not entirely accurate, and this makes them vulnerable to Crenshaw's attack. Put simply, these narrative works are not trying to impart a series of exemplary actions as witnessed in the individual deeds of the hero. Rather, the point of the stories is that the wise person, who is characterized by whatever "wise" means happen to fit the story, succeeds.[82] Rather than providence being the main theme of the court conflict legends, it is justice—a subtly but significantly different matter[83]—which is the main theme, and this is sometimes understood theocentrically and sometimes not. But either way, there is justice in the cosmos for the wise and righteous protagonist. The "wisdom elements" that von Rad and Talmon identified are generally only means to this end; they help to characterize the hero, but do not constitute the central point.

An interesting analogy to my approach is found in Alfred Hitchcock's reflections on the suspenseful techniques of his films, where he notes that the *content* of what his spies and villains are after is of no importance to the audience, as long as it is of supreme importance to the characters themselves.[84] He calls the secret plans or documents or microfilm or whatever is at issue in the movie a "MacGuffin," which is a term from an old English joke. He consciously limits the explanation of the contents of the MacGuffin, at the same time that he increases the life-or-death interest with which the characters invest it. It would be going too far to say that the wisdom elements in, for example, Esther are reduced to triviality just to show that the person who lives by them succeeds, but they are introduced indirectly to propel the story,

[82] J. A. Loader ("Esther as a Novel with Different Levels of Meaning," *ZAW* 90 [1978] 417–21) seems to be at midpoint between the two approaches. Joseph is not, in his view, portrayed as the static, proverbial wise person, but there is instead a development in the story: Joseph is unwise and fails, wise and succeeds. This is still somewhat tied, however, to the point-by-point comparison with proverbial wisdom as the criterion for success.

[83] Certain acts of God could be providential and just, but the two are still not coterminous. It might be providence if God saved the persecuted righteous person by providing food. It would be justice if God saved the righteous person and punished the wicked.

[84] François Truffaut, *Hitchcock* (New York: Simon and Schuster, 1967) 98.

and not as a catechetical end in themselves. Just as the characters in a Hitchcock film are after the MacGuffin, so also the protagonists in a court legend are "after" wisdom. It is true that one central point, the just end for both the righteous and the wicked, is also found in proverbial wisdom, but this is not focused on by the various modern commentators on wisdom narrative, and by itself hardly justifies an easy identification between the themes of the narratives and proverbial wisdom. To be sure, it is not the case that the narratives are opposed to or even indifferent to proverbial wisdom, but that the content of the wisdom schools is not merely being enacted in narrative themes. We must think of wisdom narratives as narratives and not as proverbial correlatives.

Another possible avenue of comparison between proverbial and narrative wisdom would be to see the two related as indicative proverb and extended motive clause respectively. If wisdom is the making of one's abode in the abiding truths, then indicative proverbs tell us what the abiding truths are, while narratives tell us that we should abide there.[85] This distinction between the functions of proverbs and narratives may provide a partial explanation for why Esther can so cavalierly break Jewish law: it is not so much *what* she does as *why* she does it that is important. If women followed her actual example, they would marry Gentiles and eat nonkosher food. The *reasons* for her change of heart in chapter 4, however, are closer to the main intention of the book. Her resolve to abide in the eternal truths (in this case, Jewish identity) is tested, and she decides to intercede with the king on the basis of Mordecai's appeal to her sense of belonging with the Jewish people.[86] The Scroll of Esther, then, does not tell what Jewish identity consists in, but it does tell that it is something worth prizing. The point, however, is not to prove that Esther, or other narrative figures like her, could not be exemplars of Jewish morality, but that their role as exemplar is not their chief one. Rather, they are protagonists, and in narrative, and especially in good narrative, the protagonist need not be rendered realistically or in agreement with an external code (such as the book of Proverbs, or even Jewish law).

The theme of justice, and the testing and vindication of the one "marked" by wisdom, is much clearer in court conflicts than in contests. In the Joseph story of Genesis, for example, as noted above, many of the more common

---

[85] The presence of motivating clauses in some proverbs clearly indicates two things: first, that proverbs without them lacked a clear sense of motivation, at least for some audience, and second, that a special *Sitz* within the history of proverbs may be indicated when motivating clauses are present, e.g., a special school *Sitz*.

[86] Nickelsburg ("Genre," 157–59) notes the "decision" element in court legends and related writings which he investigates, this element making explicit what is implicit throughout the narratives.

attributes of courtly wisdom are not fulfilled by Joseph's actions. Mordecai's refusal to bow in Esther does not represent any readily apparent dictum of wisdom, and indeed seems decidedly foolish; it can probably best be explained as a convenient device for complicating the plot. In *Ahikar*, as we shall see, the hero is portrayed at first as a particularly bungling court advocate who would have been well advised to hire another lawyer. What can be said for these narratives is that a protagonist, marked by wisdom in the sense that the audiences's sympathies lie with him as a just and innocent person, is tested by an unjust situation, and ultimately is vindicated in the highest court in the land. The protagonist is the one whom we identify with as wise; if we make that connection, then it is easy to "mark" him so, since we believe it of ourselves. Thus it is the narrative structure, and not the proverbial correlative, to which we should pay careful attention.

The situation in court contests is somewhat different, since the protagonist is often rewarded for his show of wisdom. However, the wisdom represented is not a distillation of the best of the inherited tradition. Here, too, it is often merely a means to characterize the hero. In 1 Esdras 3−4, for example, an older humorous riddle about "What is the strongest?" has been expanded in two ways: the third page, originally anonymous, is named as Zerubbabel, the governor responsible for the rebuilding of Jerusalem, and the speech of this third page at some point was expanded to include a hymn to truth (4:34−40). Most scholars agree that, whereas the hymn may raise the tone of the discourse from a humorous to a serious level, it is not originally Jewish, but Persian.[87] This teaching, amenable as it may be to Jewish wisdom, can hardly be considered the point of the story. Neither are Zerubbabel's tactics, especially the ridiculing of the king, normal court methods. The point, in the final form at any rate, is that *Zerubbabel* is the one who was so wise, so noble in thought, so clever and successful at court, that he was exalted in the king's eyes and allowed to oversee the rebuilding of the temple city. The one who was characterized as wise succeeds, and the hymn to truth merely serves to propel our hero to greatness.[88] The protagonist in Jewish wisdom court legends succeeds, not *through* or *by means of* wisdom, but *on account of* his or her wisdom. For the person characterized as wise, justice prevails.

[87] A representative position is found in Eric Myers, *1 and 2 Esdras* (AB; Garden City: Doubleday-Anchor,1974) 53−56. For a more detailed analysis, see William Richard Goodman, Jr., "A Study of 1 Esdras 3:1−5:6," (Ph.D. dissertation, Duke University, 1974).

[88] It is important to contrast the present application of this story with the function of an earlier version (minus the reference to Zerubbabel and the hymn to truth), which was really to entertain the reader or hearer with a tale about how a clever page could insult the king. See Goodman, "1 Esdras 3:1−5:6," esp. 124−32. In respect to this theme of boldness before the king, it is similar to the "disguised parable," to be described in Chapter 2.

Thus, in a study of wisdom court legends, new approaches to wisdom may have to be introduced to account for the peculiarities of this body of literature. The definition of wisdom in Israel is almost always derived ultimately from the Book of Proverbs or its offspring, Ben Sira and Wisdom of Solomon. It is generally felt that here, at least, we are on solid ground in determining what the tradition passed on as typically "wisdom." This is not only true for the isolation of the basic *forms* of didactic transmission and theological tenets, but for descriptions of the professional class of sages as well.[89] The other books in the Jewish wisdom canon, Ecclesiastes and Job, are considered to be rebellions in relation to the more central and conservative core of proverbial collections. Ultimately all reflections on wisdom are extrapolations from Proverbs. Studies of wisdom in ancient Mesopotamia and Egypt simply continued this approach, since in Egypt the "Instructions" genre, very similar to Proverbs, is so prevalent, and in Mesopotamia the genres of wisdom correspond for the most part with those in Israel. One might ask, however, what view modern scholarship would have had of ancient Near Eastern wisdom if, instead of the present situation, in which large collections of proverbs were preserved, the only extant examples of ancient Near Eastern literature which referred to wise people were Daniel 1–6, the Joseph story, *Ahikar*, *Life of Aesop*, legends of court sages found in Herodotus, and by analogy with these court legends, Esther. "Wisdom" might remain a difficult entity to define, but surely we would have a completely different starting point. Without references to Proverbs, an alternative method would arise which sought to isolate the ideas and ideals of wisdom based on these narratives. The case for "narrative wisdom" must be demonstrated not just in terms of "wisdom," but in terms of "narrative" as well.[90]

This thesis posits a wisdom based in popular, not professional, conceptions of what the "wise" hero is like and how he or she succeeds. Although the sage has generally been seen as the transmitter of the wisdom tradition in Israel, whether in court or in school, when the focus is shifted from proverbs as the basic form of wisdom transmission to narratives, the social milieu of the legends must be seen in broader terms. It is impossible to restrict the

---

[89] Cf. esp. Heaton, *Solomon's New Men*, 121–26; McKane, *Wise Men*, 50–52; and Blenkinsopp, *Wisdom*, 40. This practice of basing the description of the sage on proverbial collections is not limited to the early period of the Israelite court, but is used in the post-exilic period in regard to Ben Sira as well.

[90] Heaton has been very positive on the idea of narrative wisdom; see *Solomon's New Men*, 126–61; *The Hebrew Kingdoms* (London: Oxford, 1968) 165–96; *The Book of Daniel* (London: SCM, 1956) 32–47; and "The Joseph Saga," *ExpTim* 59 (1947) 134–36. However, he introduces little new in the way of innovations of method. For this, Müller, ("Die weisheitliche Lehrerzählung") is one of the few scholars to be consulted.

legends to a literary transmission; they may very well have been composed and transmitted orally before entering their literary stage. Thus, although, certain associations with learned scribal traditions may be found in these late stages,[91] in the early stages they could conceivably have been transmitted by any member of that class of people who would value education and ability, and who would look for an effective role for themselves and for fellow members of their ethnic group in the administration of the empire. These two groups—sages on one hand and the broad administrative and entrepreneurial class on the other—are not mutually exclusive. In fact, the former is really a subset of the latter.

The views of this larger class are not just found in the proverbs, collections of proverbs, and philosophical reflections, but are also expressed in the popular transmission of narrative legends.[92] The temptation, however, to demonstrate the wisdom content of, for example, Esther, by listing parallels to Proverbs, is only accomplished by warping the function and intent of the former to some extent. One of the main adjustments that we will have to make is to avoid thinking of wisdom as concepts and theology, and see it focused instead in the nature of a hero or heroine, what happens to the characters, and the affirmations that a class may see reflected in this kind of narrative. As we shall see, this function of narrative wisdom is not only found in the Jewish examples mentioned above, but also in the figures of, for example, Aesop, Ahikar, Solon of Athens, or the fallen Croesus of Lydia.[93] What is equally important is that these are not just idealized figures for the morally conscientious to meditate on, but they are almost always *cultural* heroes, protagonists who represent entire ethnic groups in the larger ruling world empires. The idea of narrative wisdom, promulgated by von Rad and Talmon and opposed by Crenshaw, will be demonstrated here not by an appeal to Proverbs and other similar ancient Near Eastern collections, but by an appeal to broader genres of narrative wisdom in Asia Minor, Persia, and Greece. This will be done by redefining the starting point for wisdom studies in ancient Judaism, to focus on the popular literary conceptions of wisdom and wise heroes and heroines.

The desire to derive descriptive terms of wisdom applicable to the interna-

---

[91] Collins, ''Court-Tales,'' is especially to be consulted on this point.

[92] Tobit, *Ahikar*, and *Onkhsheshonq* all have proverbial sections in the narrative, but this merely shows the new desires of this class to incorporate a middle-class set of maxims into their entertaining and edifying literature. For similar views of the class appeal of these works, see in addition to McKane, *Proverbs: A New Approach* (London: SCM, 1970) 117–50, 156–82 (re: *Ahikar* and *Onkhsheskonq*); also Blenkinsopp, *Wisdom*, 40 (re: Judith and Tobit).

[93] Despite the fact that Solon or Croesus are not from the administrative and entrepreneurial class, they have probably become cultural heroes of this class in the legends found in Herodotus.

tional situation of the ancient Near East, which guided previous study of wisdom, will be in evidence in this thesis as well. However, the comparisons will not be made to the same writings from other cultures which were utilized before. The proverbs, instructions, and philosophical meditations of the previous study will be set aside, and instead the method will arise from a comparison of the many extant legends which revere a wise hero or heroine. It will also be necessary to introduce other terms necessary for the study of *this* sort of wisdom. I will impose a distinction which is relevant for the study of folk literature in general, that is, the distinction between wisdom and cleverness. This distinction is often ignored in discussions of Jewish wisdom, because Jewish wisdom, at least from the Exile on, is in general morally and theocentrically bound and defined. Still, in the international context, stories of cleverness must be distinguished from stories of wisdom. The former depict a protagonist who is clever enough to get what he or she wants, and the latter a protagonist who is wise and righteous enough to get what he or she deserves. Both of these ideals exist in Hebrew literature, represented, for example, by the Jacob ideal and the Joseph ideal respectively. The extreme example of the cleverness story is the "rogue tale," wherein the clever but essentially amoral protagonist flouts all convention in the zest for living well.[94] For our purposes here, it must be emphasized that cleverness is not a characteristic of the "wisdom court legend," which is, however, not to say that the protagonist is never clever. Rather, it is the morally and often theologically defined wisdom of the protagonist which is of central concern, and not his or her cleverness, *per se*. In many cases, the main characters can seem quite obtuse—for example, Joseph (at times) or Ahikar—but they succeed on account of their wisdom and righteousness.

The standard indexes of folktale types and motifs abound with categories of narratives about cleverness, but wisdom, *as defined here*, is less common. It must be kept in mind that most indexes of folk literature are to tales and not legends, and thus focus primarily on those narratives which are not so much bound by duty and morality. Folklore studies on legends emphasize instead the moral earnestness of the narratives. A rigid correlation between tales and cleverness on one hand, and legends and wisdom on the other, would be simplistic, but there is a common tendency for legends to focus on wisdom rather than cleverness. This is not always true, however, even in court legends. Several medieval Icelandic legends exist, for example, which relate the adventures of Icelandic heroes in the courts of Norway and Denmark. At first they appear to be quite similar to the Jewish legends, especially consid-

---

[94] The definitive description of Jacob as a rogue hero is by Gunkel, "Jacob," in idem *What Remains of the Old Testament and Other Essays* (London: Allen and Unwin, 1928) 151–86.

ering their ethnic perspective of a cultural hero in a foreign court.[95] However, it is the cleverness of the hero in his ability to outwit the high kings of Skandinavia which is emphasized, rather than a morally based wisdom.

The dispute between von Rad and Talmon on one hand and Crenshaw on the other over the wisdom content of the narratives can be settled on the basis of the genre analysis presented here. The similarity of genre between the Joseph story, Esther, and Daniel 1 – 6 on one hand and *Ahikar* and the various court legends in Herodotus and Persian literature on the other is inescapable—similar plots in similar settings, presenting similar themes, are presented in a similar way. We find that in the non-Jewish stories as well as the Jewish the protagonist is often referred to as wise, generally holds the position of a wise courtier, and generally succeeds on account of wisdom. But just as the Jewish legends often fail to communicate the content of the wisdom tradition, opting instead for the affirmation that the person marked as wise succeeds, so also the non-Jewish stories communicate wisdom ideals only indirectly, by making the same affirmation. Thus the Ionian sage Thales is credited in Herodotus 1.75 with devising a clever way for Croesus to ford the Halys River. His method is absurd, and is told with the whimsical air of a humorous anecdote. "Methods of river fording" cannot be considered the wisdom teaching of this story of a great Ionian sage. It functions instead to characterize the hero as wise and able, and he is triumphant on the basis of his "ingenious" plan. From the Ionian point of view, it is "our man" Thales who was so wise before Croesus, and it does not so much matter what sort of wisdom this judgment is based on. Von Rad and Talmon missed this aspect of narrative wisdom, and Crenshaw's criticism is blunted considerably when the stories are investigated in this light.

On the basis of the broad definition of wisdom court legend which I am here proposing, that is, a legend of a revered figure set in the royal court which has the wisdom of the protagonist as a principal motif, a large number of such legends can be isolated in ancient Near Eastern literature, which will be presented in Chapter 2. Many of these are very short, but still self-contained narratives. However, the focus of this thesis will be on the longer conflicts and contests, and especially on the conflicts. Legends in these two subgenres are in general longer than the other court legends, and depend on more involved plots. They reflect a more developed narrative art, or at least a more sustained interest in the use of narrative for edifying entertainment, and a more elaborated presentation of the problems of justice and moral steadfastness in a potentially hostile world. All court legends seem to have an

---

[95] Hermann Palsson, trans., *Hrafnkel's Saga and Other Stories* (Harmondsworth: Penguin, 1970) 94 – 120.

interest in character and in demonstrating the character of the protagonist, but the conflicts and contests go beyond a mere moment in the life of the wise hero or heroine, and dramatize in greater detail the consequences of actions in a moral universe. The role of God may be debated in the court legends, but the moral view that the deserving person will succeed underlies every conflict.

2

The Court Legend in Ancient Near Eastern, Hebrew, and Greek Literature

Court Legends in the East

Although the court legend enjoyed a long history in the ancient Near East, it is not attested in every national literature nor in every historical period. A complete reconstruction of the origins and development of this genre will probably remain beyond our grasp, but it is possible to gain some idea of its use in the ancient world. It should first be noted that every post-exilic Jewish court legend is set in the Persian court, or its predecessor, the Neo-Babylonian (Esther, Daniel cycle, 1 Esdras 3–4), and the non-Jewish *Story of Ahikar* is set in the Assyrian Empire. This indicates that the genre may have arisen in this environment, and an investigation of Persian and ancient Mesopotamian literature provides some corroborating evidence of this. First, it is generally assumed that the Assyrian setting of *Ahikar* is more than just a fictitious construct, although it might be dated to one of the successor kingdoms.[1] The historical figure of Ahikar is also known from older ancient Near Eastern records,[2] and so it is quite likely that the story enjoyed some currency early on as well. Erica Reiner finds in an Akkadian inscription a reference to

---

[1] See James M. Lindenberger, *The Aramaic Proverbs of Ahiqar* (Baltimore: Johns Hopkins University, 1983) 16–17; and idem, "Ahiqar," 105–17.

[2] Max Küchler, *Frühjüdische Weisheitstraditionen* (Göttingen: Vandenhoeck & Ruprecht, 1979) 319–413.

a wise courtier who is disgraced and then vindicated, which she likens to the Ahikar story.[3] Despite the uncertainty of the dating of *Ahikar*, it is of the utmost importance for our purposes, for it proves the existence of the genre at an early date in a non-Jewish context.

In Persian literature there is also a conflict tradition concerning Zoroaster in the court of his patron-king, Vishtaspa (Hystaspes), and considering the Persian settting of several of the Jewish court legends and those in Herodotus, this attestation becomes very intriguing. Zoroaster is condemned before Vishtaspa by jealous courtier-priests who follow the older Iranian religion, but is vindicated before the king after healing the king's prize horse. In variants of the legend, the jealous courtiers are "Chaldaeans" who plant incriminatng evidence in Zoroaster's room, and Zoroaster is aided by the king's consort Hutaosa (Atossa).[4] The tensions between the ruling religious order and the witness to the new, philosophically pure, monotheistic faith are quite similar to Daniel 1–6, where the opponents are also called "Chaldaeans." The difficulty in using these legends for comparison with the early Jewish legends is the late date of the Persian collections. All of the motifs mentioned here are from medieval works, even though they probably reflect much older traditions. This will have to be kept in mind, although the picture of the genre which emerges indicates that the genre could easily have been current in Persian tradition at a very early date.

It is also tantalizing to see the Persian court as the court par excellence for the entire tradition of court legends. It was at the same time centralized and worldwide, and the Zoroaster traditions may have been adapted by various ethnic groups for their own purposes. The role of the court in the popular imagination was no doubt inspired by the Persian court. Margaret Cool Root, in analyzing the Persepolis palace friezes notes that the Greek influences are only incidental, but the Persian view of the king and the court is the central factor in the artwork.[5] Unlike older representations in the ancient Near East, the ethnic identities of the subject peoples here are clear, although no Persians are present except the king. The mutual respect of people and king, and their interrelated functions in the stability and peace of the empire are visually emphasized.[6] But behind the apparent equality of all peoples there must

---

[3] Reiner, "The Etiological Myth of the 'Seven Sages,' " *Or* 30 (1961) 1–11.

[4] *Denkart* 5.2.9, 7.5.6 and *Zardusht Nameh*. See William Darrow, "The Legends of Zoroaster" (Ph.D dissertation, Harvard University, 1981) 398. The aid of the queen is typical of the palace intrigues of Ctesias and Xenophon, which will enter into the discussion of Esther in Chapter 4.

[5] Root, *The King and Kingship in Achaemenid Art: Essays on the Creation of an Iconography of Empire* (Acta Iranica 19; Leiden: Brill, 1979) 4–8.

[6] Ibid., 131–35.

have been a good deal of competition and friction between ethnic groups in an empire which supposedly allowed for "equality of access." In fact, the most important official positions were probably controlled by the ruling Persian families.[7] We must contrast the Persian ideology of a meritocratic court, expressed in the Persepolis friezes, and a reality of ethnic competition.

Court legends with some sapiential content, unrelated to the figure of Zoroaster, can also be found in *Shah Nameh*, or *Epic of the Kings*, by Firdowsi, although this medieval collection presents similar dating problems. In particular one may notice the use of "disguised parables," or the use of a fictitious scenario by a courtier to elicit a king's better judgment. At 29:1, for example, the wise counsellor Mazdak must convince the king to allow the distribution of food during a drought, and so he tells him of several cases involving hardheartedness toward the poor and afflicted. Since the king condemns the perpetrators of injustice in each case, Mazdak uses this as justification for opening up the granary, leaving the king powerless to prosecute him. Mazdak's wisdom and abilities are explicitly noted; he is "eloquent, learned, endowed with good reason and the desire for success." He is also associated with a movement to purify Zoroastrianism and to place it back on a moral course, especially in relation to the distribution of wealth. Although condemned by the redactor of *Shah Nameh*, in this section he is presented as a wise counsellor who holds steadfastly to a "pure religion," and is especially to be compared to Daniel.

Alexander Krappe has also culled parallels to *Ahikar* from Indian literature, subsuming them all to the motif of the "disgrace and rehabilitation of a minister."[8] This widespread motif can be found in European tradition as well,[9] but it is subtly different from the court conflict as reflected in the Jewish examples. In *Ahikar* and the examples cited by Krappe, the minister is reinstated to defend the kingdom from some external threat.[10] It is this heroic element which provides the climax of the action and the resolution of the problem of the minister's disgrace, since he is reinstated because he alone can save the kingdom. Although *Ahikar* is categorized by Antti Aarne and Stith Thompson as tale type 922A, "Falsely accused minister reinstates

---

[7] Pierre Briant, in a lecture at Harvard University, November 18, 1985.

[8] Krappe, "Ahiqar the Wise," 280–84. This motif is given the number P111 in Stith Thompson, *Motif-Index of Folk Literature* (6 vols.; Bloomington: Indiana University, 1932–36).

[9] See Woislav M. Petrovitch, *Hero Tales and Legends of the Serbians* (London: Harrap, 1914) 108–10; and Isabel Florence Hapgood, *Epic Songs of Russia* (New York: Scribner's, 1886) 269–73.

[10] Cf. in this regard the court legend at 2 Kings 5, where Elisha takes the role of protector of the kingdom, with a consciousness of the imposing position of Syria. The other Jewish court legends do not reflect this element of the external threat of a single nation.

himself by his cleverness,"[11] it can probably be more closely compared to type 981 (= motif J151.1), "Wisdom of hidden old man saves kingdom," at least in regard to this manner of resolving the minister's disgrace. Even the legend of Zoroaster, in which he is reinstated by healing the king's horse, seems to reflect this same dramatic element of the eleventh hour rescue of the kingdom.

In the Jewish court conflicts, however, the focus is subtly but significantly different. There is no external threat, and the king remains the supreme power in the moral universe, capricious as he may be. The protagonist is reinstated based on some proof of wisdom or innocence, not on an act of derring-do. The dramatic landscape is not so much action as justice and morality. The adventurous plots of Esther and Daniel 3 and 6 do not detract from the fact that the charges against the protagonists are not simply dropped for the sake of a rational expediency, as they are in *Ahikar* and Krappe's Indian parrallel, but they are refuted as calumnies against the righteousness of a person unjustly condemned. This element in *Ahikar* is greatly reduced in favor of expedient forgiveness; in the Daniel cycle and Esther there is a shift in focus from the battlefield and the international relations of *Ahikar* to the moral judgments of the king's court.

Also circulating at about the same time were the fragments of the romance of Ninus and Semiramis. There are very few narrative parallels to the court legends, but it is quite possible that the social function may have been similar. Ninus, the Assyrian, and Semiramis, the Babylonian are finally allowed to consummate their love in marriage in this typical romance, which union, according to Martin Braun, represents a triumph of self-affirmation for the ethnic groups who claimed descent from the Assyrians and Babylonians.[12] This thesis will not be concerned with romances, except where they may have developed out of court legends, but it is interesting to note that the same functions fulfilled by the legends under study here are filled also by other contemporary genres of popular literature.

Court Legends in Egyptian Literature

Egyptian literature available to us from the pre-Persian period does not contain any close parallels to the court legend, although some roughly similar motifs can be found. Royal autobiographical inscriptions deal with the court,

[11] *The Types of the Folk-Tale* (Folklore Fellows Communications 74; Helsinki: Suomalainen tiedeakatemia, 1928).

[12] Braun, *History and Romance in Graeco-Oriental Literature* (Oxford: Blackwell, 1938) 8–9.

but not with the courtier or any wisdom motifs. Autobiographies of courtiers exist, but they also lack wisdom motifs and the stock plot elements that can be found in Jewish examples. In this category are included *Story of Sinuhe*, *Autobiography of Weni*, and *Journey of Wenamun*. Several wisdom genres can be discerned in ancient Egypt, and the pervasive "instructions" genre often included a narrative component.[13] In *The Eloquent Peasant*, for instance, we find something approximating a court legend, in which a dispossessed peasant bemoans his position so eloquently before the governor that his property is reinstated, while the villain is punished. Yet the fact that the protagonist is not a courtier, but a peasant, and that his loud plaints are humorous, indicates that this is a broadside, satirical tale that was not to be taken as factual, as the court legends were. The hero is not a "real" paradigm of wisdom, even though the content of his wisdom is very respectable. It is indeed the ironic contrast of great wisdom emanating from a peasant's mouth which provides the story's appeal.

By the period of the Persian conquest of Egypt, however, a document comes to light which is similar to the court legends, and this should probably be attributed to Persian influence. In the *Instruction of Onkhsheshonq* the title character visits his friend Harsiese, who has become the Pharaoh's chief physician and counselor.[14] When Onkhsheshonq hears from Harsiese that the latter is involved in a plot against the Pharaoh, he condemns the plan as foolish, but does not inform against his friend. Another courtier, however, does, and Harsiese is executed, while Onkhsheshonq is thrown into prison, where he composes a set of proverbs for his son, mostly unrelated to the narrative. The relevance of this narrative to the study of court legends, and especially to Daniel, has been noted by John Collins and Jürgen-Christian Lebram,[15] but it is of even greater import for the study of Esther, on account of some similar nuances of plot. The conspiracy against the Pharaoh is overheard by the third character in just the same way that Mordecai overhears a plan to kill Ahasuerus, and in both stories a courtier is called into the king's chambers when the latter cannot sleep. Further, in both narratives this occurs at the beginning of the revelations which serve as the climax of the story.

It is also an interesting question whether the sayings in *Onkhsheshonq*

---

[13] Many of the "instruction" documents took on narrative endings, such as *Instruction of Any*, while both in and outside of Egypt several narrative documents contained an instruction section, e.g., *Onkhsheshonq*, *The Eloquent Peasant*, *Ahikar*, and Tobit (in two recensions). The evolution of Matthew and Luke from Mark and Q should perhaps also be seen in the light of this tradition.

[14] On the date of *Onkhsheshonq*, see Miriam Lichtheim, *Ancient Egyptian Literature* (3 vols.; Berkeley/Los Angeles/London: University of California, 1973–80) 3. 159.

[15] Collins, *The Apocalyptic Vision of the Book of Daniel* (HSM 16; Missoula: Scholars Press, 1977) 33; and Lebram, *Buch Daniel*, 10.

function to communicate directly the important content of wisdom, or whether they largely serve as a contrast to the protagonist's miserable position. Above, in the *Eloquent Peasant*, the same question was raised: is there a shift in focus from the content of the sayings themselves to an ironic contrasting of the sayings and the narrative situation? Why were the sayings not merely cast in the ubiquitous Egyptian genre of ''instructions,'' without any narrative component, if they were the primary focus? This question will arise again below in regard to *Ahikar*.[16] The question can be generalized to ''wisdom narratives'' as a whole: is wisdom communicated *directly* and *explicitly*, through the content of the sayings and through the paradigmatic actions of the characters, or is it communicated indirectly, by implication only? An attempt at resolving this issue will be made in Chapter 5.

Story of Ahikar

Although the skeleton of the court conflict genre can be clearly detected in the *Story of Ahikar*, it has been greatly expanded and developed by the addition of humor, pathos, irony, and adventure, creating a work of some depth and enormous popular appeal. The latter point is proven by the wide variety of languages and versions of the story; there are extant texts in Aramaic, Syriac, Armenian, Arabic, Church Slavonic, and in Greek, assimilated to the figure of Aesop.[17] The oldest of these, the Aramaic, was found at Elephantine and is dated to about 400 BCE. It appears to be the shortest and least developed version of the story, but the fragmentary nature of the text makes this judgment impossible to confirm. Analysis of *Ahikar* will here proceed with the later versions, and only then will comparisons back to the Aramaic version be made.

---

[16] In Tobit, there is an irony between Tobit's teaching that God rewards the good, and the narrative in which Tobit appears to be abandoned by God (although he is eventually rewarded). See Nickelsburg, *Jewish Literature*, 31.

[17] The association of Aesop with the Ahikar legend is an interesting tangent to this thesis, for contemporary with the proliferation of court legends was the migration of fables into Greece via the eastern colonies. The early poet Archilochus, e.g., uses fables that are attested in Babylonian sources at an earlier date. Some scholars maintain that fables, both in the Near Eastern and Greek worlds, have an antiestablishment, antiaristocratic edge: the brutal, exploitative, and arbitrary perspective of fables reveal a resigned but bitter view of the Assyrian or Babylonian—and later Athenian-ruled Ionian—social world. If so, fables and court legends are similar in that they are both popular wisdom genres that are used for social criticism, although court legends are not as bitter. Thus the fact that they come together in the figure of Aesop seems more than just coincidental. See Albin Lesky, *A History of Greek Literature* (New York: Crowell, 1966) 154–56; and Ben E. Perry, *Studies in the Text History of the Life and Fables of Aesop* (Haverford: American Philological Association, 1936) 15–19.

The general outline of the court conflict genre can still be easily detected in the later versions, except that at key points the values of that genre are apparently overturned, creating what amounts to a satire of institutional wisdom and the hero of that wisdom, the court sage. The existence of such an "antigenre," or a satire of a genre, should not be considered unusual. The Egyptian *Instructions of Any* concludes a father's typical instructions to his son with the son's cynical response to such instruction: "It is worthless."[18] Within early Israelite and Jewish tradition, the skepticism concerning human wisdom that occasionally arises may have this satirical or critical edge; for example, Deuteronomy 30, Ecclesiastes, Baruch 3–4, and Job, especially chapter 28, reflect a critical response to the received tradition of Jewish wisdom.[19] In later Jewish and early Christian tradition, the *Testament of Abraham* and *Epistula Apostolorum* might be categorized as an "antitestament" and "antirevelation discourse" respectively.[20] The Book of Revelation has also been described as an "antiapocalypse," though with some opposition.[21] To demonstrate my reasons for considering *Ahikar* an "anti-court legend" then, I will briefly recount the story, showing in what way this program is carried out.

The courtier Ahikar is childless, and after adopting his nephew Nadan, begins to instruct him in a long-winded, formulaic collection of his best proverbs, the stock-in-trade of the courtly sage. Nadan *immediately afterward* abuses his servants, just bestowed upon him by his doting uncle, and squanders his newfound wealth. Ahikar's best wisdom, which has been so pretentiously presented, has failed to have the slightest influence on Nadan. When Ahikar rebukes Nadan (3.3–5) and rescinds his adoption, Nadan plots revenge by forging two letters. The first, written in Ahikar's hand, calls on a certain general to meet him out on the plain to start a *coup d'état*. This letter Nadan shows to the king. The second is addressed to Ahikar in the king's

[18] See Lichtheim, *Egyptian Literature*, 2.135. The shift to a more middle-class audience which Lichtheim perceives in Any may be significant for the critique of traditional wisdom, and is paralleled in, e.g., Job. On *Any* see also McKane, *Proverbs*, 92–99; and on Job, Morton Smith, *Palestinian Parties and Politics That Shaped the Old Testament* (New York: Columbia University, 1971) 158–60.

[19] There are strong eddies of skepticism and critiques of traditional wisdom in Jewish tradition, in addition to Job and Ecclesiastes. See, e.g., Von Rad, *Wisdom*, 97–110.

[20] On the former see Nickelsburg, *Jewish Literature*, 149–52; and on the latter Helmut Koester, "One Jesus and Four Primitive Gospels," in idem and James M. Robinson, *Trajectories Through Early Christianity* (Philadelphia: Fortress, 1971) 201–4; and Julian Hills, *Sayings Traditions in the Epistula Apostolorum* (Minneapolis: Fortress, 1990).

[21] See Elisabeth Schüssler Fiorenza, "The Eschatology and Composition of the Apocalypse," *CBQ* 30 (1968) 537–69; but also see the criticism of this view by John J. Collins, "Pseudonymity, Historical Reviews and the Genre of the Apocalypse of John," *CBQ* 39 (1977) 329–43.

hand, ordering him to take a regiment out to the same plain and pretend to attack, in order to impress some fictitious visiting dignitaries (3.7 – 12). Ahikar is portrayed here as the Earl of Gloucester is in *King Lear*: his credulousness will cost him much. When the king sees Ahikar in battle formation, he returns to his palace, saddened that his privy counselor has conspired against him. Nadan rides up to Ahikar and reports that the king loved the exhibition.

Although Ahikar is not explicitly depicted as inflated with hybris, the long string of proverbs which he expounds to Nadan conveys the pretentions of his conservative school wisdom, just at the point where he is about to fall. Further, when brought up before the king on charges of sedition, he stands speechless; he searches for the right words but merely stammers (4.2). Now, this is *precisely* the place where the wise courtier is supposed to excel: in speaking boldly and wisely in the court of the king![22] The two most important goals of institutional wisdom, education and success at court, lie beyond Ahikar's abilities. His silence merely serves to confirm his guilt in the eyes of the king, and Nadan calls him "foolish" and denounces him. Ahikar is condemned to death.

It is at this point that the great humanity of the character is developed, which goes beyond the one-dimensional parody of the court sage. Ahikar tells his wife (who is called "wise"), to prepare a funeral party, at which all the guards get drunk and fall asleep. Then he addresses the executioner, speaking wisely and well, and with not a little cunning, reminding him of the time when he, Ahikar, had saved him from the gallows. Here Ahikar preaches a prudence of enlightened self-interest, in contrast to the pieties of the earlier proverbs: "When I saved you from an unjust death, the king later discovered your innocence and rewarded me. If you save me he will reward you too!" (4.9 paraphrased) The executioner is swayed by the reasoning, and proposes the pit beneath the floor as a good hiding place for his prisoner. He then returns to the king to report that he has killed Ahikar as ordered. When Nadan comes to take possession of his new estate, he beats the servants and tries to rape Ahikar's wife, all within Ahikar's hearing from his secret hiding place (4.15 – 17). The charged tension of this scene is well described in a fairly realistic style, lapsing neither into callousness on one hand nor sentimentality on the other.[23]

The Ahikar who emerges from this experience is a changed character,

---

[22] Cf. Pr 16:13, 22:11, Wis 1:1 (though the pseudepigraphic author is Solomon); and Ps 45:1.

[23] One might imagine that Herodotus or Josephus might have handled a similar scene in a way that would strike us as quite unfeeling, while in the romances it would have been given over to erotic and adventurous effects that might border on the pornographic. Susan Niditch (*Underdogs and Tricksters: A Prelude to Biblical Folklore* [San Francisco: Harper and Row, 1987] 103) points out that a stay in a well or a pit often indicates a transition in traditional narrative.

although it may be reading too much into the text to see a modern, psychological view of development. He is restored before the king, but only because the capricious king has had second thoughts. As in some other parallels to the court legends, his new role does not come about as a result of being exonerated or acquitted on the basis of evidence. His importance and trustworthiness are simply reassessed (5.2 – 10), and the king, in desperation, calls upon Ahikar to answer the challenges that have been issued by the Egyptian Pharaoh. Ahikar accepts his new commission, and armed with a different kind of wisdom based on cunning and supernatural abilities, he answers the Egyptian sages' riddles and conundrums (chap. 6).[24] Ahikar now speaks boldly to the Pharaoh (6.11, 25), and even uses the same trick that Nadan has used on him—forged letters—to trip up the Pharaoh! (7.1) Finally, after his triumph and return, Ahikar asks to be allowed to take Nadan into a locked room. There he addresses him with a new teaching (7.23), consisting not of proverbs, but of *parables* (chap. 8). Regardless of our form-critical categories, or of what these sayings are called in the various versions, they are clearly different from the earlier proverbs, and were perceived to be different by the audience of the work.[25] Their effect on Nadan is also different: he swells up and bursts.

To summarize my argument, then, in four important ways the *Story of Ahikar* satirizes the pretentions of institutional wisdom:

1) Nadan is not improved by Ahikar's proverbs, but on the contrary turns on him and plots his downfall;
2) Ahikar inadvertently cooperates in the plot against himself in a hopelessly innocent manner;
3) Ahikar is speechless and helpless in the court of the king; and

---

[24] The plotline of the "Egyptian Interlude" section can also be found as tale type 981 in Thompson, *Types.*

[25] Briefly, the difference between the proverbs of *Ahikar* and the parables is that the proverbs present generalized maxims of prudence, usually in the imperative, e.g., "My son, do not tell all that you hear, and do not disclose all that you see" (2:3). The parables are short narrative similes or allegories, which carry no exhortation, but describe powerfully how brutal Nadan has been, e.g., "My son, you have been to me as an ox that was bound with a lion; and the lion turned and crushed him" (8:11). Many of these parables may have originally been more generalized didactic narratives, altered to refer explicitly or implicitly to Nadan, but many appear as short fables, carrying the same bitter view of destructive relations that is often reflected in fables. In regard to the magical power of the parables, cf. Acts 5:5,10; and see Ernst Haenchen, *Acts of the Apostles* (Philadelphia: Westminster, 1971) 239 – 41. It is interesting, however, that divine punishment plays no explicit role in *Ahikar.* Note also that in the Aesop version, Aesop near the end teaches his nephew proverbs (chap. 26), whereupon his nephew is struck *with guilt* and dies several days later. This is an interesting rationalization of the magical element.

4) Ahikar at the end loses his sage-like composure and blasts Nadan, not with "proverbs" but with "parables," which are effective.

The satire in *Ahikar* seems to be aimed at demolishing one ideal of wisdom, the pompous court sage, and replacing it with another, the cunning hero. One might say that a Joseph ideal is replaced with a Jacob ideal.

This satirical interpretation of *Ahikar* is only possible in the later "baroque" versions of the story; in the oldest version, found at Elephantine, the proverbs section appears to be lacking from the beginning of the story, and there is no indication of the redactional motifs noted above. From the fragments it appears that the sayings section came at some other point in the story, perhaps, as in the Aesop version, in Nadan's punishment scene, that is, where the "parables" are in the later versions. It appears that the Elephantine version is a straightforward court conflict story, as is the case in the Aesop rendition. The development of the *Ahikar* narrative can be seen in two phases: a straightforward court conflict (Elephantine and Aesop versions), and a complex, satirical retelling (Syriac, Armenian and Arabic versions).

In regard to this a comparison of the sayings in the different versions is instructive. The Elephantine proverbs seem to contain sayings which would be quite general and universally applicable, both where they are found in the form of proverbs (e.g., "Bend not your bow and shoot not your arrow at the righteous, lest God come to his help and turn it back upon you," [126]), and also in the form of short fables (e.g., "The leopard met a goat who was cold and said, 'Come, and I will cover you with my hide.' The goat answered, 'What have you to do with me? Do not take my skin' " [119]). These could easily have been chosen for inclusion in the Elephantine *Ahikar* story[26] because of their applicability to Nadan, and indeed the proverb above has been turned into a simile explicitly regarding Nadan in the "parables" in the satirical versions (8:5 [8:10 Armenian]). Many of the Elephantine sayings, however, do not seem capable of any reference to Nadan, and thus these were part of a general body of wisdom teaching. This is even more true in the Aesop version, where there is no conceivable specific reference to Nadan's cruelty.

In short, the Elephantine and Aesop narratives are coupled with general wisdom teachings, and may indeed be little more than vehicles for the wisdom sayings, a phenomenon noted above. The satirical versions, on the other hand, maintain a strict division of general wisdom sayings ("proverbs") and short narrative allegories explicitly likened to Nadan's behavior ("par-

---

[26] According to Lindenberger (*Ahikar*, 17–20), the dialect of the proverbs is different from that of the narrative section. I follow his reconstructions for the proverbs.

ables"). The conscious alteration of Elephantine sayings to fit two separate categories in the satirical versions can be charted easily. This becomes strong evidence that the sayings themselves are not the main focus in the late versions, but rather the position and role of the sayings in the story is crucial. A subtler didactic purpose informs the composition of the satirical versions, that is, the satirizing of institutional wisdom.

In Chapter 1 of this thesis it was noted that scholars have generally fallen under the sway of a mistaken notion about the function of "wisdom narratives." The narratives often do not convey the content of wisdom teaching, nor do they directly depict the wise person as a paradigm to be imitated; instead the narratives show that the wise hero, characterized in a number of ways, succeeds. The hero is "marked" as wise, but the content of wisdom teaching is not generally presented in the narrative. The case is somewhat different where the narrative is a vehicle for quite general wisdom sayings, as in the Elephantine and Aesop versions, but even here it is not the narrative which enacts the content of wisdom. In the satirical versions, however, it is clear that the sayings do not convey the content of wisdom, but merely serve to characterize the hero at two separate points in his career, nor does Ahikar enact wise principles in the beginning of the story. The depiction of Ahikar in the second half is perhaps closer to a direct paradigm of a newfound and more servicable wisdom, but here also the magical ability and giddy nonchalance are too romantic to be directly didactic. Ahikar should not be imitated in his deeds—that would be impossible—but the man "marked" by this cunning sort of wisdom will succeed.

Court Legends in Early Hebrew Literature

In pre-exilic Hebrew literature we find a number of sapiential court legends, and these in general provide our oldest attestations. Using the broad definition of wisdom court legend as a legend of a revered figure set in the royal court which has the wisdom of the protagonist as one of its principal motifs, there can be isolated individual pericopes in the deuteronomistic history that qualify, but they are short and seem to be used merely as a means to some other end in the narrative. Further, it is not clear whether court legend motifs, used in longer narratives, should be considered in the same category with court legends which circulated independently or in cycles of such legends. For the moment, this question will be set aside until broader comparisons can be made. Three of the legends from the deuteronomistic history should be grouped together as "disguised parables." Nathan's "parable" of the poor man's ewe (2 Sam 12:1–14), the petition of the wise woman of Tekoa (2 Sam 14:1–17), and an unnamed prophet's chastisement of Ahab

(1 Kgs 20:39–43) all demonstrate how a wise person might criticize the king without endangering his or her life. The protagonist first concocts a fictitious scenario which, though the king does not realize it, is analogous to the king's own misconduct. When the scenario is reported to the king, it elicits his passionate judgment on the issue. The courtier then points out that the king's correct judgment applies most of all to himself, in the real case which is at hand.[27]

In the first of these (2 Sam 12:1–14), Nathan is sent by God to condemn David for killing Uriah, and does so by telling David a story of a rich man who cruelly deprives a poor man of his beloved lamb. David shouts that the man deserves to die, whereupon Nathan responds, "You are the Man!" In 2 Sam 14:1–17 Joab, wanting to reconcile David and Absalom, fetches a "wise woman" from Tekoa to accomplish this. She wails before David that one of her two sons has killed the other, and that her family wants to kill him, her only heir, as punishment. David swears by God that the guilty son will receive forgiveness, at which point the woman implores him to live by his own ruling and receive Absalom back. In the last example (1 Kgs 20:39–43), an unnamed prophet tells Ahab that he, the prophet, has lost a prisoner in his keeping. When Ahab demands the punishment of death, the prophet says that God so judges against Ahab for letting go *his* prisoner, Ben-hadad.

Interestingly, the disguised parable seems to be rather rare in world literature, although it is not unknown. Herodotus, for example, makes use of this kind of narrative. The first example, 1.27, will be of some importance below for other reasons as well. After Croesus has taken nearly all the cities of Asia Minor he begins to build ships to attack the Greek islanders. Bias of Priene, one of the venerated "Seven Sages" of Greek tradition, tells Croesus that the islanders are procuring horses to attack him on land. Croesus is overjoyed to hear that they would be foolish enough to challenge him at his own game. "Just so," says Bias, "you would be foolish to attack islanders with ships." Croesus is amused by Bias's manner and takes his advice, signing a treaty

---

[27] Uriel Simon ("The Poor Man's Ewe-Lamb. An Example of a Juridical Parable," *Bib* 48 [1967] 207–42) calls this type of narrative a "juridical parable" but does not adduce any non-Israelite parallels that are convincing. Burke O. Long (*Kings* [FOTL; Grand Rapids: Eerdmans, 1984] 252) follows Simon in this nomenclature. Joseph Blenkinsopp (*Wisdom*, 36) gives the best analysis of these three stories, calling them "parables." In the Thompson motif index there are a series of somewhat similar entries, J80–99 (Wisdom learned through parables), and also cf. J1530 (One absurdity rebukes another) and J1191 (*Reductio ad absurdum* of judgment). The examples given by Thompson seem to lack the realism of the disguised parables here, however, as do those discussed by D. M. Gunn, *The Story of King David: Genre and Interpretation* (JSOT Supp 6; Sheffield: JSOT, 1978) 40–43.

with the islanders. Just like the biblical examples, this one shows a wise subject influencing the king on a delicate issue by creating a fictitious scenario and thereby eliciting the king's better judgment. Other instances can be found in Herodotus 1.159 and 3.32. In the medieval Persian *Shah Nameh* (29.1) the same narrative structure is encountered (described above).

Finally, in Philostratus's *Life of Apollonius of Tyana* (6.34), this same type of legend is reflected, although Philostratus may have robbed the narrative of some of its appeal by changing a fictitious case which the king believes to be real, to a mere supposition. When Titus refuses to hear petitions of the citizens of Tarsus because he is busy making a ritual offering, Apollonius asks him whether he would interrupt his ministrations if traitors were discovered in the city. When Titus replies that he would immediately execute them, Apollonius responds that it is disgraceful to be immediate in meting out punishments, but dilatory in conferring benefits. The emperor (here still an heir apparent) is not merely swayed, but "overjoyed." In the other disguised parables we have seen, the wise person presents the king with a case which is supposedly real, demanding a real judgment, while here Apollonius merely presents Titus with a hypothetical case. It is possible that in Philostratus's desire to render Apollonius as a true philosopher, he has altered a court legend slightly by making the interchange between the characters more like a philosophical dialogue. This would be in keeping with the contemporary western presentation of the true philosopher, but in the process the typically eastern narrative loses some of its dramatic quality. The attestations which I have found are broadly distributed, but none, not even Philostratus's source, can be associated with the west; this is likely an ancient Near Eastern genre.

Solomon is also depicted as wise king in the deuteronomistic history by means of several legends which fall outside the conflict, contest and disguised parable categories. Though still formalized and anecdotal, these are less structured and less dramatic in tone than those forms previously described, and have much less narrative depth. They do not reflect the tense and dramatic situation of a wise courtier who must function in a potentially dangerous court environment under a potentially cruel and arbitrary king, but instead they depict the relaxed and secure situation of a benevolent ruler who, through his wisdom, can keep the kingdom on a prosperous and just course. In 1 Kings 3 Solomon determines which of two prostitutes is the real mother of a disputed baby by threatening to cut it in half, and in 1 Kings 10 he answers the riddles of the Queen of Sheba. Both stories have parallels in other bodies of literature, but here their function is indicated by the context, that is, in the royal propaganda section which begins at 1 Kings 3.[28] These

---

[28] For 1 Kings 3, see John Gray, *I and II Kings: A Commentary* (OTL; 2nd ed.; London:

narratives serve to dramatize Solomon's world famous wisdom, which in 1 Kings 4:29 – 34 is stated more explicitly in non-narrative form.

Two other possible wisdom court legends in the Hebrew Bible are so long and unwieldy, and have been steeped in such controversy, that a thorough investigation is out of the question here: the Joseph story (Genesis 37 – 50) and the Succession Narrative of David (2 Samuel 9 – 1 Kings 2).[29] In regard to the Succession Narrative, these problems are prohibitive, and the question of the influence of the court legend genre on this writing will have to be taken up elsewhere. Regarding the Joseph story, however, a brief comparison with other court legends is still helpful. First, it should be noted that Genesis 37 – 50 has already been linked to the court legend genre. The major writers on court legends all note certain obvious similarities: a wise and righteous young Jew is persecuted and suffers not one but two falls, one at the hands of his brothers when they sell him into slavery, and another when Potiphar's wife falsely accuses him of sexually assaulting her. He manages, however, to rise to the level of prime minister in the court of the Pharaoh, and to be reinstated in the eyes of his family. The overall "U" pattern of fall and vindication found in the conflict legend is here complicated by a longer and more episodic narrative. Instead of one fall and vindication pattern we now find two:

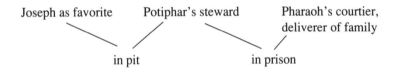

Joseph as favorite   Potiphar's steward   Pharaoh's courtier,
                                                    deliverer of family

            in pit   in prison

SCM, 1970) 120 – 22; and for 1 Kings 10, cf. *Ahikar* 6, where Ahikar solves the Egyptians' conundrums. Note the folk motif mentioned above of the hidden old man who saves the kingdom through wisdom, and cf. the *Shah Nameh* example quoted above and 2 Kings 5. Although in 1 Kings 10 Israel is not under external threat, there is the similarity of reponding to the external ruler's puzzles. The royal propaganda section which begins in 1 Kings 3 is associated with Solomon's dream revelation and gift of wisdom. The motif of the king's dream revelation at an important juncture in history has generally been compared with Egyptian parallels (Gray, *Kings*, 120 – 22), although C. L. Seow ("The Syro-Palestinian Context of Solomon's Dream" *HTR* 77 [1984] 141 – 52) stresses the Mesopotamian and Semitic parallels. See also Leonidas Kalugila, *The Wise King: Studies in Royal Wisdom as Divine Revelation in the Old Testament and Its Environment* (Lund: Gleerup, 1980).

[29] On the Joseph story see von Rad, "Joseph," 292 – 300; and on the Succession Narrative see R. N. Whybray, *The Succession Narrative* (Napierville, IL: Alenson, 1968). That either of these narratives should be classified as sapiential is sharply contested by James Crenshaw, "Method in Determining Wisdom Influence upon 'Historical Literature,'" *JBL* 88 (1969) 129 – 42.

In addition to the complication of having two episodes of fall and rise, there is the further problem of lack of moral balance in the injustice of the brothers' treatment of Joseph and the accusations of Potiphar's wife, since they are never punished and Joseph is never vindicated before Potiphar.[30] It is also unlike the court legend genre to begin the story with the persecution of the hero by shepherds; we expect courtiers, or at least palace guards. This latter problem with the genre analysis cannot be overcome, except to say that the story is now part of the patriarchal history of the foundation of Israel, and that this demands a nomadic setting for the first part of the story. Some of the problems, however, can be eliminated, and this process becomes very important for the comparative study of the court legends. One might suspect, by looking at the chart above, that a simpler story of fall and vindication had been expanded by the insertion of the episode with Potiphar's wife, and this appears to be the case. Despite the great difficulties in analyzing Genesis 37 – 50 into J, E, and P sources, most scholars agree that the entire episode with Potiphar and his wife is found in one source only.[31] The other source, usually ascribed to E, connects quite smoothly from 37:36 to 40:2 (deleting also the references to Joseph as prisoner):

> The Midianites sold (Joseph) in Egypt to Potiphar, an officer of Pharaoh, a captain of the guard. . . . And Pharaoh was angry with his two officers, the chief butler and the chief baker, and he put them in custody in the house of the captain of the guard . . . (who) charged Joseph with them.

In this version Potiphar is simply the captain of the guard with no significant role, but in the version usually ascribed to J an entire adventure involving Potiphar's wife is included, and a different captain of the guard is meant at 40:3. The simpler "E" version conforms much more closely to the court conflict pattern:

---

[30] Neither the multiple episodes nor the lack of moral balance is given sufficient attention in the genre analysis of the Joseph story. On the lack of a moral balance in the Joseph story, cf. Alberto Soggins (*Introduction to the Old Testament* [London: SCM, 1976] 53) who uses this fact, along with the humble origins of Joseph, as evidence that the story should be considered a fairy tale.

[31] Von Rad, *Genesis*, 363 – 64; E. A. Speiser, *Genesis* (AB; Garden City: New York: Doubleday, 1964) 303; Samuel R. Driver, *The Book of Genesis* (Westminster Commentaries; London: Methuen, 1904) 332 – 33; Martin Noth, *A History of the Pentateuchal Traditions* (Englewood Cliffs, New Jersey: Prentice-Hall, 1972) 26, 266; and Gunkel, *Genesis* (HAT; 4th ed.; Göttingen: Vandenhoeck & Ruprecht, 1917) 396. Donald B. Redford (*A Study of the Biblical Story of Joseph (Genesis 37 – 50)* [VTSup 20; Leiden: Brill, 1970] 251 – 53) argues that there are not two separate tellings of the story, but that the "Reuben" version, normally attributed to E, is the original story, while the "Judah" segments, normally attributed to a separate version by J, are actually expansions of the original Reuben text.

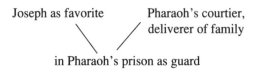

Joseph as favorite   Pharaoh's courtier,
                          deliverer of family

in Pharaoh's prison as guard

It is thus quite possible that a much more typical court legend circulated concerning Joseph, which is the so-called E version. Interestingly, it is precisely this simpler version of the Joseph story which Artapanus relates, writing about the second century BCE, without any mention of the Potiphar episode.[32] This tendency toward the expansion of court legends can be noted in Esther, *Ahikar*, Daniel, and the LXX additions to Daniel, and it may indicate the natural growth of legends into episodic romances, or at least "proto-romances," that is, longer prose narratives which grow by the accretion of the common romance motifs of adventure, dangers, women characters, travel, eroticism, and so on.[33]

Many scholars would balk at comparing the Joseph story with post-exilic court legends, simply because it is usually dated in about the eighth to tenth centuries BCE, much earlier than the others. However, there is some disagreement over the dating of this legend. Donald Redford, for example, argues for an exilic dating for this story,[34] and while not many scholars would follow him in this matter, there is no alternative which does meet with general agreement. The former consensus was based on the assumption that the story could be divided into J and E strands, which were most likely edited together in about the eighth century BCE. This furnished a terminus ad quem

---

[32] Quoted in Eusebius *Praep. ev.* 4.29b–30b. It is interesting to note how Artapanus and *Testament of Joseph* differ in relating this story: they split it between them precisely where I have hypothetically suggested the story should be split. Artapanus, ignoring completely the interlude at the Potiphars' house, tells how Joseph is betrayed by his brohers, escapes, and rises to fame in the court of Pharaoh, while the author of *Testament of Joseph* focuses solely on Joseph's resistance to the Egyptian woman's seductions, omitting almost every reference to the main plot.

[33] Gunkel (*Genesis*, liii-lv) explained the expansion of some Pentateuchal sagas as a growing novelistic tendency in pre-exilic times, which is reflected in Genesis 14, 20, 24, 32–33, and culminates in the Joseph story. W. Lee Humphreys ("Novella," in George W. Coats, ed., *Saga, Legend, Tale, Novella, Fable: Narrative Forms in Old Testament Literature* [JSOT Supp 35; Sheffield: JSOT, 1985] 93) would deny, however, that sagas are in general the kernel of later novelistic writings. I would agree, in that the Joseph story derives from a court legend, not a saga. The famous assertion of Ben Edward Perry (*The Ancient Romance* [Berkeley: University of California, 1967] 12–19) that Greek romances began as the creative act of one lone writer, and did not "evolve" on a biological model, may be applicable to the body of fully developed Greek romances, but I do not think that it accounts for the smaller pieces of somewhat similar—and earlier—Jewish literature. See also Martin Braun, *History and Romance in Graeco-Oriental Literature* (Oxford: Blackwell, 1938).

[34] Redford, *Joseph*, passim, but esp. 32–33, 65, 251–53.

for the writing, but the consensus eroded when it was realized that it is difficult to separate the two strands with certainty, or more important, to attribute them to J and E.[35] Here the Joseph story must be compared to other court legends without resolving the question of date.

Herodotus and Greek Sources

Herodotus in his *Histories* displays a wide knowledge of traditions which in many cases appear to be influenced by the court legend genre. It is especially interesting to note that most, if not all, of this sort of material derives from those sections of his work which deal with Asia Minor and Persia, and none from the Egyptian or western Greek sections. This corroborates the evidence above that the genre had little currency outside of Asia Minor and Persia. This fact is also important for making distinctions within Greek literature. It is necessary to distinguish the western Greek traditions and the eastern Greek traditions, mostly Ionian, which emanate from Asia Minor and the eastern Aegean islands. Western Greek literature contains almost nothing of interest in the way of court legends, and indeed very little in regard to popular sapiential traditions of a wise man in general. It appears that the western amphictyony, lacking a centralized and all-powerful court, produced no court legends. The rise of rhetoric in the fifth century and the descriptions of public deliberations in, for example, Herodotus's accounts of the mainland Greeks' defeat of Xerxes, should perhaps be considered the western equivalent. This is not the case, however, in the eastern environment, where we find a rich tradition of court legends in Herodotus's narratives of eastern history, in Xenophon's *Cyropaedeia*, and in the Aesop traditions.

Though the existence of legendary materials in Herodotus's *Histories* has long been recognized, these have never been isolated with precision or confidence, especially as regards their formal characteristics. Wolf Aly produced a famous study of the folk parallels in Herodotus, Karl Reinhardt spoke in somewhat general terms of the *Persergeschichten* which Herodotus used, and J. A. K. Thomson attempted to compare Herodotus's versions of

---

[35] The former consensus is found in the commentaries listed in n. 31 above. George W. Coats (*From Canaan to Egypt: Structure and Theological Context for the Joseph Story* [CBQMS 4; Washington, D.C.: Catholic Biblical Association of America, 1976] passim) denies a source division for the Joseph narrative, as does Redford, *Joseph*. Recently Frank Moore Cross (''The Epic Traditions of Early Israel: Epic Narrative and the Reconstruction of Early Israelite Institutions,'' in Richard Elliott Friedman, ed. *The Poet and the Historian* [Chico: Scholars Press, 1983] 13–39) has expressed skepticism about the possibility of a neat source division of the Joseph story, the attribution to J and E, or about the dating of any part of it.

legends with other ancient sources.[36] Arnaldo Momigliano has also compared Jewish historiography with Herodotus.[37] These studies, however, have only resulted in general comparisons between these literatures, and it is perhaps possible to be more precise.

This difficulty in differentiating Herodotus's sources and his own editorial work has led many to focus on the structure of the *Histories* as a whole, in order to determine the author's method. Certain recent studies have increased the appreciation for Herodotus's own literary ability in reshaping the sources. Among these the works of Henry Immerwahr, Richmond Lattimore, and Robert Drews deserve special attention.[38] The redaction criticism of Herodotus is certainly a valid approach, and the conclusions of these studies should not be minimized, but a strong redactional hand does not necessarily mean that sources are obliterated in the process of collection and editing. The analogy of the interplay of form and redaction criticism in the study of the gospels is very appropriate here. As a result, the conclusions of

---

[36] Aly, *Volksmärchen, Sage, und Novelle bei Herodot und seinen Zeitgenossen* (Göttingen: Vandenhoeck & Ruprecht, 1921); Reinhardt, "Herodots Persergeschichten," in Walter Marg, ed., *Herodot: Eine Auswahl aus der neueren Forschung* (München: Beck, 1965) 320–69 (also in Reinhardt, *Vermächtnis der Antike* [Göttingen: Vandenhoeck & Ruprecht, 1960]; and Thomson, *The Art of the Logos* (London: George Allen and Unwin, 1935). Thompson, (*Folktale*, passim) also notes some of the more important folk traditions in Herodotus. Reinhardt's attempt to distinguish Persian and Greek sources has occasioned some criticism, e.g., Walter Burkert, Review of *Vermächtnis* in *Gymnasium* 67 (1960) 549; Richard Harder, "Herodot 1, 8, 3," in Marg, ed., *Herodot*, 374; and Hartmut Erbse, "Tradition und Form im Werke Herodots," *Gymnasium* 68 (1961) 253–57. Reservations regarding Aly's conclusions on identification of eastern sources are also expressed by Ludwig Huber in the afterword (p. 321) to the second edition of Aly, *Volksmärchen*.

[37] Momigliano, "Fattori orientali della storiografia ebraica post-esilica e della storiografia greca," *Rivista storica italiana* 77 (1965) 456–64.

[38] Immerwahr, *Form and Thought in Herodotus* (Cleveland : Case Western Reserve University, 1966); Lattimore, "The Wise Adviser in Herodotus," *CP* 34 (1939) 24–35; and Drews, *The Greek Accounts of Eastern History* (Cambridge: Harvard University Press, 1973). Other notable recent studies are Hans-Peter Stahl, "Learning Through Suffering? Croesus' Conversations in the History of Herodotus," *YCS* 24 (1975) 1–36; Erbse, "Tradition"; Fritz Hellmann, *Herodots Kroisos-logos* (Berlin: Wiedmann, 1934); and Stewart Flory, *The Archaic Smile of Herodotus* (Detroit: Wayne State University, 1987). John Van Seters (*In Search of History* [New Haven/London: Yale University, 1983] 45–46), in his comparison of Hebrew and Greek historiography, also follows in general the redactional approach to Herodotus. Herodotus is certainly capable of subsuming eastern stories of courtiers under his own rubric of the wise adviser. Cf., e.g., the role of the courtier Artabanus in advising Darius and Xerxes at 4.83, 144, 7.10–52. Herodotus has reshaped the last of these into a "tragic" *logos* of Xerxes' fall. Interestingly, this is the only place in Herodotus that I have found where a prophecy, oracle, or dream (Artabanus's dream of Xerxes' success) proves to be wrong. Croesus's misunderstanding of the Delphic oracle shows, however, a similarity between the two *logoi* attributable to Herodotus.

the redaction-critical studies of Herodotus should be kept in mind when one investigates the question of sources, but they should not be considered proof against the existence of recoverable sources, nor did these scholars likely intend such a judgment.

In addition to the larger folk tales that have been noted by previous scholars, such as the rogue tale of the temple robbers (Herodotus 2.121), the legend of Arion saved from drowning and carried to Athens by a dolphin (1.24), and the death of Croesus's son Atys (1.34–45), we should recognize that many of the smaller bits of "historical" tradition are probably also derived from widely circulating popular stories, and should be analyzed as such. It is unfortunate that discussion of eastern sources in Herodotus has hinged on a few of the larger *logoi* only, often with the conclusion that they are "Herodotean" after all. A. T. Olmstead could argue confidently that the story of Gyges' founding of the Mermnad dynasty through treachery (1.8–14) was definitely eastern in origin, as was the tragic story of the death of Croesus's son Atys, but Hartmut Erbse and Richard Harder have pointed out a thoroughgoing western redaction in the Gyges story.[39] Olmstead could equally argue that the story of the temple robbers derived from an Egyptian source, but Walter Burkert associates the narrative with a Greek cult legend.[40] The Magophonia, or the revenge on the Magi by the Persians after one of their number impersonates the king (Herodotus 3.61–79), was considered eastern by Momigliano and Gunkel, based on its close parallels to Esther, but Alexander Demandt has shown that a central motif, the concealment of the pretender's missing earlobe under the royal headdress, is only possible in the western context, since only there are Persian kings depicted with their ears covered.[41] The debate over the "easternness" of the sources has thus been limited in general to individual motifs in these favorite *logoi*, with only slight attention to recurring narrative patterns and questions of genre.

In fact, a number of story types are repeated often in Herodotus, giving the impression that within this work alone one could reconstruct several genres

[39] Olmstead, *The History of the Persian Empire* (Chicago: University of Chicago Press, 1948) 321–22; Erbse, "Tradition," 256; and Harder, "Herodot," 374.

[40] Olmstead, *History*, 322; and Burkert, Review of Reinhardt, *Vermächtnis*, 549.

[41] Momigliano, "Fattori," 457; Gunkel, *Esther* (Tübingen: Mohr, 1916) 115; and Demandt, "Die Ohren des falschen Smerdis," *Iranica Antiqua* 9 (1972) 94–101. Momigliano (*Alien Wisdom: The Limits of Hellenization* [Cambridge: Cambridge University, 1975] 131) admits the correctness of Demandt's conclusions, but the circulation of these traditions in Asia Minor—not in the East or the West—may be the most important factor to consider. The "missing ears," or some similar identifying characteristic, recur often in folklore; cf. Thompson's motif numbers F511.2.4, D702.1, D712.1.

of oral legends, both eastern and western. We note, for instance, that on
several occasions people are invited to a banquet, only to be slaughtered at
some prearranged point in the evening's entertainment (e.g., 2.100, 107, 111,
5.18 – 20). One wonders why anyone in the ancient Near East would accept
a dinner invitation! It must be assumed that this was a common story type
that circulated in a culture which, ironically, valued hospitality.[42] Herodotus,
of course, seems to accept these as historical accounts. Another common
motif could be tentatively called the "strategem," with its subcategory, the
"communication strategem," which glorify the quick-witted strategems of
people at court, in the context of international diplomacy or in warfare. One
such strategem (4.146) concerns the Minyae, who are imprisoned by the
Spartans for threatening to usurp too much power in the city government.
Awaiting execution, they send for their wives, who exchange clothes with
them once inside the prison. The men then leave the jail undetected and
escape. This same type of story can be found at 1.21 – 2, 3.4, 4.1 – 4, and
95.[43] The communication strategem, which specifically involves the clever
ways which various people devise to pass secret messages to each other, can
be found several times as well.[44] In addition, there are also in Herodotus
many pronouncement stories or anecdotes—short narratives culminating in
pithy sayings[45]—and in one case it is also indicated that these stories were
collected and valued. At 7.226 it is said that Dieneces was the most valiant
of the Spartans and Thespians who fought at Thermopylae, because when he
was told that the Persians would fill the sky so full of arrows that the sun
would be hidden, he replied, "Wonderful! We will have our fight in the
shade!" Herodotus then adds, "(Dieneces) is said to have left on record
other sayings, too, of a similar kind, by which he will be remembered."

This somewhat random selection of popular motifs from Herodotus

[42] Jack Martin Balcer (*Sparda by the Bitter Sea: Imperial Interaction in Western Anatolia* [BJS 52; Chico: Scholars Press, 1984] 433) associates these with Thompson's motif number K811.1.

[43] There existed an ancient genre of strategem stories, an example of ὑπομνήματα. Polyaenus published a large collection of military and diplomatic strategems for the education of the Antonine emperors in the second century CE, and Plutarch's *Sayings of Kings and Emperors*, dedicated to Trajan, belongs to the same genre. Strategems, which are amusing stories of quick-wittedness, are to be differentiated from Herodotus's much longer accounts of military engagements and the delliberations involved with them. In the latter, Herodotus is probably tapping peculiarly western genres of historiography and rhetoric.

[44] For example, Histiaeus once shaves a slave's head, pricks a message on his scalp with a needle, and then waits for his hair to grow back before sending him to an ally (5.35). Other such communication stratagems are at 7.239 and 8.128.

[45] Reinhardt, "Persergeschichten," 326. He sees the anecdote as a peculiarly Greek form, not eastern. Within the limits of this thesis, that question will have to be put aside.

merely illustrates that he in large part catalogued popular traditions—whether eastern or western—regardless of how much he may have judged between them or redacted them in the process of composing his *Histories*.[46] On the face of it there is no way to tell whether a particular story type arises mainly in the East or the West, but in some cases a comparison with other bodies of literature reveals a predominance of a certain narrative structure and group of motifs in one region or the other. This is certainly the case with the legendary materials under study here, the wisdom court legends. Some of those attested in Herodotus fall into categories we have already seen reflected in literature of the ancient Near East, but the main characteristics of this genre, a central, all-important court and a revered wise courtier, are lacking in the western Greek sources.

We should begin by analyzing the court legends in Herodotus by focusing on the protagonists in the stories. Greek advisers to the eastern monarchs figure prominently in Herodotus's narrative. The experience of the Ionian colonists in Asia Minor proved to be similar in some respects to the Jewish experience under the Persains. Although the Ionian and other Greek colonies kept up constant contact with the Greek homeland, their political existence was determined by their place in eastern kingdoms, first the Lydian and then the Persian. The Ionians were thus an ethnic minority in Asia Minor, and their "diaspora" consciousness is reflected in many of the legends in Herodotus. According to Lionel Pearson, the Ionians turned their attentions more to the Persians than to the mainland Greeks.[47] The Ionian historians, and especially Herodotus, had a thirst for eastern lore and ethnographic and historical traditions, and Herodotus went so fas as to describe Persia from the *Persian* point of view. At the same time that there is a strong ethnographic interest, there is little interest in Persian religion, and a cynical attitude toward the gods pervades the work, which is quite different from the Athenian piety.

The Ionian perspective can especially be seen in legends that I will group together as an "Ionian court legend" cycle. We find three figures from the Seven Sages of Greek tradition (Solon, Thales, and Bias) who are wise counselors in the court of Croesus. Thus, although Solon is not an Ionian hero as such but an Athenian one, he has been enlisted—inaccurately—as a representative Greek wise man to instruct Croesus on happiness (1.29–33).[48] Thales

---

[46] Cf., e.g., Stewart Flory (*Archaic Smile*, 16): "Herodotus stands alone midway between the two cultures, oral and written: his book was definitely composed and written for readers, but its substance and its approach are largely oral."

[47] Pearson, *Early Ionian Historians* (Oxford: Clarendon, 1939) 19–20, 76–77, 118.

[48] The story of Solon in the court of Croesus (Herodotus 1.29–33) shares motifs with other court legends, especially an Indian example quoted by Krappe ("Ahikar the Wise," 283) as a parallel to *Ahikar*. The historical difficulties of placing Solon in Croesus's court have long been

is mentioned at 1.75 in what Herodotus calls a "common Greek story," as
the author of an ingenious plan to divert the Halys River into two channels to
allow Croesus's troops to cross. Bias of Priene appears at 1.27 in the "disguised parable" I described above. There he wisely leads Croesus to the
conclusion that it would be foolish for a cavalry general to attack the Greek
islands.[49]

In all three cases the narratives have a formalized nature that more likely
arises from popular tradition than from sound historical sources Herodotus
may have had. Although there is no hard evidence that the three legends
were composed by Ionians, they clearly have a propaganda value for this
group in asserting their ethnic identity vis-a-vis the Lydian rulers. This use
of the court legend—to depict the wise exploits of a revered cultural hero in
the ruling court—is identical to the use put to the genre in the Jewish examples. What sort of ethnic consciousness might have given rise to these court
legends? The great Ionian achievements in nearly every field of intellectual
endeavor during the late seventh and early sixth centuries must have given
this conquered people a distinct sense of intellectual superiority over the
Lydians who came to rule them by 550 BCE. Evidence suggests that the
Ionians looked upon Croesus with some ambivalence as a benign but self-
indulgent dictator.[50] Indeed we find this air of intellectual superiority combined with a grudging obedience to an acceptable emperor as a parallel to
most of the Jewish court legends.[51] Under Persian rule, however, the grudg-

---

recognized by scholars, but the evolution of the story in popular tradition has not, to my
knowledge, been thoroughly investigated. The motif of the wise adviser in Herodotus has been
noted by Lattimore ("Wise Adviser"), and John Van Seters (*In Search*, 46) assumes that because
Herodotus utilizes it often to structure various sections of his work, it could not in general be
derived from older traditions. I believe, however, that the motif is traditional and has also
become part of Herodotus's redaction in his choosing, ordering, and editing of legends.

[49] Other disguised parables can be found at 1.159 and 3.32.

[50] The Ionian views of the Lydian and Persian empires differed greatly. In general the Greeks
were disdainful of the Lydians' luxurious way of life, but were not particularly negative, nor did
they view Croesus as a tyrant. See William E. Mierse, "The Persian Period," in George M. A.
Hanfmann, ed., *Sardis from Prehistoric to Roman Times: Results of the Archeological Explora-
tion of Sardis 1958–1975* (Cambridge/London: Harvard Univesity Press, 1983) 103; John
Griffiths Pedley, *Sardis in the Age of Croesus* (Norman, OK: University of Oklahoma, 1968)
134; and J. M. Cook, *The Greeks in Ionia and the East* (London: Thames and Hudson, 1962) 98.
Croesus was in fact a popular figure in western Greek art; for instance, he was the only personage
from contemporary history to be depicted on vase paintings, and was famous for his gifts of gold
to Delphi. Herodotus's anti-Ionian bias is a good example of his redactional role in composing
his history, yet it does not obscure pro-Ionian sources at some points, where they can be
identified by popular formal characteristics.

[51] Even Daniel 1–6 is not consistently negative regarding Nebuchadnezzar. The author or
redactor is for the most part not interested in Nebuchadnezzar's role in the fall of Judah.

ing obedience of the Ionians was put aside during the Ionian Revolt of 499 BCE. It is perhaps significant, then, that we have no Ionian court legends from the early Persian period, though by Xenophon's time this situation had changed. The genre is evidently not very incendiary, and was only appropriate to the less oppressive situation under the Lydians. The Ionian Revolt reflected an anti-Persian and pan-Hellenic spirit, although the motives of the rebels, or even the outline of the events, is unclear.[52]

If we turn to those court legends concerning Croesus, however, we find that these bear the closest resemblance to the Jewish legends, and may have been derived from a cycle or cycles of court legends. Although the Croesus stories fall into different categories, a pattern emerges which allows a fairly certain reconstruction of their use. They must be considered from several perspectives, depending upon how Herodotus used them. Most of the Croesus material has been unified and redacted by Herodotus into the so-called Croesus *logos* of book one, outlining the rise of this eastern monarch and his fall as a result of *hybris*.[53] The stories of Croesus lying within this *logos* reflect Herodotus's redactional stamp much more than those outside it, so much so that we should consider them separately. At the same time, stories from the period of Croesus's kingship seem quite different from those depicting his role *after* his fall, when he becomes a wise adviser to the Persian kings Cyrus and Cambyses. We can thus divide the Croesus stories into a quadrant of four groups using two different criteria of division—within/outside the *logos*, and before/after Croesus's fall from kingship:

	Before fall	After fall
Within *logos*	A	B
Outside *logos*	C	D

Category A (before fall, in *logos*) includes:

1) Introduction of Croesus (1.6);
2) Croesus attacks Ephesus (1.26);

---

[52] Hermann Bengtson ("The Ionian Rebellion and the Persian Wars to the Battle of Marathon," in idem, ed., *The Greeks and the Persians From the Sixth to the Fourth Centuries* [New York: Delacorte, 1968] 38–44) and John V. A. Fine (*The Ancient Greeks: A Critical History* [Cambridge: Harvard University, 1983] 269–76) give brief descriptions of the Ionian Revolt. The latter attributes the rebellion to antityrant motives, and notes the Ionian union of cities as possible evidence of a pan-Hellenic spirit in western Asia Minor.

[53] See Immerwahr, *Form*, 81–88; and Hellmann, *Kroisos-logos*, passim. Herodotus's perspective on Croesus in the *logos* is much more tragic than in the Croesus references outside the *logos*. By "tragic" is meant the depiction of the rise and fall of a great figure as a result of *hybris* and competition with the gods. Hengel (*Judaism and Hellenism*, 2. 75, n. 29) also posits the existence of a Croesus cycle which arose in Asia Minor or Persia.

3) Croesus and Bias's "disguised parable" (1.27);
4) Summary of Croesus's conquest (1.28);
5) Croesus and Solon of Athens (1.29–33);
6) Death of Croesus's son Atys (1.34–35);
7) Croesus loses Lydia (1.46–85); and
8) Croesus advised wisely by Lydian Sandanis (1.71).

Category B (after fall, in *logos*) includes:

1) Croesus remembers Solon's words (1.86);
2) Croesus saved from fire by Apollo (1.87);
3) Croesus talks with Cyrus, speaks wisely (1.87–88);
4) Croesus advises Cyrus wisely re: spoils (1.89–90); and
5) Croesus questions oracle at Delphi (1.90–92).

Category C (before fall, outside of *logos*) includes:

1) Croesus's powerful and effective threat to Lampsacus (6.37); and
2) Croesus grants gold to quick-witted Alcmaeon (6.125).

Category D (after fall, outside of *logos*) includes:

1) Croesus advises Cyrus re: subduing Lydia (1.1555–56);
2) Croesus advises Cyrus re: Massagetae (1.206–11);
3) Croesus weeps over Psammenitus (3.14);
4) Croesus compliments Cambyses wisely (3.34); and
5) Croesus criticizes Cambyses' excess, is condemned to death, but is hidden
   by executioner and is later reinstated (parallel *Ahikar*) (3.35–36).

Categories A and B belong to the *logos* and reflect more of Herodotus's redactional hand in unifying them into one "tragic" story of Croesus than do categories C and D. The introduction, summary of conquest, and account of Croesus's loss of Lydia (segments A-1, 4, and 7) were probably for the most part composed by Herodotus, and especially in the latter case contain a good deal of western material. They provide the skeleton for the rise and fall motif. However, contained within the long summary of Croesus's loss of Lydia we find a story of Croesus receiving wise counsel from the Lydian Sandanis. This story seems identical in intent to the stories described above of wise Greeks advising Croesus: the king receives good advice from a cultural hero, but this time a hero of his own people. Herodotus states that Sandanis "was already known for his good sense, and by the opinion he then expressed greatly increased his reputation among the Lydians." Just as above in the case of Dieneces, where Herodotus indicates that his wise sayings were well known, here also the impression is given that such court legends about Sandanis were common, and that Herodotus probably learned them from native Lydians. This will be important below as evidence that Lydians were among those who transmitted court legends.

The two short narratives of Croesus's attack on Ephesus (A-2) and conversation with Bias regarding the islanders (A-3) likely arise from Ionian traditions of western Asia Minor where the stories are set. The latter is likely an etiological legend explaining why Croesus formed a treaty with the islanders. The former story is left unresolved in Herodotus, and its intent and conslusion are unclear, although in Polyaenus *Strategems* 6.50 it is told as an etiological legend explaining how Croesus was persuaded to make an agreement with Ephesus. Herodotus likely knew two etiological treaty legends from his home area of western Asia Minor, one of which (A-2) loses its original point when incorporated into the *Histories*.

The story of Solon's disquisition on happiness in the court of Croesus (A-5) has received considerable attention in the secondary literature,[54] but its closest parallel can be found in the Persian court legend of Buzurdjmihr in *Shah Nameh* (31:3).[55] There the wise counselor is falsely accused of stealing the king's prize jewels, but from his prison cell he sends word to the king three times in succession that, although he is being cruelly punished, his state is happier than that of the king. The courtier's pronouncements insult the king's high estate, and as a result each time he is moved into a worse confinement, until an execution is ordered. When a neighboring monarch propounds difficult riddles to the king, he repents of his decision and reinstates the courtier, so that the latter may respond, as in *Ahikar*. The dramatic tension and denouement of the *Shah Nameh* story is much more artistically executed than in the Solon story, giving the impression that in Herodotus we see an eastern legend assimilated to the figure of Solon.[56] Greek historical traditions contained no reference to an eastern imprisonment of Solon, and so Herodotus or his source was forced to have Solon simply leave after insulting the Lydian king. The ending of the story is as a result undramatic and unsatisfying, and one may conclude that the *Shah Nameh* version is more typical of the way the story circulated as a popular oral legend in the Ancient Near East. The account of the death of Croesus's son Atys (A-6) begins the tragic fall of the king, and thus serves to structure the narrative according to Herodotus's redactional scheme within the *logos* of the rise and fall of this monarch. However, the story itself is also attested in such places as Aesop and the Egyptian *Doomed Prince*, and is likely a popular tale type.

---

[54] Wolf Aly, *Volksmärchen, Sage, und Novelle bei Herodot und seinen Zeitgenossen* (Göttingen: Vandenhoeck & Ruprecht, 1921) 36–38; Hellmann, *Kroisos-logos*; and Immerwahr, *Form*, 148–88.

[55] Retold in Krappe, "Ahikar the Wise."

[56] Alongside this Persian parallel to the story frame, we note that the poems of Solon betray a similar caution against the danger of wealth (1.7–32, 71–76, 5.9–10), and the view that the Persian king is not happy is found at *Gorgias* 470E.

In category B, again within the *logos*, but after Croesus's fall, the presence of eastern sources is less likely. Croesus's recollection of Solon's words, once the bitter truth of them is obvious (B-1), is likely Herodotean, and the relation of Croesus to Apollo and Delphi (B-2 and 5) is a Greek tradition.[57] Whether the story in B-4 of Croesus advising Cyrus on how to restrain his men from plundering Sardis is an eastern tradition or Herodotean is unclear.

The situation in category C, outside the *logos* and before the fall, is similar to B, in that there is no clear pattern of provenance of sources or particular Herodotean usage. The story of Croesus's reward to the clever Alcmaeon (C-2) more than likely emanates from Alcmaeon's home of Athens, where both the tradition of Croesus's generosity and that of Alcmaeon's adventures were likely at home.[58] The origin of Croesus's artful threat to Lampsacus (C-1) is difficult to determine. When the city of Lampsacus holds Croesus's ally Miltiades prisoner, Croesus threatens to cut down the city "like a pine tree" unless they release him, which threat the residents of Lampsacus are unable to understand. Finally, an elder citizen interprets the threat to mean that, since a pine tree alone sends out no new shoots when it is cut down, Croesus must intend to wipe the city off the face of the earth. The city capitulated immediately. Whether Croesus is revered in this story as a potent king who can send terror into his enemies with a well-chosen expression, or feared as a tyrant who could subjugate the city, is not clear, but the point and origin of the story may have more to do with the elder citizen. This motif, the old man coming forward to save the town, is very similar to Thompson's motif number 981, "Wisdom of Hidden Old Man Saves Kingdom." The fact that the protagonist is hidden or discredited in the type index is all that differentiates it from the narratives mentioned here. In some respects 2 Sam 20:14–22 is even more similar. There a "wise woman" of Abel convinces her townspeople to chop off the head of the rebel Sheba and throw it out to Joab, David's general, rather than lose the city to his relentless siege. Although the relation of the person held in the city to the attacking general is the opposite in the two cases (an ally in Herodotus, an enemy in 2 Samuel), the role of the wise figure who effectively intercedes is the same.

It is, however, in category D—references to Croesus outside the logos and after his fall, where he is depicted as the wise courtier of the Persian kings—which come closest to the ancient Near Eastern court legends.[59] The traditional nature of several of these could be debated; D-3, for instance, which

---

[57] On the former, see Immerwahr, *Form*, 160, and on the latter, Fine, *Greeks*, 248–49.

[58] Thomson, *Logos*, 41–44. Alcmaeon was of a famous Athenian family.

[59] Xenophon takes a royal Persian perspective in *Cyropaedeia*, by depicting Cyrus saying sage words to his courtier Croesus (7.4.11–13; 8.2.15–19).

simply mentions Croesus as an important courtier who wept over Psammenitus, may not reflect an eastern legend. In D-1, however, where Croesus advises Cyrus on how to subdue the Lydian rebels, the pithy advice is parallel to Cyrus's in his court at the end of the *Histories*: soft living will produce soft people. Although this could reflect Herodotus's own views, the highly stylized presentation of essentially the same advice found in three other court legends set in the East, B-4, A-8 and D-2, indicate that it arises in the East, or possibly from the ethnographic interests of the Ionians.[60] In D-2, Croesus advises Cyrus to cross the Araxes River to attack the Massagetae, using as a stratagem a variation of the "banquet slaughter." This turns out to be wise advice, since the stratagem works and the Persians defeat the Massagetae in this first battle. Cyrus is killed soon afterward, however, by the Massagetae, and this fact is thrown up in Croesus's face later by Cambyses, in story D-5. It is important to note here that, despite Cambyses' opinion on the subject, which may very well be Herodotean, the immediate effect of Croesus's advice was a complete success.[61] The tradition reflected here is one of Croesus as a wise courtier, although in Herodotus's treatment the good advice ironically leads to disaster.

The court legend of D-4 clearly reflects an eastern setting and courtly interests, and has no relation with the known western Greek traditions about Croesus. In this story Cambyses asks his court who is greater, he himself or his father Cyrus. The other courtiers reply that he is greater, since he has kept his father's dominions and added others to them. Croesus, however, avers that of the two, Cyrus was more to be revered. When Cambyses asks how so, Croesus reponds that Cyrus left a great son behind in Cambyses, which the latter had not done. The audience's interest in this anecdote is aroused because the response of Croesus skirts dangerously close to insulting the king, but at the last moment, before the king's wrath is felt, Croesus turns the insult into a compliment. Something like the mirror image of the disguised parable, this story depicts the wisdom of Croesus through his ability to speak more directly and frankly with the king than could the average courtier.

---

[60] Ironically, in Croesus's advice regarding Lydia (D-1) and Cyrus's at the end of the *Histories*, it is averred that luxuries will soften people's military resolve, while in D-2 (concerning the Massagetae) and A-8 (Sandanis's advice to Croesus), the desire for luxuries is considered a powerful motive to fight. What is common to both positions is the insight that human nature can be understood and manipulated, and the application of this anthropological knowledge, by the courtier, in state policy. Hippocrates (*Aer.* 12–24) gives a lengthy analysis of the theory that geographical features of a region affect the peoples who live there.

[61] Lattimore, "Wise Adviser," 29.

The story of Croesus running afoul of Cambyses and being sentenced to execution (D-5) is especially important for our study, because it is closely parallel to *Ahikar*: the courtier who is truly wise and loyal is condemned to death by an impetuous king, is hidden by the would-be executioners, and is restored to honor when the king perceives that he has acted rashly and regrets his decision.[62] It is difficult to determine what in this story or in the previous story should be ascribed to Herodotus's hand. Above it was stated that Cambyses' criticism of Croesus's advice to Cyrus is likely Herodotean. The description of Cambyses' excesses in general also run through this entire section, and it is conceivable that this theme is composed by Herodotus, whether or not he learned of this from eastern informants. An interesting aspect of this legend is the counsel of prudence that Croesus gives Cambyses which causes the king's anger:

> My Lord, do not always act on the passionate impulse of youth. Check and control yourself. There is wisdom in forethought, and a sensible man looks to the future. If you continue too long in your present course of killing your countrymen for no sufficient cause—and of killing children too—then beware lest the Persians rise in revolt.

The court legend which just precedes this one, in which Croesus cleverly compliments Cambyses, focuses on the wit and aplomb of the courtier, but here he is depicted as delivering a set of very conventional maxims, and without being clever enough himself to avoid the judgment of execution. This unexpected element in the court legend can perhaps be explained as an influence of the Ahikar legend, since that story begins with Ahikar's instructions to his nephew in the form of proverbs. In the "baroque" versions of the story, the conventionality of these maxims was probably intended, but in this early variant of the story there is less irony—the maxims merely reflect Croesus's good counsel. In neither story is this advice the final criterion of the hero's wisdom, but it merely establishes his role and character; the point of the story in both cases lies in what happens to the wise man, and how he arises vindicated in the end.

It seems likely, then, that there existed in the Lydian and Persian empires cycles of wisdom court legends concerning Croesus. Various types of legends and a mixture of eastern and western traditions can be found in categories A through C, and in these groups the legends are more profitably considered from the point of view of the other figures present, such as the Ionian sage-heroes, the old man of Lampsacus, the Lydian wise counselor

---

[62] Cristiano Grotanelli, "Aesop in Babylon," in Hans-Jörg Nissen and Johannes Renger, eds., *Mesopotamien und seine Nachbarn* (2 vols.; Berlin: Reimer, 1982) 2. 559.

Sandanis, or the irrepressible Athenian Alcmaeon. Croesus never appears as the unmistakably wise king in a "ruling ethnic perspective" court legend, as Solomon and Cyrus were often presented.

In category D, however, we find several wisdom court legends which depict the conquered Croesus planting wise advice in the ear of the Persian kings. Whereas above I hypothesized an Ionian cycle with the representative Greek sages Solon, Thales, and Bias in the court of Croesus, here we find the defeated Lydian performing the same role in the Persian court. While the legends of Ionian heroes are the cultural affirmations of that group, the Lydian stories are likely ruled ethnic perspective legends of the Lydians. Although there is no hard evidence that stories about Ionians were composed by Ionians and stories about Lydians by Lydians, this is certainly a reasonable hypothesis here, considering the obvious propaganda value they have. Both the Ionian and Lydian cycles are generically identical—ruled ethnic perspective court legends, in which the ruled assert their greater wisdom over the rulers—but they must be attributed to two different ethnic groups. The story concerning Sandanis in Croesus's court (A-8) certainly seems to refer to a group of court legends revolving around Sandanis, and it is just as likely that those who transmitted that tradition to Herodotus also told him the stories of their fallen king in the Persian court.

It is, of course, also possible that Greeks would have composed legends about the fallen Croesus in Cyrus's and Cambyses' court, or that Herodotus himself thought fit to introduce narratives about Croesus following these famous monarchs about giving wise advice.[63] Although the genre is eastern, it could be argued that the attribution of these legends to Croesus is western. However, this is not likely. There are many western traditions about Croesus, but they are quite different from group D both in terms of motifs and of genre. In the west Croesus was seen as a benefactor of Delphi who was transported by Apollo from the pyre erected for him by Cyrus to the Isles of the Blessed.[64] In the East he was remembered in the first place as an important imperial ruler, but just as important, as a wise courtier to the Persian kings.[65] The latter tradition is incompatible with the view that he was spirited away on his pyre, but Herodotus merged the two traditions by having Croesus saved from the flames by Apollo, not to be transported to the Isles of

---

[63] Lattimore ("Wise Adviser," 34–35) suggests the latter.

[64] In western Greece Croesus is one of the few roughly contemporary mortals who is represented in Greek vase painting, evidently because of the belief that Apollo rescued him from the pyre. Croesus, like Midas, was also one of the main eastern patrons of the Delphic oracle, and is correspondingly associated on the mainland with great gifts of gold.

[65] Xenophon *Cyropaedeia* 7.4.11–13; 8.2.15–19 reflect the tradition of Croesus before Cyrus, but as a hearer, and not a speaker, of wise sayings.

the Blessed, but to become a Persian courtier. The stories hypothetically isolated here as western all concern his relationship with Delphi and Apollo, and
are generically quite different from the eastern legends where he is either the
king in a court legend, being advised by Ionian (and on one occasion,
Lydian) sage-heroes, or the Lydian sage-hero who advises the Persians.
Although it is not impossible that Ionian Greeks composed and transmitted
wisdom court legends about Croesus, it is more likely that similar kinds of
court legends emanating from both Ionians and Lydians can be distinguished.

The existence of such cycles has important implications for an understanding of Jewish court legends, especially the Daniel cycle of stories. In
both the hypothetical Croesus cycle and in Daniel we find a defeated nobleman (compare Dan 1:3) who becomes a wise courtier to a succession of
kings, and whose wise sayings and deeds are transmitted by fellow members
of his ruled ethnic group in a cycle of wisdom court legends. Although
Daniel serves Neo-Babylonian kings and "Darius the Mede," he also serves
Cyrus as well (Dan 1:21, 10:1, and Bel and the Dragon), so there is some
intersection in the kings served in the two traditions. In addition, both the
Croesus and the Daniel cycles make use of the court conflict subgenre (Herodotus 3.35 – 6 or D-5 above, Daniel 3, 6, and Bel and the Dragon).

We thus find Ionian stories composed under Lydian domination (Solon,
Thales, and Bias instructing Croesus), Lydian stories composed under Persian domination (the fallen Croesus instructing the Persian kings) and Jewish
stories probably composed under the Persian or Hellenistic empires (Daniel,
Esther, 1 Esdras 3 – 4). In all three cases the ruled ethnic perspective court
legend is used to the same effect: to assert the wisdom and statecraft of the
cultural hero of the ruled ethnic group. These stories should not be seen,
however, as providing a didactic *content* in terms of statemanship (e.g.,
"how to succeed in a foreign court"), nor would they appear to be useful as
case studies in a court school of the Persian Empire, a gymnasium in the
Ionian cities, or a Jewish academy. The wise instructions that are found in,
for example, the story of Croesus and Cambyses are hardly significant, and
would not give sufficient reason for the story to be saved and transmitted.
They also do not seem merely to provide a "role model for success" in the
diaspora, as Humphreys has suggested, although this function should not be
totally excluded. Instead, they generally serve to affirm the value and identity of the ruled ethnic group, just as many of the court legends mentioned
earlier affirm the ethnic identity of the ruling group in the person of the great
king who represents the nation, such as Cyrus or Solomon.

To be sure, court legends do not always contain this component of ethnic
propaganda; *Ahikar* seems to lack this.[66] In the case of the ruled ethnic

---

[66] The "Egyptian Interlude" in which Ahikar defeats the Egyptian wise men in contests of

perspective legends there is included the added drama of challenge and persecution, and eventual vindication: the confused but well-meaning great king
is forced to recognize the crucial role that a member of an ethnic minority
plays in the functioning of the empire. The wisdom to be found in these
legends is not something to be distilled and practiced—the disguised parable,
for example, could hardly be effective in a real court situation, and certainly
not on a regular basis—but wisdom is a part of these legends in the value that
is affirmed: the cultural hero who is "marked" by wisdom, who lives by
wisdom, succeeds.

Legends which promulgate the wisdom of the ruling ethnic group are also
found in Herodotus. As in the case of Solomon legends noted above, Cyrus
is often depicted as the wise ruler and protector of his people. Herodotus's
Histories end with a court legend of Cyrus's prescient statement about the
inadvisability of invading rich countries. The courtiers begin by asserting
that extending the empire seems a wise move. Cyrus is the last to speak, and
gives a word of advice, not as a command, but as a warning that is so wise
that it has authority without need of a royal order: "Soft countries breed soft
men."[67] The courtiers then agree that ruling over luxurious countries will
render them unable to continue to defeat opposing armies, and they drop the
plan. Cyrus here is the embodiment of Persian superiority, the benevolent
ruler who holds authority through his wisdom and not through tyranny. His
resistance to the temptation of luxuries also makes him a great king who protects his country's welfare through virtue.

The similarity here to many passages in Xenophon's *Cyropaedeia* also
deserves attention. The same qualities of wisdom and an unforced authority
are found time and again in the stories about Cyrus, although Xenophon has
rewritten whatever sources he had in his own style, and independent legends
are not nearly so easy to isolate. Cyrus's preference for rugged and austere
living is demonstrated often, but especially in 1.3.4–7; 1.6.8, 17; 4.2.40–47;
4.5.1–4, 7, 54; 5.1.1–8; and elsewhere. Cyrus often makes wise decisions
or pronouncements, for instance at 2.2.1–10; 2.4.5; 7.5.37–47; 8.2.10–11,
15–19; 8.4.32; and 8.6.10. There are also in Xenophon many passages about
foreign advisers in Cyrus's court, but it is difficult to distinguish any traditional court legends; in this regard we note especially 2.3.7–16; 5.2.15,
29–30; 7.2.9–14, 29; 8.3.5–8; and 8.3.26–40. The themes of these ruling

---

wisdom, and thus saves his kingdom from a heavy tribute, may not be original to the story; it is
lacking in the Elephantine version. It should also be noted that the proposed Mordecai/Haman
source of Esther does not appear to have an element of ethnic competition, although this was possibly excised and modified in the Jewish redaction.

[67] Lattimore, "Wise Adviser," 32. Cf. Aeschylus, *Persae* 623–80, 703–8 for a western view
of the wisdom of Cyrus.

ethnic perspective court legends are the same as those in the final pericope of
the *Histories*: Cyrus rules by wisdom and virtuous self-abnegation, and thus
protects the people of a great empire.

It may also be the case that affirmation of ethnic identity on a more subtle
level is found in later Greek tradition as well. After the Greeks repelled the
Persian invasion, the new Athenian league gained control of most of the
Greek cities in western Asia Minor. There was evidently quite a bit of
resentment of these new rulers, and *Life of Aesop* reflects an anti-Athenian,
anti-Apollonian tendency which may have resulted from this situation.
Although it would be difficult to prove that the composition of this layer of
the Aesop story coincided with the disaffection of the Asia Minor Greeks
with their mainland liberators, it remains an intriguing possibility.[68]

The parallel between the *Life of Aesop* and *Ahikar* indicates that the entire
Aesop tradition, with its anti-Athenian perspective, may be closely related to
the interests and methods of the court legend genre. In addition to the parallel just mentioned, Aesop also comes before Croesus as an adviser, and only
then becomes the adviser of Lykeros (= Nebuchadnezzar) in the *Ahikar*
parallel.[69] The antiaristocratic perspective must also be emphasized. The
misshapen and tongue-tied Aesop borrows from the image of the φάρμακος:
he is ugly, slandered, and ultimately killed by Apollo as a scapegoat.[70]
He becomes the cult figure of the lower classes and oriental slaves in Ionian
culture.

Final Stages of the Court Legend Genre

What can be known about the outlines of the history of the court legend
genre has now been sketched, beginning with their cloudy origins in the
ancient Near East, and their much clearer proliferation in the Persian and
Hellenistic empires. The genre perhaps remained current in the East, as witnessed by the reinterpretation of *Ahikar* in Syriac, Armenian, and Arabic versions, by the appearance of court legends in the Persian *Shah Nameh* and in

---

[68] Ben E. Perry (*Studies in the Text History of the Life and Fables of Aesop* [Haverford: American Philological Association, 1936] 15–19), in fact, traces this tendency in the *Life* to the earliest known layer. The Athenian point of view is evident in Euripides' *Ion*, which subordinates the
Ionian founder to the western ideology. See J. M. Cook, *The Greeks in Ionia and the East* (London: Thames and Hudson, 1962) 121–22.

[69] Aristotle, *Rhet.* 2.20. See Ben E. Perry, *Babrius and Phaedrus* (LCL; Cambridge: Harvard
University Press, 1965) xxx-xlvi; Francisco R. Adrados, "The 'Life of Aesop' and the Origins of
the Novel in Antiquity," *Quaderni urbinati di cultura classica* 30 (1979) 93–112; and Grotanelli, "Aesop," 562–63.

[70] Adrados, "Aesop," 94–95.

the Zoroaster legends, and in the Indian collections of legends, although in all these cases the date of composition of the stories could be quite early. In the West, however, this genre seems never to have gained any real popularity except in the *Histories* of Herodotus. As was noted above, the Greek amphictyony did not seem an appropriate context for court legends. The western ideal of kingship remained in general unelevated. Alexander already reflects a democratization and decentralization of kingship when compared with Cyrus, and the Roman emperor was not automatically even attributed dynastic status, but was *primus inter pares*.[71] An intriguing question is whether there are in the Roman period any offspring of the court legend, and certainly several narrative genres suggest this possibility.

The first possibility to be considered are the Jewish and Christian parables concerning the king. David Stern has analyzed the rabbinic examples closely, and his study provides little evidence of a similar use of the court motif there.[72] Generally in the rabbinic *meshalim* the king is a metaphor for God. The allegorical meaning of the *mashal* is crucial to their use, as is the *nimshal*, the application of the parable in preaching. The parables were often originally about a certain man (*adam*), which in the retelling is assimilated to a king, or to be more emphatic about the allegorical world of the parable, a "king of flesh and blood."[73] A courtier does on occasion figure in the parables, but as an allegorical figure, representing, for example, Moses and his intervention for Israel.[74] Similar conclusions can probably also be applied to the early Christian parables. Although some of the parables in their earliest form were probably not allegorized—Lk 14:16–24 is much less allegorized than the parallel at Matt 22:1–14—they still have an application far different from the older court legends. Some, such as the Matthean passage here, are even assimilated to the royal palace from a more general rich man's estate, just as occurred in the rabbinic traditions. Thus in some cases the royal court remains the dramatic setting for wisdom teaching in court legends and in Jewish and Christian parables, but little else is similar.

A more promising genre is the meeting of the wise man with the emperor. This development of the Hellenistic and Roman periods is never set in court, but in the emperor's travels to the provinces, where he is usually arriving to

---

[71] The author of *De mundo*, a work written about the turn of the era and falsely attributed to Aristotle, could use the ancient Persian court as a metaphor for God's removal from direct involvement in the world, but the author evidently felt western kings were not appropriate for such a metaphor.

[72] Stern, "Interpreting in Parables: The Mashal in Midrash, with Special reference to *Lamentations Rabba*," Ph.D. dissertation, Harvard University, 1980.

[73] Ibid., 50–51.

[74] Ibid., 61, 106–7, 167.

subdue unruly subjects. This genre derives from the stories of meetings of wise men with Alexander the Great, and there is no hard evidence that it has anything to do directly with the court legend genre. However, the similarities are interesting. For instance, in the story of the meeting of Alexander the Great and Diogenes, the directness and candor of the latter is treated as an admirable trait, indicative of the true philosopher.[75] The same type of story is told about Jewish sages, most notably concerning Johanan ben Zakkai's meeting with Vespasian, where Johanan prophesies that Vespasian will become emperor.[76] Alexander and Vespasian appear to have been favorite figures for this genre; other traditions concerning meetings of sages with Vespasian are told by Jewish and pagan historians.[77]

A motif found in some of these is common to the ruled ethnic perspective court legends. The Jewish examples listed above certainly affirm the prophetic authority of the Jewish sage, and the rightful role of Judaism in the Roman Empire.[78] Two of the stories of Vespasian's latent supernatural abilities may also serve to promulgate Serapis worship. Tacitus (*His.* 4.81–84) recounts two incidents in which Vespasian, while still a general, approaches the Serapis temple of Alexandria, and from this encounter successfully heals two men and has a vision which foretells his coming to power. Although Tacitus may use these stories for his own purposes—documenting Vespasian's abilities—the legends may have originally arisen from Serapis cult propaganda. Like Johanan ben Zakkai, devotees of Serapis insure their own religion's success by recounting their relation to the emperor.

A somewhat similar genre has been analyzed by W. E. Tarn, which consists of a dialogue between a king and a sage on kingship.[79] In the fourth-third centuries BCE, many dialogues "concerning kingship" (περὶ βασιλείας) were composed, and Indian parallels were also found by Tarn, including the story of the meeting of Alexander with Indian gymnosophists.

---

[75] Plutarch, *Alex.* 14.2; Diogenes Laertius, *Vit. phil.* 6.38. David Aune ("Greco-Roman Biography," in idem, ed., *Greco-Roman Literature and the New Testament* [Atlanta: Scholars Press, 1988] 110–14) traces a similar development in the biographical tradition about Secundus.

[76] ARNA 4; ARNB 6; *Lam. Rab.* 1.5; *b. Git.* 56a–b.

[77] Josephus *Bell.* 3.8.9, §§ 399–408; Suetonius *Ves.* 5–6; Tacitus *His.* 2.78; Philostratus *Vit. Apol.* 5.27ff.

[78] Others are perhaps less civic-minded, and depict either a Jewish sage refuting a Roman official publicly (Johanan ben Zakkai: *Num. Rab.* 4:9; *Bek.* 5a; Akiba: *Gen. Rab.* 11:5; *Sanh.* 65b; *B. Bat.* 10a), or a sage answering wisely the barbed insults of the emperor (various sages: *Ruth Rab.* 3:2; *Exod. Rab.* 30:12; *Hag.* 5b; *Eccl. Rab.* 1:9, 11:1). See Moshe David Herr, "The Historical Significance of the Dialogues Between Jewish Sages and Roman Dignitaries," *Scripta Hierosylimitana* 22 (1971) 128–33, 141–49.

[79] Tarn, *The Greeks in Bactria and India* (Cambridge: Cambridge University Press, 1951) 414–36.

Other examples of this genre are the *Letter of Aristeas* and Plutarch's *Banquet of the Seven Sages*.

Within the category of dialogues with the emperor are also found the *Acta Alexandrinorum*, accounts of philosophers' opposition to some of the early emperors. This tradition of a dialogue or debate between a sage and the emperor obviously shares some similarities with the court legend. The high stakes of the setting, that is, the inherent risk in engaging in a verbal exchange with an absolute monarch, is common to both, as is the focus on "wisdom,"[80] and in many cases, the role of the protagonist in representing a group is also similar, be he or she a Jew, a "philosopher," a follower of Serapis, or whatever. Herbert Musurillo proposes that they originated among the leaders of the Alexandrian clubs, and have a pro-Alexandrian and anti-Roman *Tendenz*.[81] This might indicate that they do in fact carry on the tradition of the ruled ethnic group court legend, although the genre is strongly influenced by that of the western dialogue, and also by rhetorical tradition. The important narrative aspect, so typical of the eastern legends, is as a result lost. The joyous imbibing of a good story is scarcely to be found, doubtless as a result of the seriousness of the persecutions.

The court legends that had long been transmitted in Jewish tradition were also undergoing editorial changes, which indicate the new needs of the popular audience. Briefly, we should note that the Joseph story was retold in several different versions. Artapanus begins his recounting of the story in the fashion of a very neat but summary court conflict:

> Joseph was a descendant of Abraham and son of Jacob, and because he surpassed his brethren in understanding and wisdom, they plotted against him. But he became aware of their conspiracy, and besought the neighboring Arabs to convey him across to Egypt, and they did as he requested; for the kings of the Arabians are offshoots of Israel, being sons of Abraham, and brethren of Isaac. And when he had come to Egypt and been commended to the king, he was made administrator of the whole country.

Omitted in this retelling of the story is the entire episode between Joseph and the wife of Potiphar—just the segment which was missing in the so-called "J" version and which obscures the basic "U" pattern of the conflict legend. However, Artapanus merely uses this summary as a base on which

---

[80] Wisdom must be defined somewhat differently in the Roman and Jewish settings, but in both cases, where "witnessing" is involved, it is here broadly construed to mean philosophical principles for which one is prepared to risk one's life.

[81] Musurillo, *The Acts of the Pagan Martyrs: Acta Alexandrinorum* (Oxford: Clarendon, 1954) 273–77.

to launch a "national hero romance" of Joseph's adventures in Egypt and his contributions to Egyptian civilization. The *Testament of Joseph* takes the very episode which Artapanus omits and turns it into an extended erotic scene of attempted seduction and resistance, as an edifying model of sexual morality. Jospehus also develops this scene, but in a much more polished literary romance, as Braun has noted.[82] Last, *Joseph and Asenath* enlarges the role of the heroine and the love between the two protagonists. What all of these versions have in common, regardless of overall genre, is the addition of romance motifs, attesting various permutations of the development of a popular romance tradition about Joseph.

The Book of Esther undergoes similar stages of development, both in the pre-MT stages, as we shall see below, and also in the LXX, where the relation of Esther and Ahasuerus is played up considerably. The court legends of Daniel 1 – 6 and the LXX additions are also interpreted in directions which lie outside the normal court legend genre, since they are combined with the visions of Daniel 7 – 12, but only in the LXX additions is there any change in the direction of romance. The complicated question of how the court legends are reinterpreted in Daniel will have to wait until chapter 4. The court contest of Zerubbabel in 1 Esdras 3 – 4 is very likely excised from its original setting in the first edition of the Chronicler, although it does survive in its present home in the Greek translation.[83] Outside of Jewish tradition, *Ahikar*, as we noted above, is also enlarged beyond the bare court legend genre and becomes something of a satire on the original intent of a court legend. In most of these cases we find that the short and direct narratives of the court legends have been expanded by the addition of romance motifs, fulfilling the needs of a bourgeois audience.

Aside from several undatable eastern exemplars of the court legend, then, we have no evidence that the simple genre was still current by the Roman period, although the *Acta Alexandrinorum* may carry on a similar, but essentially non-narrative, tradition. Older court legends were transmitted in the Roman period, some as sacred literature, and were elaborated upon in some instances, but the high period of the genre was clearly over. Herodotus was read by later authors, and many writers mentioned the ancient courts which he described, but no one, it seems, was reproducing wisdom court legends.

---

[82] Martin Braun, *History and Romance in Graeco-Oriental Literature* (Oxford: Blackwell, 1938) 88 – 90.

[83] Frank Moore Cross, "Aspects of Samaritan and Jewish History in Late Persian and Hellenistic Times," *HTR* 59 (1966) 201 – 11.

3

The Cycle of Daniel Court Legends

By the turn of the common era a number of court legends and visionary materials were gathered around the figure of Daniel,[1] a wise Jew who counseled the great ancient Near Eastern kings of the sixth century BCE. The MT Book of Daniel contains six such stories (chaps. 1 – 6), and the Greek translations of Daniel add two more, Susanna and Bel and the Dragon. Some fragments from Qumran are also associated with Daniel, but they are mostly visionary materials which have more in common with the visions of Daniel 7 – 12 than with the legends of 1 – 6.[2] The *Prayer of Nabonidus* (4QPrNab) is certainly related to the court legend, though it is not, as it stands, about Daniel; it concerns instead an unnamed Jewish seer. The figure of Daniel is

[1] In the Ugaritic texts Dan'el was a mythical king closely associated with Baal. In Ezek 14:14, 20 Daniel is mentioned with Noah and Job as an ancient legendary figure. Ezek 28:3 also invokes Daniel as a venerated wise figure, but one who is otherwise unidentified. Tying the various references together into one figure is tempting, and is done by some scholars, e.g., John J. Collins, *The Apocalyptic Imagination* (New York: Crossroad, 1984) 69; and idem, *Vision*, 2 – 3; but others, e.g., Walther Zimmerli (*Ezekiel* [Hermeneia; 2 vols.; Philadelphia: Fortress, 1979 – 83] 1.314 – 15), are hesitant to see these texts referring to the same traditional figure. If there is continuity between these depictions of Daniel/Dan'el, then the hero of the MT Book of Daniel has been reduced in stature from a larger-than-life ancient king to a Jewish nobleman of the more recent past, i.e., based on the definitions of Chapter 1 of this thesis, he has been demythologized from myth to legend. The literary-critical analysis of Daniel 1 – 6 by Danna Nolan Fewell (*Circle of Sovereignty* [JSOT Supp 72; Sheffield: Almond, 1988]) became available to me too late to be used in this study.

[2] See J. T. Milik, " 'Prière de Nabonide' et autres écrits d'un cycle de Daniel," *RB* 63 (1956) 411 – 15.

not precisely the same in all these writings, as John Collins has pointed out.³ The figure of Daniel in MT chapters 1–6 is a wise and righteous courtier-sage who witnesses to true Jewish piety, while in Daniel 7–12 his visions are much more emphasized, as is the case in most of the Qumran fragments. The two sections were not considered incompatible by the final redactor, however, since, as several scholars have recently observed, it is *mantic* wisdom which provides a point of intersection between the two.⁴ Although in many respects Daniel in chapters 1–6 is like the protagonist in other court legends, his mantic abilities are in general the key to his success. There are enough common motifs in the Danielic materials, including *Prayer of Nabonidus*, to justify the hypothesis of a "Danielic school," through which these materials have passed.

Danielic legends come down to us in the MT and in two different recensions of the Greek text, the Old Greek (OG) and the Theodotionic translation (Th) which supplanted the OG in the standard Greek manuscripts. The Th is a faithful, even slavish, translation of a Hebrew and Aramaic text which was then current and which was nearly identical to MT, but the OG was quite different in parts of the Book of Daniel, and contrary to the views of many scholars, should be considered a valuable witness to the original text of Daniel. Where there is no MT version (in Susanna and Bel and the Dragon), the OG is also for the most part to be preferred to the Th recension as a better witness to the original text. These text-critical issues will be discussed below.

Susanna

Both Greek translations of Daniel are introduced with Susanna, a story in which Daniel figures as a young man. It is here that God first bestows wisdom on him to save the beautiful young woman, Susanna, from an unjust execution. The story, however, was probably not originally about Daniel, but about an unnamed "young man" (νεώτερος) who was only secondarily identified with Daniel. The story has evidently been assimilated to the figure of Daniel and placed at the beginning of the corpus of legends to introduce the hero with a fuller biography, beginning with his youth.⁵ It is very

---

³ Collins, "Court-Tales," 232–33.

⁴ Collins (ibid., 229–34) has maintained this, influenced by Hans-Peter Müller ("Magisch-mantische Weisheit und die Gestalt Daniels," *UF* 1 (1969) 79–94; and idem, "Mantische Weisheit und Apokalyptik," VTSup 22 (1972) 268–93.

⁵ Robert H. Pfeiffer, *History of New Testament Times* (New York: Harper, 1949) 454; and Carey Moore, *Daniel, Esther, and Jeremiah: The Additions* (AB; Garden City: Doubleday, 1977) 90, n. 23.

interesting that the main plot elements of the court conflict are all here—persecution of the innocent righteous person (here Susanna, not the ''young man''), and final vindication before the governing powers—but the setting has been transposed from the royal court to the local Jewish court of elders.[6] For our purposes, this is a very interesting development, as it indicates the adaptation of the standard court legend genre to a Jewish middle-class audience, which in this case is not particularly concerned with the issues of the position of Jews *qua* Jews in the pagan empire.[7] The story begins and ends completely within the confines of the self-governing Jewish community, with no mention of the Gentiles whatsoever.

It is important to note, however, that the story of Susanna can be divided into two halves: the first recounts the making of Susanna's predicament, while the second describes Daniel's interrogation and unmasking of the villains. Folklore motifs can be discerned in both halves. The first half is the motif of the falsely accused chaste wife,[8] but it has been blended with typical court conflict elements. We find a righteous Jew who is conspired against and suffers a fall from an honored position, and also a focus both on the psychological state of the persecuted person and her vindication before the same body which had earlier condemned her, all of which are typical of conflicts.[9] The second half reflects the popular folktale motif of the wise child who prevents an unjust action of his elders.[10]

The OG and Th versions betray slightly different redactional intentions, and the consensus of scholars is that OG attests an older version of the story. Joachim Schüpphaus and Helmut Engel have both argued for OG priority, and have isolated a number of redactional tendencies of the Th version.[11]

---

[6] Nickelsburg, *Jewish Literature*, 26. Like the Book of Ruth, it is a story which takes as its main characters the local citizenry.

[7] Much of the popular Jewish literature from the post-exilic period seems to be aimed at a broad, middle-class audience and reflects a trend toward some degree of social realism and the use of characters from normal walks of life. Although this is nowhere carried to completion, Ruth perhaps comes closest. See Morton Smith, *Palestinian Parties and Politics that Shaped the Old Testament* (New York: Columbia University, 1971) 158–60; and idem, ''Jewish Religious Life in the Persian Period,'' in W. D. Davies and Louis Finkelstein, eds., *Cambridge History of Judaism* (Cambridge: University of Cambridge Press, 1984) 1. 248–57.

[8] Moore, *Additions*, 88–89; Pfeiffer, *History*, 453; and cf. Thompson, *Motif-Index*, no. K2112. However, Thompson (*Folktale*, 110) insists that type 883A, Innocent slandered maiden, originated in literary treatments, from where it has at times entered into oral transmission.

[9] Cf. Nickelsburg, *Jewish Literature*, 23; also idem, *Resurrection*, 49–58; and idem, ''Genre,'' 155–63.

[10] Moore, *Additions*, 88–89.

[11] Schüpphaus, ''Das Verhältnis von LXX- und Theodotion-Text in den apokryphen Zusätzen zum Danielbuch,'' *ZAW* 83 (1971) 49–72; and Engel, *Die Susanna-Erzählung: Einleitung, Übersetzung und Kommentar zum Septuaginta-Text und zur Theodotion-Bearbeitung* (Freiburg: Universitätsverlag; Göttingen: Vandenhoeck & Ruprecht, 1985).

Whereas OG Susanna, which probably began at vs 5b, focuses on the elders as the model villains, Th shifts the focus of the story to Susanna.[12] In Th one can also detect an increased focus on the erotic aspects of the story and a psychologizing and historicizing tendency, accomplished by filling out more of the thoughts of the principal characters and by providing more details of Susanna's home and lineage.[13] Susanna's daily walk in the garden in OG becomes an erotic bath scene in Th, described at some length for such a short story. The endings of the two versions also differ. The OG concludes with a sermonic application of the lesson of the story, an exhortation to watch over young men so that they may grow up to be men of worth.[14] In this conclusion the original anonymity of the hero is evident, because Daniel is not mentioned and the application has nothing to do with his life story. In the Th conclusion, on the other hand, it is stated that this event in Daniel's life elevated him to importance in the Jewish community. There is no sermonic application, but instead Daniel's first great achievement remains the focus of the biographical legend. Engel also concludes that the Th version comes closer to Müller's genre designation "weisheitliche Lehrerzählung," but his argument for the particular intention of the OG version (anti-Hasmonean) versus the generalizing intention of the Th (weisheitliche Lehrerzählung) may be overdrawn.[15]

There are several reasons for taking the OG version to be the better witness to the original text. The secondary identification of the young man is

[12] One wonders, however, between the two versions, whether the elders, Susanna, or Daniel is the "true" focus of the story. Note especially the review of Engel's book by Zipora Talshir (*Bib* 67 [1986] 582) who holds that Daniel is the dramatic focus in both Sus and Th. A modern parallel is interesting here. John Ford's "Young Mr. Lincoln" fills in Lincoln's early years and first test, just as Susanna does Daniel's. In Ford's movie, two rural innocents are accused by a city-slicker of a murder he had committed. The country hick Lincoln acts as the defence attorney of the two young men, and uncovers the cityslicker's treachery in cross-examination. Just as Sus OG opposes youth/elders, "Young Mr. Lincoln" opposes rural/urban, but it is nevertheless a "Lincoln" movie.

[13] Engel, *Susanna*, 181–82. Richard Valentasis (unpublished seminar paper at Harvard University, 1983) has also noted that some of these motifs are found in romance, as has Richard I. Pervo (*Profit With Delight* [Philadelphia: Fortress, 1987] 152 n. 105). We shall see that the tendency toward romantic elements can be found in many popular Jewish narratives of this period.

[14] That the OG conclusion of Susanna is a sermonic application was pointed out in seminar discussion by John Strugnell, Harvard Divinity School, spring 1983. The genre of this sermon corresponds to the "word of exhortation" (λόγος παρακλήσεως), a sermon form I have isolated in "The Form of the Sermon in Hellenistic Judaism and Early Christianity," *HTR* 77 (1984) 277–99, esp. 294.

[15] Engel, *Susanna*, 180–83. If an anti-Hasmonean position is present in OG in the critique of elders and institutions, then it is a very mild affair.

more awkward in OG, and has evidently been smoothed over in Th.[16] The greater interest in the bath scene in Th, mentioned above, would also not likely have been excised and toned down in every detail in OG; it is more likely that the Th expanded the story at this point, although an expurgation by the OG editor for a sermonic use is conceivable. The strongest evidences, however, for the priority of the OG are found in the endings of the two documents, since the OG would not likely have so thoroughly eradicated Daniel's name from the ending, nor would it have eliminated the connection with the rest of the legends of Daniel.

The story of Susanna, then, reflects a remarkable history of literary development. The plot line of the court conflict is adapted to a local setting, and also betrays the influence of one or more folk motifs. It focuses on the issues of moral purity within the Jewish community, without any reference to the pagan world. This is used in the OG as a sermon illustration or example story, with an exhortation to the community to respect the young. One wonders why it should be so important to assert the need for respecting youth, and here we are probably getting at the intention of the OG story: a desire to affirm the education of young men in Jewish wisdom, corresponding, for instance, to Ben Sira 51:13–30, and also to Daniel 1. The Th version, however, drops any hint of a sermon application and ends with an assimilation of the story to the corpus of legends about Daniel. We shall see that, aside from the incorporation into the Danielic corpus and the focus on wisdom and youth, there are very few specific redactional themes in OG or Th Susanna which correspond to those in Daniel 1–6. This is understandable if we assume that the story had little to do with Daniel 1–6 in its formative stages, and was only associated with those legends later.

Daniel 1

Nickelsburg's view that Daniel 1 was written by the person who collected the independent stories of chaps. 2–6 has much to be said for it. Here the characters of all the stories are introduced, and it is told how they came to be in Babylon and in Nebuchadnezzar's administration.[17] Other issues are also

---

[16] OG: νεωτέρῳ ὄντι Δανιηλ / Th: νεωτέρου ᾧ ὄνομα Δανιηλ. The difference is slight, but the OG merely *identifies* the youth with Daniel; Th *introduces* the new character, using the normal dative of respect.

[17] Nickelsburg, *Jewish Literature*, 20, 38. Louis Hartman and Alexander Di Lella (*The Book of Daniel* [AB; Garden City: Doubleday, 1978] 131–33) leave the issue open. The corpus which Daniel 1 introduces could also have been Daniel 2–7, as Lebram (*Daniel*, 20–23) has argued, following A. Lenglet, "La structure littéraire de Daniel 2–7," *Bib* 53 (1972) 169–90.

presented here which appear later in the other stories; however, the similarities do not necessarily imply that Daniel 1 *presupposes* chaps. 2–6. Verse 2b mentions the temple vessels which appear later in chap. 5, but they have no real role in chap. 1, and could have been added by the editor of chaps. 1–6, as indeed they appear to be in chap. 5. Likewise vs 17 introduces Daniel's ability to interpret dreams, but it interrupts the flow of the story, and also could have been inserted when chap. 1 was placed with 2–6.

Müller turns to other evidence to argue that Daniel 1 presupposes 2–6. The particular kind of wisdom which is displayed by Daniel and his companions is not the same in each legend. In chaps. 3 and 6 it is specifically *courtly* wisdom which is their stock-in-trade, while in chaps. 2, 4, and 5 it is *mantic* wisdom.[18] Both of these types of wisdom are represented in chap. 1, which would indicate that here the later chapters are being introduced. However, Daniel 1 is in its general conception only concerned with courtly wisdom; only in vs 17—the verse which may have been inserted—is the mantic wisdom of the heroes affirmed, and it appears quite possible that a story more concerned with Jewish observance in a courtly context, with an emphasis on courtly wisdom, has been modified by the addition of the element of mantic wisdom. In opposition to this view it could be argued that vs 20 also uses "mantic" titles for the court officers: the king "found them ten times better than all the magicians and astrologers (הַחַרְטֻמִּים הָאַשָּׁפִים) that were in his realm." However, even here the possibility of an insertion should be considered. The main problem of the story, the health of the Jews who remain kosher, is resolved in vs 15, where they appear healthier to the steward who is set over them, and in vs 19 where the king conversed with them and they "stood before the king" (cf. 2:2). This phrase seems to conclude their exaltation, yet vs 20 repeats it in different terms. Even considering Müller's arguments, then, the issue appears to be unresolved.

Lebram's recent commentary on Daniel, however, put forth another set of arguments for taking Daniel 1 to be an editor's introduction to an already existing collection of legends.[19] In keeping with his theory that the Hebrew portions of Daniel were additions to the older Aramaic Daniel (a theory which need not be followed to evaluate his arguments about chapter 1), he notes that the first chapter betrays a different orientation from chapters 2–7: it is conerned with the Exile and the Palestinian motherland and lacks the perspective of the diaspora. Its intention is to bind the diaspora figure of Daniel to a Jerusalem temple consciousness, using Hebrew instead of Aramaic.[20]

[18] Müller, "Mantische Weisheit," 279.

[19] Lebram, *Daniel*, 22–23, 43, 48, 51–52.

[20] If, as I argue below, the Jerusalem temple consciousness is added in Daniel 5, then this

There is considerable evidence, then, that Daniel 1 was placed at the beginning of a Daniel corpus to introduce what followed. This, however, does not rule out the possibility that Daniel 1 also depends upon an older source which was adapted for just this purpose. The original story in that case would have concluded with the resolution of the issue of their kosher status, and vs 20 would have also been added to extend their exaltation into the realm of mantic wisdom as well. Without the passages listed above, Daniel 1 could have been an independent court legend, just as the other chapters were. The "witnessing" aspect, that is, Daniel's insistence on remaining loyal to the laws of God at all costs,[21] would in that case have been a theme of the original story, while the mantic wisdom aspect would have been inserted by the redactor. I will return to this issue below.

In addition to the questions raised above regarding a source of Daniel 1, the dating of the story by the reign of a king in vs 1 ("In the third year of the reign of Jehoiakim king of Judah. . . .") may also reflect an attempt to give these stories the semblance of historical accounts, a redactional tendency which occurs also in Esth 1:1. This method of dating corresponds very closely to the chronicles genre, and is likely a result of the collecting and editing of Daniel 1–6, rather than part of the source stories. Independent court legends do not have this dating formula, but often acquire it in the process of expansion into larger works.

Daniel 2

Chapter 2 is a court contest in which Daniel surpasses all the other courtiers in dream interpretation. When the king has a troubling dream, he demands that his wise men must not only interpret it, but must first tell him the content of the dream. This unusual requirement serves to increase the task to a

---

would strengthen Lebram's hypothesis. There are also several contradictions noted by Lebram (*Daniel*, 48, 51–52) between chapters 1 and 2–7, but these should not be pushed too strongly as evidence of a separate literary history of the two, since contradictions exist among the various legends in 2–7 also.

[21] See also Collins, *Vision*, 32–33; and Hartman and Di Lella, *Daniel*, 196. I prefer not to use the term "martyr legend" here because a distinct genre is not yet crystalized, despite the application of this term to Daniel by Aage Bentzen (*Introduction to the Old Testament* [7th ed.; 2 vols; Copenhagen: Gad, 1967] 1.238; and "Daniel 6: Ein Versuch zur Vorgeschichte der Märtyrerlegends," in Walter Baumgartner, et al., eds., *Festschrift Alfred Bertholet* [Tübingen: Mohr-Siebeck, 1950] 58–64). Lebram (*Daniel*, 47) notes that the self-imposed restrictions on diet in the narrative literature of this period often exceed the probable kosher laws of that time, and in fact are usually vegetarian. Cf. Tob 1:10–12; Esth 14:17 OG; Jud 9:5, 12:1–4; 2 Macc 5:27; and Jub 22:16.

superhuman level, for as vss 10–11 state, this lies beyond the abilities of even the wisest Babylonian sage.[22] Indeed it is stated that "none can show it to the king except the gods, whose dwelling is not with flesh" (vs 11). Daniel's ability to relate the content of the dream as well as its interpretation shows that the nature of his wisdom is different from the Babylonians', and is directly revealed by God.

Daniel 2 readily reveals several redactional levels. To begin with, the oracular dream itself probably originally derived from a wholly different context. Collins notes that King Nebuchadnezzar is amazed at Daniel's *ability* to interpret dreams, but is not concerned about the *content*.[23] In view of the condemning, prophetic tone which predicts imminent destruction for Nebuchadnezzar's kingdom, this seems odd. Collins shows that the original oracle was probably Babylonian, not Jewish, and prophesied the "future restoration of a Babylonian kingdom by a god (presumably Marduk)."[24] The last part of the vision and interpretation, the stone which destroys the image and thus the kingdoms, is in Collins's view of Jewish redaction.[25] The adulation that Nebuchadnezzar bestows on Daniel was perhaps in the original bestowed upon a seer who predicted the future rise of a *Babylonian* kingdom.[26]

In the narrative sections Hartman and Di Lella also point out several passages which they suggest derive from a second, independent version of the story,[27] although it is perhaps more likely that, rather than representing a second source, the passages are later insertions into a single version. The first of these is a seam which can be detected in the doublet of vss 13–16 on one hand and vs 24 on the other, which both depict Daniel requesting an audience with the king. A redactor has inserted Daniel's first exchange with Arioch and his request for a delay in the judgment (vss 13–16), and his pious

[22] See Collins, *Vision*, 35; and A. Leo Oppenheim, "The Interpretation of Dreams in the ancient Near East," *Transactions of the American Philosophical Society* 46 (1956) 179–255. The extreme difficulty of the task is made more oppressive by being kept within the bounds of what the audience thinks is possible for a witness to God's law. In *Ahikar*, for instance, the problems posed for him by the Egyptian king are completely unreal and whimsical, and were not likely believed by the audience. Daniel and his three friends are Jewish noblemen, heroic to be sure, but not larger than life. They are nevertheless increased in stature beyond the normal person's ability precisely because they are witnesses and servants of God.

[23] Collins, *Vision*, 34.

[24] Ibid., 42.

[25] Ibid. 42,44. Note also Lebram's (*Daniel*, 48) analysis of redactional layers within the dream. Here I am more interested in the court narrative.

[26] Hartman and Di Lella, *Daniel*, 139–45. See also Gustav Hölscher, "Die Entstehung des Buches Daniel," *Theologische Studien und Kritiken* 92 (1919) 117–18; and Otto Plöger, *Theocracy and Eschatology* (Oxford:Blackwell, 1968) 12.

[27] Hartman and Di Lella, *Daniel*, 139, 145. Lebram (*Daniel*, 48) agrees in regard to 2:13–24.

meeting with his three companions (vss 17 – 19), along with the prayer (vss 20 – 23). Leaving out vss 13 – 23 makes the text read much more smoothly, and eliminates the difficulty of having Daniel introduced to the king in vs 25, when he had already spoken to him in vs 16. Second, vss 29 – 30, Daniel's insistence that his wisdom is a gift of God, essentially repeats in different words what was stated in the two preceding verses, and also intrudes between the explicit announcement of Daniel's report and the report itself (vss 28 and 31 – 45). Daniel's attribution of his ability as a diviner to God is increased as a theme, or at least emphasized more strongly.[28] Third, vs 49 was also added by the same redactor who added vss 13 – 23; only in these two places do the three companions appear. An emphasis on mantic wisdom and the "vertical" relationship of witness to God can thus be detected in the redactional layer, extended somewhat beyond the hypothetical source.[29]

Daniel 3

Chapter three, a court conflict, is the only one in the Danielic corpus which does not mention Daniel; it focuses solely on Shadrach, Meshach, and Abednego (only their Babylonian names are used). Whereas Daniel 2 as received contains several digressions which interrupt the natural flow of the story, Daniel 3 in general moves forward smoothly from one plot element to the next. Indeed, chapter three exhibits many indications of oral transmission, and in this case, moreso than in the other legends of Daniel 1 – 6, we are very close to the original oral source.

The oral nature of the legend can be argued first of all by noting that it conforms to the tendencies of such narratives delineated by Axel Olrik:[30] Olrik's "laws," which should not really be considered laws, but tendencies of oral narratives, will be listed, and noted afterward will be the ways in which Daniel 3 does or does not conform to them:

[28] Cf. also Gen 41:16 regarding Joseph, although in Daniel it is stated even more strongly. This differs from the more common view of courtly wisdom in Israel, where limitations on human knowledge are often expressed (e.g., Pr 16:1 – 10, 12 – 15; cf. Proverbs 30 and Job 28.) Even when court wisdom allowed for a correspondence between knowledge of God's ways and success and insight in the world, the focus is not exclusively on revealed wisdom and the vertical relationship of witness to God, as it is in Daniel 1 – 6.

[29] Collins (*Vision*, 33) notes this tendency in regard to conflicts, but a shift can be discerned in the contests as well. "Courtly wisdom" and "mantic wisdom" are not mutually exclusive properties; a court prophet or seer would need both. However, it is the difference in emphasis that must be kept in mind here.

[30] "Epic Laws of Folk Narrative," in Alan Dundes, ed., *The Study of Folklore* (Englewood Cliffs: Prentice-Hall, 1965) 129 – 41.

1) Law of calm opening and closing: folk narratives do not begin or end with sudden action, but in a stable state of affairs. Although Daniel 3 begins with an ominous action—the construction of an image—it is not sudden or violent, and the plot develops quite slowly, considering the overall length of the legend. The ending, though shorter, portrays the youths' elevated status at court which presumably will continue.

2) Law of dramatic duality: only two characters or unified groups appear in active or speaking roles at any one time. This law is in evidence, even when more than two groups are in the court at the same time. Nebuchadnezzar talks to the Chaldaeans in vss 8 – 12, and to the three youths in vss 13 – 18. However, a slight confusion of characters results around the furnace scene, as the characters multiply. The Chaldaeans are forgotten at this point, but the three youths, the court strong men, the king, and now an angel are all in close association here. The king is the only speaker from among the antagonists, however, and below I will attempt to clarify this scene somewhat.

3) Law of contrasts: main characters, such as the protagonist and antagonist, often appear as polar opposites in every attribute. Since Shadrach, Meshach, and Abednego have three different opponents here—the "Chaldaeans" of vss 8 – 12, King Nebuchadnezzar, and the "mighty men of the army" of vss 20 – 22—it is difficult to pin down a single set of contrasts, but of the three, the king does most of the talking, and so we should consider him first. Here we note that the king's bluster and fury indicate a character opposite of the three youths, who give calm and reasoned discourses in the face of death. The outspoken independence of the Jews can also be contrasted, however, with the depiction of the other courtiers as servile toadies. The latter are in fact slain by the fire for carrying out the king's orders (vs 22).

4) Law of repetition of events: important actions are often repeated, usually three times. In longer narratives plot repetitions are conducive to building the expectations of the audience of what will finally lead to a climax and resolution of the plot. In shorter narratives such as this one, there is no need for such a repetition in the plot structure, and the repetitions we do find—not of plot elements but of names, titles, etc.—serve another purpose. Repetitions and lists, often repeated verbatim, are certainly found in oral compositions, and here this phenomenon occurs in the lists of the officials (vss 2, 3, and 27 with a slight change), musical instruments (vss 5, 10, 15, and 7 with a slight change). But the repetitions in this chapter go far beyond that, since Shadrach, Meshach, and Abednego are mentioned as a group thirteen times. We note that nearly everything that is

mentioned in this legend is repeated mechanically, to a very comical effect.[31]

The repetition is in fact found in almost every verse of the story, except at two places: in the apologia of the Jews, which implies a contrast of their character with that of the other actors, but also strangely at vs 8, which states that "Chaldaean men" (גברין כשדאין) came forward to accuse the Jews. Not only is this plot element presented simply and unmechanically, but even stranger, these villains are not punished in the end. In verse 20 it is the "mighty men of his army" (גברין גברי־חיל די בחילה) who are commanded to bind the three Jews and throw them into the furnace, and they are the ones who are punished in vs 22. These characters are mentioned with the repetition typical of the story: their designation consists of two different roots repeated twice each. The moral imbalance and the lack of repetition are both remedied if we assume that originally it was the mighty men of the army who acccused the Jews, and then suffer for their perfidy. With this solution the moral balance is returned to the story, and the characteristic repetitions are associated with the antagonists. The fact that "Chaldaeans" appear so often in Daniel 1 – 6 merely serves to confirm this as a redactional gloss.[32]

5) Law of contact in denouement: at the climax of the action the protagonist and antagonist are in close contact. In vss 22 and 26 we see this tendency reflected, when first the mighty men and then the king are literally in close contact with the three Jews, so close that the heat is felt. The fact that the Chaldaeans are no longer present in this scene is only more evidence that they were originally not part of the story.

6) Two laws which I will place together are the law of the single strand and the law of concentration on the leading character: a single strand of plot development is followed in oral narratives, with no subplots, and a single character or group remains the focus throughout. The latter of these is considered by Olrik the "greatest law of folk tradition."[33] Here we also find Daniel 3 in accord with the indicators of oral tradition.

---

[31] Hector Avalos (unpublished seminar paper at Harvard University, fall, 1986) notes the many repetitions in Daniel 3 and ascribes them to an attempt on the part of the author or redactor to satirize pagan authorities. At the very least, they are comical, if not satirical.

[32] In court conflicts concerning Zoroaster, it is also sometimes "Chaldaeans" who conspire against him, not Magi, as one might expect. A Persian/Babylonian tension is perhaps reflected here too, just as an anti-Median tension may be reflected in the Magophonia tradition. For Daniel 3, however, Hartman and Di Lella (*Daniel*, 159, 163) suggest that the Greek text of vss 46 – 50 reflects the original story line, in which the ones who are slain are "Chaldaeans."

[33] Olrik, "Laws," 139.

Only in vss 22–25 are difficulties encountered. Verses 22–23 (the demonstration of the heat of the furnace) strikes the reader as being superfluous and melodramatic, and worse yet, involves an awkward plot repetition: the heroes are thrown into the furnace twice (vss 21 and 23). However, in view of the use of repetitions for comic effect, this may be original to the story. The introduction of the angel in vss 22–25 also distracts from the single focus of the narrative, coming as it does right at the climax, and it has been suggested that this element has been added to the story.[34] In the LXX additions, of course, this subplot is carried much further at the written stage of redaction, and the reader is transported into the furnace for what seems to be an eternity.[35]

Whatever approach is taken to the angelophany, the story is in general well constructed and does not betray many evidences of redactional activity (other than the addition of Chaldaeans). It was probably orally composed, and follows the typical pattern of the court conflict fairly closely: there is a conspiracy against the heroes, instigated by Chaldean courtiers or mighty men of the army (vs 8), but the three companions of Daniel are saved from the decreed punishment through the intervention of God, and are acclaimed by Nebuchadnezzar as worthy counselors. Certain differences can nevertheless be noted between this story and the standard court conflict as witnessed in non-Jewish sources and in Esther. First, the conspiracy of the Chaldeans is tied up with an edict that would force idolatrous worship of a gold image upon Jews. This adds the element of religious persecution to the plot structure which is missing in, for example, the story of Croesus before Cambyses (Herodotus 3.35–6), Ahikar, and Esther, in all three of which the personal antagonisms at court provide the motive for the persecution.[36] Second, and related to this, is the negative view toward the king, at least up until the very end, which is also not generally a part of the court conflict. The king in the court conflict is usually depicted as falling under the influence of villainous courtiers and his own unwise decisions, as in the legends mentioned above, but as Collins notes, in Daniel 3–5 the king is much more antagonistic.[37] We thus find here an adaptation of the common genre plot structure to a more pointed critique of imperial institutions (whether of the Babylonian, Persian, or Hellenistic empires), with an increased tension in regard to the religious demands of the ruling society and the necessity of the hero to witness to

---

[34] R. H. Charles, *A Critical and Exegetical Commentary on the Book of Daniel* (Oxford: Clarendon, 1929) 72–75.

[35] Hartman and Di Lella (*Daniel*, 159) suggest another solution to the problem, which is to prefer the slightly longer reading of the LXX (minus the inserted prayers).

[36] Collins, Vision, 50–52.

[37] Ibid., 47, 52.

Jewish piety. The essentially comic nature of the story, however, should be kept in mind when assessing the view of the king. In tone, this narrative is similar to the final layer of MT Esther.

Daniel 4

With Daniel 4, 5, and 6, the analysis of possible redactional stages of the Daniel legends is given a major impetus by the fact that the Old Greek text (OG) of these chapters differs from the MT and the Theodotionic translation much more than it does in the rest of Daniel 1 – 12. This has led some scholars to suggest that, since two separate recensions exist for these three chapters only, they may have once circulated independently of the rest of the corpus, either as the older, original core of the Daniel tradition, or as a later, apocopated version of Daniel 1 – 6.[38] The former point of view has recently been given a thorough investigation by Ernst Haag in a study which bears heavily on the present analysis.[39] By beginning with the observation that the difference between the MT and the OG in Daniel 4 – 6 indicates that these chapters may have formed an early, independent corpus, Haag develops a thorough source analysis of these chapters with many useful insights. He ignores, however, another implication of this difference between the OG and the MT: the OG may be a better witness than the MT to the *Vorlage* of these chapters.

Because of its conflated and disjointed nature, most scholars have considered the OG to be inferior to the MT. Reading the OG version of Daniel 4 – 6 is like wandering through an attic, full of old and discarded fragments. R. H. Charles, G. Jahn, and Paul Riessler,[40] however, have argued that in

---

[38] James A. Montgomery (*The Book of Daniel* [ICC; New York: Scribners, 1927] 24 – 57, esp. 37) discusses the question and takes the latter position. The Theodotionic recension replaced the OG of Daniel in the LXX version transmitted to us. For a discussion of how this process came about, see Sidney Jellicoe, *The Septuagint and Modern Study* (Ann Arbor: Eisenbrauns, 1978) 84 – 90; and the major commentaries.

[39] Haag, *Die Errettung Daniels aus der Löwengrube* (Stuttgart: Katholisches Bibelwerk, 1983).

[40] Charles, *Book of Daniel*, lvi – lvii, 79 – 82, 119 – 124; and G. Jahn *Das Buch Daniel nach der Septuaginta hergestellt* (Leipzig: Pfeiffer, 1904) passim; and Paul Riessler, *Das Buch Daniel* (Stuttgart/Wien: Roth'sche, 1899) 28 – 44. The superiority of the MT was promulgated by August Bludau, *Die alexandrinische Übersetzung des Buches Daniel und ihr Verhältnis zum massorethischen Text* (Freiburg: Herder'sche, 1897) 31, 143 – 54; and later by Montgomery, *Daniel*; the latter's views can be found in three excurses at the end of his commentary on chaps. 4, 5, and 6. Most other scholars follow Montgomery, and especially to be noted is David Satran, "Early Jewish and Christian Interpretation of the Fourth Chapter of the Book of Daniel," (Ph.D. dissertation, Hebrew University, 1985). Recently, however, Sharon Pace ("The Stratigraphy of the Text of Daniel and the Question of Theological *Tendenz* in the Old Greek," *Bulletin of the*

many readings it represents an older and better text. Wandering through this attic is in fact like wandering through the attic of Queen Elizabeth or Abraham Lincoln: it is full of historical treasures and first drafts. I will present new evidence here in support of this position, and try to show that the OG text is not just to be preferred for individual readings, but is throughout the better witness to the original text. By comparing Haag's source analysis of the MT with the OG text—here focusing on Daniel 4—we will be able to derive much surer and more detailed insights into proposed sources of these chapters. This process also then provides a basis for isolating redactional tendencies in the MT.

At the risk of over-simplifying Haag's minute analysis of the texts, his view of the development of Daniel 4 – 6 follows along these lines: at the core of these chapters lie two stories with similar structure and intent concerning Nebuchadnezzar and his "son" Belshazzar which circulated together, with no mention of Daniel. They are Dan 4:25 – 30 MT (Nebuchadnezzar's pronouncement from his palace wall) and Daniel 5 (with many phrases excised).[41] Haag's reconstruction of Dan 4:25 – 30 is as follows:

> King Nebuchadnezzar walked along the roof of the royal palace of Babylon. The king said: "Is not this Babylon great, which I have built with my mighty power as a royal residence, to the glory of my majesty!" While the words were still in the king's mouth, a voice fell from heaven: "To you, King Nebuchadnezzar, it is decreed: Your majesty is removed from you! You will be driven out of human society; you will live with the beasts of the field, and be fed grass like the cattle." At that moment this pronouncement was fulfilled against Nebuchadnezzar. He was expelled from human society. He ate grass like the cattle; his body was moistened with the dew of heaven, and his hair became as long as eagle feathers and his nails like a bird's talons.

Haag's reconstruction of Daniel 5 results in a short narrative of an unearthly hand which interrupts Belshazzar's feast to write a condemning inscription on the wall. Immediately after, Belshazzar dies, with no role for Daniel nor with any interpretation of the writing. Although one may find it hard to believe that there is no figure to interpret the writing in Daniel 5, his hypothesis concerning these two stories possesses an intriguing logic. They can stand alone as two similarly structured stories of revealed judgment against the first and last kings of the neo-Babylonian empire (as understood

---

International Organization for Septuagint and Cognate Studies 17 [1984] 21) has allowed that the OG may represent some older traditions. See also her new book (under the name of Sharon Pace Jeansonne), *The Old Greek Translation of Daniel 7–12* (CBQMS 19; Washington: Catholic Biblical Association of America, 1988).

[41] Haag, *Errettung*, 23 – 25, 49 – 62, 72 – 73.

by the author). They both begin by demonstrating the *hybris* of the king of Babylon, then recount a sudden and mysterious intervention from heaven with a message of judgment, and close with the fulfillment of this judgment on the king. The focus of these two stories is on the fall of Babylon, not on the return of Jews from Exile, and there is no sense of an eschatological expectation. The orientation is not on the future, but on the lessons of the past. These stories were then combined, according to Haag's theory, with two sapiential legends about the wise courtier Daniel, Dan 4:1–23 (Daniel interprets a dream as a warning to Nebuchadnezzar) and 6:4–27 (again, with many excisions).[42] The reconstruction of Dan 4:1–23:

4:1 I was lying content in my house
    and happy in my palace.
  2 I saw a dream which terrified me,
    dream-visions from my bed.
  5 Then Daniel entered,
    in whom is the spirit of the holy gods,
    and I told him the dream.
  7 I beheld from my bed:
    Behold, a tree stood in the middle of the earth
    and was very high.
  8 The tree grew and became strong,
    its top reached up to heaven
    and its boughs to the end of the earth.
  9 Its foliage was beautiful;
    it brought forth fruit bountifully,
    and nourishment for all was found in it.
    Under it the beasts of the field sought shade,
    the birds of heaven lived in its branches,
    and all flesh took nourishment from it.
 10 Behold, a Watcher and holy one
    descended from heaven
 11 and called with a loud voice:
    Cut down the tree
    and chop off its branches!
    Cast off its leaves
    and scatter its fruit!
    Let the animals flee from it
    and the birds leave its branches!
 12 Leave only the stump in the earth!

---

[42] Ibid., 73–88. Haag (p. 83) rejects the term ''court legends'' for these narratives.

14 The order derives from the decree of the Watchers;
     the judgment has come through the word of the holy ones.
15 I, the king, saw this dream.
16 Then Daniel began and said:
17 The tree, which you saw,
19 O King, was you.
21 But this is the meaning, O King:
23 The decree to leave your stump
     (means): your kingdom remains reserved for you,
     provided you recognize that Heaven is Lord.

The other sapiential legend about Daniel is Daniel 6, which Haag edits to a more economical story, but without major changes. The two sapiential Daniel stories were then placed as an envelope around the two stories of pronouncements against Babylonian kings, and were further redacted into a compositional unity.[43] In the process the original intention of the pronouncement stories is sometimes lost, as for example, when the negative judgment against Nebuchadnezzar is softened and his repentance allows for a recovery from his affliction (Dan 4:31 – 34 MT). Haag is probably correct to consider Daniel 4 – 6 as an independently circulating corpus which had as building blocks—among other things—these four separate units, but this does not exhaust the possible source analysis.

Daniel 4 is seen by most scholars to be based on an account similar to *Prayer of Nabonidus* from Qumran (4QPrNab), though Haag would rather see the direction of influence reversed.[44] Most of the parallels between 4QPrNab and Daniel 4 are, in Haag's source division, to the redactional stages of the latter and not to his purported sources. Thus Haag would prefer to look elsewhere for background influences on Daniel 4, and these he finds in Jeremiah 27 and 50 – 51. Before we consider this possibility, however, we should compare 4QPrNab with the two stories which Haag posits as the sources of chapter 4; we shall also consider the OG version of these stories, a step which Haag did not take.

In 4QPrNab, Nabonidus reports in the first person that he failed to find relief from skin lesions until he prayed to the "God Most High." The struc-

---

[43] Ibid., 99 – 128, esp. 99 – 108.

[44] David Noel Freedman ("The Prayer of Nabonidus," *BASOR* 145 [1954] 31 – 32) and Rudolf Meyer (*Das Gebet des Nabonid* [Berlin: Akademie, 1962] 111 – 12) represent the common view. Haag's position is found in *Errettung*, 63 – 69. Werner Dommershausen (*Nabonid im Buche Daniel* [Mainz: Grünewald, 1964] 84 – 85) occupies a middle ground on this issue. Other broad parallels should perhaps also be considered, e.g., the Famine Stela from Egypt, where a first-person inscription of a king reports a seven-year famine, which is brought to an end through the efforts of an efficacious priest.

ture of *Prayer of Nabonidus* is quite similar in some respects to Daniel's involvement with Nebuchadnezzar in Daniel 4, although the Jewish seer in 4QPrNab is unnamed, the name of the king is different, and the problem in the Qumran fragment is a disease, while in Daniel, a dream which defies interpretation. Ultimately, 4QPrNab and other Danielic fragments from Qumran must be placed in the context of a "Danielic school."[45] Even where that figure does not appear, we are likely dealing with a set of motifs and phrases which emanate from the same group. This issue will be raised again below. *Prayer of Nabonidus* reads:[46]

1 The words of the p[ra]yer which Nabonidus, king of the land of [Ba]bylon, the great king, pray[ed when he was stricken]
2 with an evil disease by the decree of G[o]d in Teman. [I Nabonidus] was stricken with [an evil disease]
3 for seven years, and from [that] (time) I was like [unto a beast and I prayed to the Most High]
4 and, as for my sin, he forgave it (or: my sin he forgave). A diviner—who was a Jew o[f the Exiles—came to me and said:]
5 'Recount and record (these things) in order to give honor and great-[ness] to the name of the G[od Most High.' And thus I wrote: I]
6 was stricken with an evil disease in Teman [by the decree of the Most High God, and, as for me,]
7 seven years I was praying [to] gods of silver and gold, [bronze, iron,]
8 wood, stone (and) clay, because [I was of the opini]on that th[ey] were gods
[   ].

This document can be divided into three parts. Lines 1–2a are a title in the form of a short, third-person introduction, which names the king and summarizes some of the events. Lines 2a-5 are a first-person summary of most of the events of Nabonidus's story, taking the form of an inscribed decree, ending with a Jewish sage's instructions to proclaim what God has done by means of this decree, and lines 5–end are the recounting of his experiences. The question of overall genre is not easily answered, but after the long title, it is essentially an idol parody narrative (described below in regard to Bel and the Dragon) disguised as a royal decree. Note that, despite what is said in line 1 and the name that has been given this writing, there is no prayer actually contained here, but only the *report* of a prayer. *The Praying of Nabonidus* would be a more accurate title.

---

[45] On the subject of a "Danielic school," I am indebted to many suggestions by Professor Frank Moore Cross.

[46] I follow here the reconstruction and translation of Frank Moore Cross, "Fragments of the Prayer of Nabonidus," IEJ 34 (1984) 260–64.

The scholarly concensus that 4QPrNab reflects an older tradition than Daniel 4 was based on several observations. First, the assimilation of a story concerning the more obscure Nabonidus to the legendary king Nebuchadnezzar seemed more likely than the reverse. Second, since the Jewish seer in 4QPrNab is unnamed, it seems more likely that the figure gains a name in Daniel 4 than that he loses one in 4QPrNab. Third, the historical traditions in 4QPrNab reflect accurate historical information about Nabonidus known from the Haran inscription. There are also indications that Daniel 4 represents an expansion of an account similar to 4QPrNab: elements of the latter are found in Daniel 4 in the two halves of the chapter. The Jewish seer comes to play in the king's first-person account of a dream interpretation, while the afflictions of the king for seven years are found only in the third-person account of the second half (Dan 4:25 – 30).[47]

The comparison of 4QPrNab with Daniel 4 must be broadened, however, to include the OG verson of Daniel 4; Daniel 4 OG has several points of comparison with 4QPrNab which are lacking in MT. Specifically, a first-person account of events in 4:30a-36/33 OG[48] is formally very similar to its counterpart in 4QPrNab. The section of Daniel 4 OG which is parallel to 4QPrNab can stand as an independent story, and is probably a much closer variant of 4QPrNab than is the rest of the OG or MT version. Here I present a translation of this section of Daniel 4 OG, with those parts attributed to redaction in italics.

> 30a I, Nebuchadnezzar, king of Babylon, was shackled for seven years.
> I was fed grass like a bull,
> and from the fields of the earth I ate.

---

[47] Haag (*Errettung*, 67 – 69), however, sees the combined form of Daniel 4 as more original. Since he splits the two halves of the chapter into two separate source stories, the fact that parallels are found in both halves indicates that 4QPrNab must have known the combined version. If Daniel 4 is divisible into two source stories as Haag suggests, then, to his mind, it is unlikely that both are dependent on 4QPrNab, and any direct influence must result from familiarity with the redacted form of Daniel 4 on the part of the composer of 4QPrNab. Further, it is the redactional layer of Daniel 4 (according to Haag's analysis) that contains the parallels with 4QPrNab, not the source layer. Daniel 5 can perhaps also be presumed: the list of materials of which the idols are made in 4QPrNab is almost identical to the list in Dan 5:4. Haag (ibid.) is, however, forced to argue that the accurate historical traditions concerning Nabonidus in 4QPrNab enter in late, when the king's name is changed.

[48] I will use the verse numbers of Joseph Ziegler's edition of the LXX of Daniel (*Susanna, Daniel, Bel et Draco* [Septuaginta, Vetus Testamentum Graecum 16:2; Göttingen: Vandenhoeck & Ruprecht, 1954]), which where possible follows the MT numbering, and places the LXX numbers second. Note that the numbering in Alfred Rahlfs' edition (*Septuaginta* [2 vols.; Stuttgart: Deutsche Bibelstiftung, 1935]) will sometimes correspond to the latter, but not consistently.

And after seven years I devoted my soul to prayer
and made supplication concerning my sins before the Lord God of heaven,
and concerning my transgressions I prayed to the Great God of Gods.
30b   *And my hair became like the feathers of a bird*
and my nails like a lion's.
My flesh and my heart were changed,
and I walked about naked with the beasts of the earth.
I saw a dream, and dark forebodings came over me,
and eventually a great sleep overcame me
and a drowsiness fell upon me.
30c   *And at the end of the seven years the time of my redemption came,*
and (the expiation of) my sins and my ignorances was fulfilled
    before the God of heaven.
I prayed concerning my transgressions to the Great God of Gods,
when an angel called to me from heaven and said,
"Nebuchadnezzar, serve the Holy God of Heaven
and give glory to the Most High.
The palace of your people is returned to you.
36/33   At that time my kingdom was returned to me,
and my glory was given back to me.

Like Daniel 4 in general, this section *as it stands* is a morass of conflicting images and logical difficulties. Not only are the images of the affliction mixed, but the order of events is very difficult to reconcile:

1) I became like a bull;
2) after seven years I prayed;
3) I was changed into an unreal beast and had dreams;
4) at the end of seven years my sins were expiated;
5) I prayed;
6) an angel said to praise God; and
7) at that time I was returned to the throne.

The descriptions of the afflictions are duplicated (numbers 1 and 3 here), as are the prayers (2 and 5), which gives a disjointed and repetitive account of the king's experience. A long and confused collection of doxological fragments also follows at this point. However, within this farrago of story fragments, a source can be recovered with a fair degree of certainty. My reconstructed version of 4:30a-36/33 (hereafter called "Bull Sojourn"), is given here. The doxological fragments which conclude Daniel 4 OG are difficult to disentangle, but it is likely that at least the last half of vs 34b was once part of the conclusion of this source, since it matches closely the theme of repentance, and is included also:

I, Nebuchadnezzar, king of Babylon,
was shackled for seven years.
I was fed grass like a bull,
and from the fields of the earth I ate.
And after seven years I devoted my soul to prayer
and made supplication concerning my sins
before the Lord God of Heaven, . . .
I prayed concerning my transgressions to the Great God of Gods,
when an angel called to me from heaven and said,
"Nebuchadnezzar, serve the Holy God of Heaven
and give glory to the Most High.
The palace of your nation is returned to you."
At that moment my kingdom was returned to me
and my glory was given back to me. . . .
I, king of kings, publicly give thanks to him,
because he dealt with me thus:
on the same day he returned me to my throne,
and I regained control of my authority
and my kingdom among my people,
and my majesty was returned to me.

This reconstruction requires some explanation. Like 4QPrNab, it takes the pseudepigraphic form of a royal decree, but executes it more consistently. The coherence and completeness of this account indicate that it could have stood as an early independent account—much like 4QPrNab—which was then combined with other similar accounts into a larger story. Corroborating this observation is the fact that it does not fit well in its present context. Immediately preceding this is Nebuchadnezzar's statement from his palace wall, recounted in the third person, which has just been answered by a voice from heaven condemning Nebuchadnezzar to a seven-year exile and punishment. At this point the account switches back to the first person, which is the beginning of what I have reconstructed here, and introduces the king anew: "I, Nebuchadnezzar, king of Babylon...." The new introduction could be ascribed to the king's public decree, and it is also balanced by the first-person narration at the beginning of Daniel 4, but it is significant that the account as a whole presumes nothing from the preceding narrative. The MT at this point places the description of the afflictions in the third person (vs 30), which accords with the third-person narrative of vss 25–29 MT (28/25 – 33/30 OG).[49]

---

[49] This should not be overlooked as yet another piece of evidence that the OG is closer to the *Vorlage*. It is more likely that the MT brought the various sections into mutual conformity than that OG disrupted the narrative flow.

Within the Bull Sojourn the verses were removed with the following rationale. Verses 30a–36/33 are a jumble of repetitions and conflations, especially between vss 30a and 30c, and we find this marked by a seam between the end of 30a and the middle of 30c. In both cases it is stated: "concerning my sins I prayed to the great God of gods."[50] It is quite common for a redactor to pause in copying a text, insert material, and then continue, repeating the identical line of the original text which preceded the insertion. The seam thus created is helpful in discerning added material. Although doublets such as this can also arise in orally transmitted narratives, in this case the more likely alternative is that a literary seam has resulted from the insertion of glosses into the narrative. The material between these two almost identical phrases is a series of disorganized images of the affliction: my hair became like the feathers of a bird, my nails became like a lion's, my flesh and heart were changed, I walked naked with the beasts of the earth, I saw dreams and visions, a great sleep fell upon me. In contrast with this, the description of the affliction from before the seam is simple and coherent, even exhibiting synonymous parallelism (as do some of the other stichoi): "I was fed grass like a bull, and from the plants of the earth I ate" (vs 30a). The king here appears to have become like a domesticated bull, and not like a wild and grotesque creature.[51] This is a crucial distinction, as we shall see below, despite the fact that in the MT the images of domestic and unreal creatures are totally interwoven (vs 30).

By removing the material between this seam, we not only arrive at a coherent array of images, mostly in parallel members, but the problems of logical order mentioned above are neatly removed: King Nebuchadnezzar is afflicted for seven years, prays, an angel comes and gives instructions, Nebuchadnezzar follows them and praises God. The beginning of vs 30c, which states that after seven years his sins were expiated and "the time" of his redemption had come, is now seen to be a prophetic fulfillment introduced by the redactor of Daniel 4 as a whole, and not part of this original source.

---

[50] περὶ τῶν ἀγνοιῶν μου τοῦ θεοῦ τῶν θεῶν τοῦ μεγάλου ἐδεήθην. Only the position of the verb differs in the two verses.

[51] Wild oxen still roamed in this period, but the image of feeding (Semitic ersatz passive: "they fed me" = "I was fed") implies that the king is meekly domesticated. David Marcus ("Animal Similes in Assyrian Royal Inscriptions," *Or* 46 [1977] 86–95) notes that in Assyrian inscriptions a wild bull (*rēmu*) simile is usually used in regard to crushing one's enemies, while the domesticated ox (*alpu*, *šūru*, the latter cognate to Hebrew *šôr*, Aramaic *tôr*) signifies a subjugated people, led by a rope placed through the nose. The Aramaic *tôr* which likely lies behind the Greek βοῦς of our text could mean either, and its use in 4QPrNab implies a wild animal, but its use here, which may be pre-"Danielic," leans more in the direction of a domesticated animal.

The doxological hymn and decree fragments at the end of Daniel 4 have arisen from the original sources that make up the chapter, as well as from the redactor's hand. For the source of the Bull Sojourn, the last half of vs 34b is the most likely hymnic conclusion, and is included in the reconstruction above. It is a concise statement of the king's new confession,[52] and confirms that he was placed again on his throne.

The relation between the Prayer of Nabonidus and this part of Daniel 4 is thus much closer when the OG text of Daniel 4 is used. Their relation can be seen more clearly with a tabular comparison of motifs:

4QPrNab	Bull Sojourn (30a – 36/33, 34b)
3rd-person intro	
I, Nabon., was stricken	I, Nebuch., was shackled
seven years	seven years
I was like [a beast]	I became like a bull
	after seven years
I prayed to Most High	I prayed to Great God of Gods
God forgave me	
Jewish seer said:	angel said from heaven:
Recount in writing and	
	serve God of Heaven and
praise name of Most High	give glory to God Most High
	kingdom returned
Thus I wrote:	
I was stricken	
by decree of God Most High	
seven years I prayed to	
gods of silver, gold, etc. . . .	
	I, King of Kings, give thanks;
	he returned me to throne

In the Daniel source, the king states in the first person that he was afflicted seven years, prayed to God, and that an angel came, who, like the seer in 4QPrNab, said to give praise to God. In addition to the similarities in the statement of the afflictions of these two accounts, it should also be noted that the function of the seer in 4QPrNab and the angel in Daniel 4 is quite parallel, in that they instruct the king in the proper worship of God. The reasons that were given above for supposing that the Qumran fragment attests the older and more accurate historical tradition still apply: it is more likely that

---

[52] Although in the original God was probably named rather than referred to pronominally (cf. τῷ ὑψίστῳ ἀνθομολογοῦμαι in vs 37/34, beginning). It is also possible that the doxology begins one phrase earlier, κυρίῳ τῷ θεῷ.

the king's name was changed from Nabonidus to Nebuchadnezzar than the other way around. Although the name of Nabonidus could have been added relatively late in the transmission, along with the pertinent facts of this king's departure to Teman, it is generally conceded that a change from a major figure to a minor figure is unlikely.

However, in other respects this hypothetical source of Daniel 4 reflects some elements that have a different function. The seer in 4QPrNab is awkwardly inserted and has little role in the account, entering only after the king is healed,[53] but is roughly equivalent in the structure of the narrative to the angel in the Daniel source, who has the crucial role of instructing the king in the means of being cured. Further, the doxological hymn at the end of the Daniel source follows perfectly in the narrative order. The decree in 4QPrNab, on the other hand, seems unnecessarily repetitive, both in its content and in its use of the inscription form, and involves the introduction of a new motif: the inability of the idols to heal him. This appears to be a separate redactional element, paralleled in Daniel 5, pushing the writing in the direction of an idol parody narrative. This may have caused the repetitiveness of the decree. Last, the Daniel source lacks the short third-person introduction of 4QPrNab; in this respect it is more like the beginning of Dan 4:1–24 as Haag reconstructs it. The third-person introduction detracts from the pseudepigraphic device of the inscription form.

The two documents in question probably do not exhibit direct literary dependence either way; it is sufficient to point out that they are closely related accounts. But for the study of the court legend, the intriguing possibility presents itself here that the Daniel 4 source reflects the earlier tradition (except for the name of the king), in which case we could discern an evolution of thinking about the role of Jews' relations with the king. First, in some accounts, such as 4:29/26–33/30 OG (analyzed below), God acts or speaks directly to the great Babylonian monarchs; in the Bull Sojourn of OG an angel speaks; in 4QPrNab it is an unnamed and nearly superfluous Jewish seer who speaks,[54] and finally, in the combined version of Daniel 4 OG, it is the Jewish courtier-hero Daniel, whose role is then increased in the MT. In terms of genre, it is an evolution from prophecy against the king to court

---

[53] The seer is unnecessary for the central declaration of King Nabonidus who, it should be noted, finds the God Most High, and thus his cure, with no help from the Jewish seer. The seer merely serves to suggest to the king that he proclaim his cure after the fact. This presumes the translation offered here. The other possible reading in line 4 is "the Jewish exorcist forgave. . . ." This is read by, e.g., A. Dupont-Sommer, *The Essene Writings from Qumran* (Gloucester, MA: Peter Smith, 1973) 322.

[54] As Professor Cross has cautioned me, however, we cannot tell whether this shadowy figure has any further identification later in the account, perhaps even as Daniel.

legend. But whatever the developmental order of the documents, it is clear that there are a variety of roles for the interlocutor of the king.

The Wall Pronouncement of Daniel 4

Next we may turn to the middle section of Daniel 4, Nebuchadnezzar's pronouncement from his city wall (hereafter referred to as the "Wall Pronouncement"), and again, working with the hypothesis that the OG is a better witness to the Vorlage than is the MT, I shall address the former version first. We shall also see that, like the "Bull Sojourn," the Wall Pronouncement likely derives from an independent source. Daniel 4:29/26–33/30 OG is translated here with proposed redactional glosses in italics:

29/26   *And after twelve months*
         The king was strolling about on the walls of his city in all his glory,
         and on the towers of the city he walked.
30/27   And he said: "Is not this Babylon great, which I have built,
         and the house of my kingdom which is in my firm control
            shall redound to my glory."
31/28   And when he finished speaking he heard a voice from heaven:
         "Take heed, King Nebuchadnezzar,
         the kingdom of Babylon has been taken away from you
            and given to another, a man hated in your house.
         Now I will set him upon your throne,
         and he will receive your authority and your glory and your riches,
         so that you will know that the God of heaven has authority
            in the human realm,
         and he will give it to whomever he wills,
         By morning[55] another king will reside contentedly in your house
         and will take control of your glory and your might
            and your authority.
32/29   *And the angels will pursue you for seven years,*
         and you will not be seen nor will you speak with anyone,
         and you will be fed grass like a bull,
         and your portion shall be from the grass of the earth.
         And, indeed, instead of receiving glory, you will be bound,
         and the house of your riches and your kingdom another will have.

[55] The Greek would mean "until morning" or "as far as the east," but neither of these quite fits. F. F. Bruce ("The Oldest Greek Version of Daniel," OTS 20 [1977] 28–31; followed by Satran, "Fourth Chapter," 77) translates ἕως δὲ ἡλίου ἀνατολῆς as "by morning," and although this is an unlikely translation, it seems the only possibility here.

33/30 By morning all these things will be visited upon you,
Nebuchadnezzar, king of Babylon,
and not one of all these things will be lacking.

The argument for an independent source here is partially based on the parallel to the Wall Pronouncement found in Eusebius *Praep. ev.* 9.41.456d – 457b, and attributed to Abydenos, who in turn quotes the Ionian historian Megasthenes:

Now Megasthenes says that Nebuchadnezzar was braver than Hercules, and made an expedition against Libya and Iberia, and, having subdued them, settled a part of their inhabitants on the right shore of the Pontus. After this, it is said by the Chaldaeans, he went up on his palace and was possessed by some god or other, and began to utter the following: "I, Nebuchadnezzar, O, Babylonians, am going to prophecy to you the coming calamity, which neither Belus my forefather, nor Beltis my queen was able to persuade the Fates to avert. A Persian mule will come, aided by alliances with your gods, and lead you into slavery. An ally of his will be a son of a Mede,[56] the Assyrian glory. How I wish that, before he gives over the citizens, some Charybdis or sea swallow him up thoroughly out of sight, or having turned in some other direction, he be carried through the wilderness, so that he be where there are neither cities nor human footprint, where beasts have their dwelling place, and birds roam, wandering as an outcast among the rocks and ravines. I wish I might have had a better end before all these things came into his mind." And when he had finished prophecying, he immediately disappeared, and his son Evil-Merodach began to rule.

The similarities with the Wall Pronouncement of Daniel 4 are striking,[57] especially when the OG version of these verses is compared:

Abydenos	4:29/26 – 33/30 OG
Nebuchadnezzar	Nebuchadnezzar
on roof of palace	on walls and tower of city:
	"Is not Babylon great?"

---

[56] I follow the well-accepted emendation of Μήδης to υἱός Μήδης. See Charles, *Book of Daniel*, 83.

[57] Several commentators note the relevance of the Abydenos fragment, but none pays it sufficient attention. Cf. Charles, *Book of Daniel*, 82–83; Norman Porteous, *Daniel* (OTL; London: SCM, 1979) 70–71; Aage Bentzen, *Daniel* (HAT; Tübingen: Mohr-Siebeck, 1937) 21; Eberh. (sic) Schrader, "Die Sage vom Wahnsinn Nebukadnezzar's," *Jahrbücher für Protestantische Theologie* 7 (1881) 618–22; and Montgomery, *Daniel*, 221–22.

revelation; king prophecies:	revelation; angelic voice:
Persian and "son of Mede" (Nabonidus?) will take kingdom	kingdom will be taken by "one hated in your household" (Evil-Merodach or Nabonidus?)
curse:	afflictions:
	angels will punish 7 years
Charybdis or sea swallow banished to wilderness no cities or people where beasts and birds live wander in rocks and ravines	eat grass as bull
	they will bind you kingdom to another
king disappears	king will be punished

The OG version probably reflects a source with a totally negative judgment on the king, in that his downfall at the hands of a usurper is obviously the culmination of the prophecy, while the possibility of repentance and reinstatement derives from the redaction of Daniel 4 as a whole. This reconstruction is similar to what Haag suggested for the source of the MT text, but had he made reference to the OG evidence, a somewhat different conclusion to the story might have resulted. In Haag's reconstruction, there is still a judgment against the king in which he becomes like a wild and unreal beast, and there is nothing said about what happens thereafter. This is possible; according to Haag, both this account and Daniel 5 are very short and end in enigmatic judgments.[58] However, in the OG, it seems more likely that the sojourn as a bull is not part of the original judgment. The loss of the kingdom by "one hated within your household" is the predicted judgment, and the seven-year sojourn as a bull is completely intruded from the Bull Sojourn source. The Wall Pronouncement source of Daniel 4 OG, a negative prophecy against the king, evidently used the same or nearly the same tradition as the pro-Babylonian version which Abydenos attests, but overturns it in a polemical critique.[59] Although the source of the Wall Pronouncement in OG is totally negative in its judgment on the king, Abydenos's source was not. There the king is treated sympathetically, even heroically, is inspired by a god to prophesy, and is not humiliated at the end, but disappears. This disap-

---

[58] Cf. above, pp. 87–89; and Haag, *Errettung*, 23–25, 49–62.

[59] The Abydenos fragment also contains animal images which are paralleled in the Bull Sojourn section of Daniel 4 OG, but the Bull Sojourn, as reconstructed, portrayed the king as becoming like a domesticated bull, not like a wild or unreal beast.

pearance may reflect the hope of an eschatological restoration. The sudden disappearance of a revered figure, often to appear elsewhere, is a well-attested motif in the ancient Near East.[60] If, as Collins suggests, the original prophecy which lay behind Daniel 2 looked forward to the restoration of the Babylonian Empire,[61] then one can easily imagine Abydenos's source, identified as coming from the Chaldaeans through the Ionian historian Megasthenes, as holding out the same hope.

The OG version of these verses of Daniel 4, then, yields up a plausible separate tradition, which suggests an independent source, and this is accomplished without a great degree of hypothetical reconstruction. All that was required was the removal of the two parallel lines which included the bull motif, presumably intruded from the verses of Daniel 4 analyzed in the previous section. Viewing the Abydenos fragment side-by-side with the parallel part of Daniel 4 OG only reinforced this conclusion. The real issue in both the Abydenos fragment and *this* part of Daniel 4 is usurpation, not a sojourn as a wild beast.

The Dream Interpretation Account of Daniel 4

Where Haag found one source at the end of Daniel 4, through an analysis of OG I have postulated two, the Bull Sojourn and the Wall Pronouncement. Evidence that the OG is the better witness to the *Vorlage* will continue to mount, as we begin to investigate the beginning of chapter 4, the Dream Interpretation account. Only here is there a courtier who is identified as Daniel, and this account is perhaps closer in structure to Daniel 2, another dream interpretation account, than it is to the other proposed sources of Daniel 4. The Dream Interpretation section is translated here, with the proposed redactional sections in italics (numbers are the verse numbers as given in the Göttingen LXX):

> 4:4/1 In the eighteenth year of his rule, Nebuchadnezzar said:
> "I was happily residing in my house
> and resting contentedly on my throne.
> 5/2 I saw a dream and was dumbfounded,
> and fear seized me.

---

[60] Cf. Herodotus 4.14–15; Ovid *Fasti* 2.481–509; Livy 1.16; Plutarch *Romulus* 27–28; Philo *Vita Mos.* 2.51 288–91, Philostratus *Apollonius of Tyana* 8.10–11, 30–31 and the gospel empty-tomb narratives.

[61] Collins, *Vision*, 42.

10/7   I was sleeping, when before me there appreared an exceedingly tall tree
growing up out of the earth.
The appearance of it was great,
and there was none other like it.

12/9   *Its branches were about thirty stadia high,*
and in its shade were all the beasts of the earth,
and the birds of heaven were nesting in it.
Its fruit was plentiful and ripe
and it provided nourishment for all the animals.

11/8   And the appearance of it was great.
The foliage of it reached to heaven
and the shade-area up to the clouds,
filling the whole area under heaven,
and the sun and the moon dwelt in it
and illuminated the whole earth.

13/10   I was watching this dream before my eyes,
when, suddenly, an angel was sent with all authority from heaven

14/11   and he called and said concerning it,[62] "Cut it down and destroy it,
for it has been decreed by the Most High to uproot it and demolish it."

15/12   *But thus he said: "Leave one of its roots in the earth,*
so that it may graze on grass like an ox in the mountains with the beasts
of the earth,

16/13   *and from the dew of heaven its body may be changed,*
and for seven years it may be pastured with them,

17/14   *until it knows that the Lord of Heaven has authority over all*
things in heaven and on earth,
and whatever he wills, he does to them.

14a   Before me it was cut down in one day,
and it was destroyed in one hour of the day.
The branches were spread to all the winds,
and it was dragged off and thrown away.
And it ate grass with the beasts of the earth
and was taken under guard,
and was bound by them in shackles and bronze manacles.
I was awestruck by all this,
but then the dream disappeared from before my eyes.

18/15   And when I arose early from my bed,
I summoned Daniel,
the leader of the sages
and the head of those who interpret dreams.
I described the dream to him,
and he showed me the entire interpretation of it.

---

[62] Montgomery (*Daniel*, 249) notes (quoting Bertholdt) that the Greek αὐτῷ must translate
Aramaic לה, "in regard to it."

19/16   *Daniel was greatly amazed,*
        and dark forebodings gripped him,
        and he grew frightened and began to tremble,
        and his appearance changed,
        and his head bobbed up and down for an hour,
        and awestruck, he answered me in a soft voice:
        O King, may this dream be for those who hate you,
        and may its interpretation come upon your enemies.
20/17   The tree which grew up in the earth,
        whose appearance was great,
        is you, O King.
21/18   *And all the birds of heaven which were nesting in it,*
        they are the greatness of the land and of the nations
        and of all the tongues to the ends of the earth
        and all the regions which serve you.
22/19   And that the tree rose up and approached heaven
        and the foliage of it touched the clouds:
        you, O King, were raised up over all the people
        who are on the face of the whole earth,
        your heart was raised up in arrogance and might
        through all the acts against the holy one and his angels.
        Your deeds were seen, in that you made desolate the house
        of the living God on account of the sins of the sanctified people.
23/20   And the vision, which you saw,
        that an angel was sent with all authority from the Lord and
        that he said to pull out the tree and cut it down:
        The prophetic word of the Great God will come upon you,
24/21   and the Most High and his angels are pursuing you.
25/22   *They will lead you away under guard*
        and will send you away to a deserted place.
26/23   *And the root of the tree which was left,*
        since it was not thrown away:
        The place of your throne will be safeguarded for you
        for a time and an hour.
        Indeed they are preparing themselves against you
        and will whip you
        and will bring on the things judged against you.
        The lord lives in heaven,
        and his authority is over all the earth.
27/24   *Pray to him concerning your sins*
        that in his mercy he may pardon all your wickedness,
        in order that it may go easily for you
        and you remain on the throne of your kingdom for many years,
        and not be destroyed.
        Heed these words,

> *for my accounting is accurate,*
> *and your time is at hand.*
> 28/25 *And at the conclusion of these words,*
> *Nebuchadnezzar, when he heard the interpretation of the vision,*
> *took these words to heart.*

The OG begins the story with a chronicles-style dating in the year of the reign of the king: "In the eighteenth year of the reign of Nebuchadnezzar. ..." This is identical to the dating which is found at 3:1 in both OG and Th, but not in MT. This manner of introduction is often found at the beginning of the popular writings of this period, when they take on historicizing pretentions,[63] and may indicate the original introduction to the early corpus of Daniel 4–6, just as its presence in Dan 3:1 OG, and then 2:1 and 1:1 may indicate the transferral of this element to these chapters as they were added on at the beginning of the original corpus. The letter and doxology with which the MT of Daniel 4 begins is lacking at the beginning of Daniel 4 OG, but an almost identical one is found at the end (vs 34c). Haag rightly eliminates these verses from the beginning of the MT to restore the source, but this step is unnecessary in the OG.[64]

The first-person narration of events by Nebuchadnezzar which then follows draws our attention to the possibility of formal similarity with the Bull Sojourn, but whereas the Bull Sojourn takes the form of a royal decree, the Dream Interpretation presents these words as part of the chronicles of the king. Since Daniel has such a limited role in Daniel 4 OG, it is perhaps better to classify the entire chapter in this way, that is, as a chronicle of Nebuchadnezzar's reign. Nebuchadnezzar states that he has had a terrifying dream (vs 5/2), and in the OG immediately proceeds to recount it (vss 10/7–17/14a). In the MT, however, before the king recounts the dream, he summons by decree all the sages of Babylon (vs 3). They are unable to interpret the dream (vs 4), but Daniel then enters (vss 5–6), and only then is the dream recounted (vss 7–14 MT). Haag excises the other courtiers and their failure from the source, pointing out that they have no further role in the story, but leaves vs 5 detailing the entrance of Daniel.[65] A comparison with

---

[63] See Chapter 4 for a discussion of this formula, regarding Esth 1:1. Cf. Dan 1:1, 2:1, and 7:1 MT; and Jud 1:1. Montgomery (*Daniel*, 247) notes that this year would correspond to Nebuchadnezzar's despoiling of the Jerusalem temple, mentioned also at 4:22/19 OG.

[64] Satran ("Fourth Chapter," 62–94) observes this difference between MT and OG, and argues that it indicates that OG is a secondary redaction of MT. Some of the other chapters of Daniel 1–6 have doxologies at the end, and so it is more likely that OG has moved the doxology to conform to that pattern than that the MT would disrupt it. His argument is valid, but to my mind not strong enough to outweigh the other arguments for the priority of the OG.

[65] Haag, *Errettung*, 15–16.

the OG, which lacks this verse as well, indicates that all mention of Daniel is postponed until after the dream is recounted.[66]

In the dream description of OG a doublet is found between vss 10/7 and 11/8 (vs 12/9 lies in between these two verses, as the numbering is based on the MT order); both verses have identical statements concerning the tree: "The appearance of it was great" (ἡ ὅρασις αὐτοῦ μεγάλη). Both lines introduce visions of the tree which are quite different conceptions. The first (vs 12/9) says that the branches of it are thirty stadia (three miles) tall, and in its shade are all the beasts of the earth, in its branches are all the birds of the air, and it provided fruit for all the creatures.[67] This pastoral metaphor for the Great King's life-giving abundance for his people can be contrasted with the more mythological conception found in vs 11/8 (which *follows* vs 12/9): the top of the tree reached to heaven and the shade-area of it reached up to the clouds, encompassing the area under heaven; the sun and the moon dwelt in it and illuminated all the earth. There is nothing here concerning the bounty of the tree or the protection of animals, but the cosmic height of it is emphasized instead.

Both depictions are derived ultimately from notions of a world tree which is planted by the waters of the underworld, and whose top reaches to heaven, but they lack some of the stock elements of these parallels, such as a mountain or a Garden-of-Eden setting, roots leading down to the subterranean waters, or a comparison with the forest of lesser trees which surrounds the

---

[66] Charles, *Daniel*, 82.

[67] A Babylonian inscription, found at Wadi Brissa, also makes use of an image of Babylon as a great tree: "Under (Babylon's) everlasting shadow, I have gathered all the peoples in peace" (Stephen Langdon, *Building Inscriptions of the Neo-Babylonian Empire* [Part I; Paris: Leroux, 1905] B. Col. VIII. lines 17–35, 45–50, pp. 171–72.) Rudolf Meyer (*Das Gebet des Nabonid* [Berlin: Akademie, 1962] 44–45) and Aage Bentzen (*Daniel* [HAT 19; Tübingen: Mohr-Siebeck, 1937] 19) have utilized this as a parallel to the tree in Daniel 4, although it must be granted that it is a vague use of the metaphor. (Note that Bentzen gives the reference incorrectly.) However, other aspects of this inscription also recall Daniel 4. "Vast peoples" of the empire are said here to live in peace, which reminds us of the circular decrees in Daniel 4 to "all the peoples, languages," etc., and it has a closer reference to the interpretation of the pastoral image of the tree in vs 21/18 OG: "the might of the land and of the nations and of all the languages to the ends of the earth and all the regions. . . ." The importance of the palace in this inscription also calls to mind the centrality of that motif in vs 34c OG, and the many references to the "great gods" (*ilâni rabûti*) in this inscription may account to some extent for the presence of the epithet "the great god" in the same doxological fragment. The column just before this one at Wadi Brissa describes the great feast which Nebuchadnezzar gave at the Babylonian New Year Festival. This festival, as I shall try to show below, is the fictitious setting of the feast of Daniel 5. This particular inscription only constitutes a distant parallel, and should not be overinterpreted; it is not the source of the imagery in Daniel 4, but rather, as a pseudepigraphic inscription, the Dream Interpretation source of Daniel 4 utilizes these same stereotyped formulations.

one great tree.[68] What differentiates the two descriptions in Daniel, however, is the way that they utilize this myth: the second description of the tree in vs 11/8 taps more of the mythological content than does the first in vs 12/9.[69] Here there is very little of the mythological conception of the world tree left. Parallels of a cosmic figure, not necessarily a tree, which eclipses the sun and moon can also be sought in Jewish and Christian mythological descriptions of the coming of the redeemer (or of the law), especially in Ignatius *Ephesians* 19, where it is said that the great star (redeemer) is surrounded by the sun and the moon and all the stars.[70]

In OG these two separate conceptions are juxtaposed, and the seam which probably resulted from the insertion still remains. In the MT, however, the editing of these two different conceptions into one smooth text has been quite artfully accomplished: the tree grew and reached up to heaven and the shade-area of it reached to the ends of the earth; the leaves were full and the fruit of it provided food for all; beneath it lived the beasts of the field and in the branches lived the birds of heaven. Elements are present here from both versions in the OG. It could, of course, be argued that since these elements were all mythological commonplaces, the order of composition is not neces-

---

[68] See Geo Widengren, *The King and the Tree of Life in Ancient Near Eastern Religion* (King and Saviour IV; Uppsala: Lundequistska, 1951) 45–58, esp. 42–43; Walther Zimmerli, *Ezekiel* (Hermeneia; 2 vols.; Philadelphia: Fortress, 1979–83) 2. 146; and Susan Niditch, *The Symbolic Vision in Biblical Tradition* (Chico: Scholars Press, 1980) 108–12. For the Hebrew Bible parallels to this image, see Louis F. Hartman, "The Great Tree and Nebuchodonosor's Madness," in J. L. McKenzie, ed., *The Bible in Current Catholic Thought* (New York: Herder, 1962) 75–82; Hartman and Di Lella, *Daniel*, 176; and Montgomery, *Daniel*, 228–29. Cf. esp. Ezek 31:2–18, 17:2–24; Is 6:13; and also 1QH 6:14–19 and 8:4–15. Cf. also Herodotus 1.108, 3.30, and 7.19, and on later parallels, esp. Christian, see Richard Bauckham, "The Parable of the Vine: Rediscovering a Lost Parable of Jesus," *NTS* 33 (1987) 84–101.

[69] It should be noted, however, that Ezek 31:2–18 contains a set of motifs which I have separated in Daniel 4 into two distinct visions—a tree touching heaven, with large branches in which the animals and birds reside, and which is overcome with arrogance. Hence it could be argued that the visions need not be separated. My argument, however, is not that these motifs cannot be found together, but that two distinct visions emerge in the vision and the interpretation.

[70] Very similar mythical conceptions to Ignatius *Ephesians* 19 can be found in the Nag Hammadi documents, and Jewish attestation can be seen in *Testament of Levi* 18 and Baruch 3:33–4:3, which are perhaps also influenced by Num 24:17. The depiction of Yahweh as the Divine Warrior also utilizes a chorus of the sun and moon (Ps 148:3), which has influenced Rev 12:1; see Cross, *Canaanite*, 168–69. I hope to pursue a further investigation of this mythical motif at some future time, but see Jean Daniélou, *Primitive Christian Symbols* (Baltimore: Helicon, 1964) 120. Helmut Koester (*Synoptische Überlieferung bei den Apostolischen Vätern* [TU 65; Berlin: Akademie, 1957] 31–32) also notes that the star in Matthew 2 may be an historicized version of the myth in Ignatius *Ephesians* 19, and it also seems that Justin *Dial.* 45 is a semihistoricized midpoint between these two. The advent of Zoroaster is also symbolized by a tree in *Shah Nameh* 13.2, with the leaves representing counsel and the fruit wisdom.

sarily two descriptions in OG combined into one in the MT; the MT version might, in fact, have preceded the OG version. That the MT redactor may have had the broader mythological pattern in mind is not to be denied, but the separation of motifs in OG would then have to be explained. The possibility that the OG version has resulted from a separation of the motifs found in MT into royal/pastoral on one hand and cosmic on the other, each introduced with an identical phrase, is not likely. It is more likely that the version attested in the OG came about first. The identical introductory verses indicate the seam which was produced when the royal/pastoral image was inserted into the more mythological vision. Furthermore, a reason for inserting these verses can be propounded: they were added to bring a totally negative symbol of royal hybris into line with a less condemning view of a king who is to be chastized, and who holds sway over the varied ethnic composition of the empire, a motif found elsewhere in Daniel 4. In addition, we shall see that each of these two visions corresponds to a separate stratum in the further composition of the Dream Interpretation in the OG. The MT redactor has evidently smoothed out the vision by combining the two into one coherent account, keeping the cosmic magnitude of the tree from the more mythological conception, and the pastoral metaphor of the tree's abundance.

The fate of the great tree in the dream is also presented differently in OG, and here too a separation can be made in the text into strata. First, we should consider the section which describes the announcement of judgment, broken down here into the separate parts of the punishment (taken from vss 14/11 – 17/14):

1) cut it down and destroy it;
2) it has been decreed by the Most High to uproot it and destroy it;
3) leave its root in the earth;
4) with the beasts let it be fed grass like a bull;
5) from the dew of heaven its body will be changed;
6) seven years it will be fed with them; and
7) until it knows that Lord of Heaven has authority.

The judgment in the dream is then enacted (from vs 14a):

8) it was cut down in one hour of the day;
9) its branches were spread to all the winds;
10) it was dragged out and thrown away;
11) it ate grass with the beasts of the field; and
12) it was placed in prison in shackles and manacles.

The abrupt mixing of different sorts of images indicates that several hands are at work. In the announcement of judgment section (numbers 1 – 7), a tree is destroyed, but the root is saved and eats grass like a bull for seven years.

Several separate images are obviously mixed here; the destruction of the tree goes with the original dream interpretation, while the fate of the root is added, and the seven-year sojourn as a bull is introduced from the Bull Sojourn story.[71] The dream-image of destruction has been transformed into an actual physical transformation into a beast. This mixture is then placed in the context of the king's edification concerning God's authority. In the enactment of judgment the same abrupt mixture of images occurs, but is made even more eggregious when suddenly the root is bound in prison.

The total destruction of the tree, the earliest layer, corresponds to the part of the dream where the tree reaches all the way to heaven and has divine pretentions. In the depiction of the fate of the tree, the condemnation of the Most High (element no. 2) is probably part of this first layer of redaction, an anti-Babylonian polemic. The interpretation of the root as a transformation into a beast, along with the images which follow, can easily be removed, and the root left behind is probably also not part of the original dream;[72] the destruction of the tree originally implied complete destruction. In a later layer, there is a role for the root: it symbolizes the restoration of the Babylonian king, much as the shoot functions in Isa 11:1 and Ezek 17:22–24. The dream vision of the tree as a pastoral image, the interpretation of it as the extent of the empire in terms of peoples, and the fortunes of this root all probably derive from the same redactional layer.[73]

The MT has more neatly combined these images of destroyed tree, root, bull, and binding in the judgment (vss 12–13): "Leave the stump of his roots in the earth, with a band of iron and brass, in the grass of the field, and let it be wet with the dew of heaven, and let his portion be with the beasts in the grass of the earth; let his heart be changed from a person's, and let him be given the heart of a beast. . . ." The images are more successfully and sensibly interwoven. For instance, there is no immediate change from a stump to a bull, and the inexplicable binding in OG becomes a band of iron and brass on the stump. But more important, in the MT the courtier Daniel divides this

---

[71] Meyer (*Gebet*, 47) also separates the tree and beast motifs in his analysis, as does Collins (*Daniel with an Introduction to Apocalyptic Literature* [FOTL 20; Grand Rapids: Eerdmans, 1984] 63).

[72] Note how easily it can be excised: at vs 15/12 a new sentence is awkwardly begun to describe the root, and it is precisely at this point where we find the abrupt change of images to the grazing as a bull.

[73] But concerning this root it is said (vs 26/23 OG): "The place of your throne will be safeguarded for you for a time and an hour." The "time and an hour" does not correspond to the "seven years" found at vs 16/13 in the dream vision, and may indicate that two levels of redaction are in evidence here: an early redactor's attempt to make allowances for a repentant Nebuchadnezzar, and the later redaction of Daniel 4 as a whole, in which the seven years are introduced from the Wall Pronouncement.

part of the dream into dream-symbol and its interpretation or *pišra'*, wherein the stump sitting in the field is a dream-symbol, but becoming like a bull is what will actually happen to the king (vss 21–22). A successful union of the two images of tree and bull is thus achieved, using the stump as the symbol of the restoration of the king after a seven-year affliction. Despite imperfections in the MT imagery, it is a great improvement over the OG, and the relation of the two is best explained as an attempt on the part of the MT redactor to make sense of illogical images in the OG. Once again, Haag rightly eliminated all references to the bull image from his source,[74] but his task is made much easier if the OG is utilized, where the separate images are not yet interwoven.

Only after the dream is recounted is Daniel introduced in the OG, troubled by the import of the dream, just as he is in MT (vss 18–19). There is, however, no short dialogue in OG between the king and Daniel in which the former urges him to continue, as there is in MT. Haag's reconstruction of the source of this story is ended quite abruptly. Daniel gives no interpretation of the dream, except to say that the stump remains so that the king may repent, even though it is presumed that he does not. In Haag's view, this negative source story about the king only allowed for the possibility of repentance after it was incorporated into the corpus of Daniel 4–6.

The OG, however, proceeds from this point quite differently from the MT, and may reflect the original ending of this source. The tree image is interpreted in two different ways: first, the birds in the tree are the extent of Nebuchadnezzar's empire in land and peoples ruled (vs 21/18); second, the height of the tree approaching heaven is Nebuchadnezzar elevated over all the peoples of the earth, but also bloated with arrogance (vs 22/19): he has "left destitute the house of the living God on account of the sins of the sanctified people."[75] The first of these corresponds to the part of the dream-vision which was probably added, that is, from within the seam; the second from the anti-Babylonian source. The original ending of the Dream Interpretation, as far as we can tell, was probably vs 26/23: "The Lord lives in heaven, and his authority is over all the earth."

Conclusions Concerning Daniel 4

A review of the conclusions of this foray into the sources of Daniel 4 would be helpful at this point. Analyzing only the MT, Haag postulated a short

[74] Haag, *Errettung*, 105–6.
[75] The implication that Nebuchadnezzar was working God's will in punishing Jerusalem, but went too far and had to be punished also, is found at Is 47:6.

negative judgment story in 4:25 – 30 concerning Nebuchadnezzar, which was coupled with a similar legend in the source of Daniel 5, concerning Belshazzar, supposedly Nebuchadnezzar's son. In addition, he isolated two legends of Daniel in the court of the king, Dan 4:1 – 23 and Daniel 6, which were placed at the beginning and end respectively of the other two to form the corpus of Daniel 4 – 6. This theory I agreed with in part, but I suggested some important modifications. Turning to the OG as the older and better witness, I isolated three different sources in Daniel 4:

1) Using 4QPrNab as a comparison, I isolated 4:30a-36/33,34b (with excisions) as the "Bull Sojourn," a somewhat positive view of the repentant Nebuchadnezzar, analogous to the repentant Nabonidus of the Qumran fragment. Here Nebuchadnezzar's seven-year sojourn as a bull is introduced, from which he manages to recover.
2) Using the Abydenos fragment as a point of comparison, I preferred the OG version of Haag's proposed source in 4:25 – 30 MT (4:29/26 – 33/30 OG), the Wall Pronouncement. Where the Abydenos fragment reflects the positive hope of the Chaldaean source for a Babylonian restoration, the Jewish redaction of Nebuchadnezzar's pronouncement from his city wall is thoroughly negative: he will lose his empire to a hated member of his household (probably Nabonidus).
3) In the first part of Daniel 4 I used the OG text to separate the Dream Interpretation story into a source which is thoroughly condemning of Nebuchadnezzar, and a redactional layer which mollifies the tone somewhat, allowing for Nebuchadnezzar's restoration after a period of punishment. This layer is probably to be identified with the redactor of the chapter as a whole.

The long, muddled doxological section at the end of Daniel 4 may result from the combination of doxological conclusions from the sources, along with the elaborations by the redactor of the chapter as a whole. However, it is very difficult to arrive at a convincing source analysis for most of it. The doxologies have so few specific references or terms, that finding correspondences to the source accounts is a tentative process. Some observations can nevertheless be made.

First of all, we should note that part of the conclusion of Daniel 4 (vs 34c) is not muddled at all, and is not a doxology; it is a letter, rendered very precisely:

> Sender: Nebuchadnezzar
> Addressee: to all the nations, etc.

Thanksgiving: May your well-being be increased. . . .[76]
  Connective: And now. . . .[77]
       Body: I shall recount. . . .

This is a fictitious letter, since the body only alludes to the events in question; it nevertheless adheres to the letter form. It is found in MT in essentially this form at the beginning of Daniel 4. Montgomery uses the future tense "I shall recount to you" in the OG as evidence that the letter originally preceded the chapter, as in the MT.[78] However, the arrangement of the OG letter is quite logical. The recounting refers to what the letter is to contain, not to the recounting of events that has preceded in the narrative, as the conclusion of the chapter makes clear: Nebuchadnezzar sent letters which would detail "everything that had happened" to him; thus "I shall recount" (ὑποδείξω) is appropriate in its OG position near the end of Daniel 4.

But to what layer is this pseudepigraphic letter to be attributed? I would propose that this model of clarity, precision, and terseness fits better with one of the sources than it does with the windy doxological section. The doxologies are better understood as the redactor's expansion of the short narratives. The source that this letter fits best is the Bull Sojourn, since it is the only source that provides for a repentant king. The similarities between the Bull Sojourn and *Prayer of Nabonidus* which were noted above might also be invoked here, since *Prayer* ends, as far as we know, with the king's public recounting of events.

The sources of the three separate accounts in Daniel 4 are originally independent, despite some interesting similarities. The heavenly voice in the Wall Pronouncement and in the Bull Sojourn at first would seem to stem from the same tradition, but in the former case it is the condemning pronouncement which heralds an end to the king's reign, while in the latter it is the voice of a heavenly intermediary who exhorts Nebuchadnezzar to repent. The redactor of chapter four has altered the condemning voice to have it bear a message of repentance. The transformation into a bull in the Bull Sojourn would also seem at first sight to be influenced by the curse in the Abydenos fragment, where Nebuchadnezzar hopes that Cyrus will wander as a wild

[76] According to Joseph A. Fitzmyer ("Some Notes on Aramaic Epistolography," *JBL* 93 [1974] 215), a common thanksgiving in Aramaic letters is שלמכון ישׂגא, which is precisely what MT has at the new location of the letter (3:31 MT), and what the Greek must be translating: εἰρήνη ὑμῖν πληθυνθείη.

[77] A common feature of Aramaic letters is a transitional formula such as כעו or וכעו, used at the beginning of the body or when a new topic is introduced (Fitzmyer, "Aramaic," 216). Here it is translated by καὶ νῦν, but is lacking at 3:32 MT.

[78] Montgomery, *Daniel*, 248; followed by Satran, "Fourth Chapter," 70.

beast, but this is probably only a coincidental similarity to the very different image of a domesticated animal in the Daniel 4 source.

It is clear that only some of the source writings mentioned here can properly be called wisdom court legends. Where a king is condemned by a heavenly voice, as in the Wall Pronouncement, there is little court or wisdom element. Also, where the content of the dream is more important than the role of the courtier, as in the source of Daniel 4:4–29 OG, it is best not to place the legend in this category.[79] The Bull Sojourn, along with 4QPrNab, should likewise not be considered wisdom court legends. In some court legends it is the king who is the wise figure, but in those cases it is the king's own ethnic group who propagate the story. Here the wisdom of the king is not clear, and more to the point, the story is not told by the king's ethnic group. Do the *Prayer of Nabonidus* and the Bull Sojourn communicate a wisdom teaching through the character of the foreign king? It is uncertain to what extent Jews would have interpreted the king's change in this way. The role of the king is merely as a vehicle for the demonstration of God's rule, although he is not negatively viewed. The wisdom teaching, if one is present, is that despite the king's illusion of world rule, it is the God of Heaven, always described with some such universalizing epithet, who rules. It is thus a "ruled-ethnic-perspective" court legend, without a large role for a cultural hero to speak the part of the Jews.

Whatever the state of the source stories of Daniel 4, the resulting process of editing reflects an incorporation of various kinds of stories into a connected account. The OG version of Daniel 4 begins with a chronicles-style dating and an account of the king's distresses which evidently purports to be history. The pseudepigraphic device of a royal decree is not present at the beginning of Daniel 4 OG, as it is at the beginning of the Bull Sojourn, and neither is the device of the letter present at the beginning, as it is in MT. There is little attention to the Jewish courtier Daniel in OG (compare only vs 18/15), but in the MT redaction there is a movement in the direction of court legends: the other courtiers are ceremoniously called in at the beginning of the story, but are unable to interpret the dream (MT 4:3–4, lacking in OG). Not only does this increase the impression made on the audience of Daniel's ability, but it also places him in a certain milieu and in a certain official context: he is the best of the wise men. Only after the other courtiers fail to interpret the dream does Daniel enter the scene. This order of events is the

---

[79] Collins (*Daniel*, 46) makes this distinction. Haag (*Errettung*, 73–88, 99–108) differentiates between Dan 4:25–30 and Daniel 5 on one hand, and Dan 4:1–24 and Daniel 6 on the other, but rejects the term "court legend" for any of the sources. He uses the genre term *weisheitliche Lehrerzählung* for the latter two.

same as in Daniel 2, and corresponds more closely to the narrative type of the contest as outlined by Niditch and Doran.[80]

The list of wise men is also practically identical to Dan 5:7 MT. In both cases an assimilation to the rest of Daniel 1−6 seems to have motivated this change, and the court contest element heightens the drama of the Jew's role in advising the king.[81] The deletion of references to angels by the redactor of MT can only sharpen this focus on Daniel the courtier.[82]

The tendency to emphasize the courtier's role evolved gradually: in the Wall Pronouncement, there is a voice from heaven, in the Bull Sojourn an angel, in 4QPrNab (a parallel tradition), an unnamed Jewish seer, and in the dream story, the courtier Daniel, whose role increases as the cycle of legends grows. At the same time, events which were originally described in short accounts with little plot are now recast as a connected series of adventures, in other words, as narrative. This suggests a separate audience from that of the source accounts, and probably a different set of attitudes toward, for example, foreign kings as well. Haag and others, including Niditch and Doran, have reservations about the use of "court legend" and related terms as a genre classification,[83] but its usefulness and validity is here borne out. The redaction of Daniel 4, especially in the MT, is clearly conditioned by this genre. The reservation that more than one narrative structure or set of motifs, that is, more than one morphological structure, is placed under the same rubric "court legend," would be a problem if we were to limit "genre" to one such discreet narrative structure, but genre here must be taken in a broader sense, to include other factors which constitute a work and condition an audience's response, including setting, stock characters, and theme.

---

[80] "Success Story."

[81] Haag (*Errettung*, 103−4) notes some of the redactional intentions of the combination of stories, specifically that the dream interpretation story, which stood as a general warning to pagan rulers not to ignore the true God, now has a prophetic fulfillment in the story of Nebuchadnezzar's seven-year affliction. Thus a more particular interest in prophecy and fulfillment can be noted. At the same time, the sources of Daniel 4, which both ended with the fall of the Babylonian king, are now reinterpreted with a return of the king to power. Haag also notes that the letter and decree forms serve to emphasize the hope of peaceful coexistence. Also see John G. Gammie, "On the Intention and Sources of Daniel I-VI," *VT* 31 (1981) 283.

[82] Satran ("Fourth Chapter," 78−79) notes the changes in the references to angels, but considers it as part of the OG redactor's interpretation of MT.

[83] Haag, *Errettung*, 83; Niditch and Doran, "Success Story" (see the discussion in Chapter 1 concerning their views); and see Klaus Koch, *Das Buch Daniel* (Darmstadt: Wissenschaftliche Buchgesellschaft, 1980) 90.

English Translation[84] of
the Old Greek of Daniel 4

4/1 In the eighteenth year of his rule, Nebuchadnezzar said:
"I was happily residing in my house
and resting contentedly on my throne.

5/2 I saw a dream and was dumbfounded, and fear seized me.

10/7 I was sleeping, when before me there appeared an exceedingly tall tree
growing up out of the earth.
The appearance of it was great,
and there was none other like it.

12/9 *Its branches were about thirty stadia high,*
and in its shade were all the beasts of the earth,
and the birds of heaven were nesting in it.
Its fruit was plentiful and ripe
and it provided nourishment for all the animals.

11/8 And the appearance of it was great.
The foliage of it reached to heaven
and the shade-area up to the clouds,
filling the whole area under heaven,
and the sun and the moon dwelt in it
and illuminated the whole earth.

13/10 I was watching this dream before my eyes,
when, suddenly, an angel was sent with all authority from heaven

14/11 and he called and said concerning it, "Cut it down and destroy it,
for it has been decreed by the Most High to uproot it and demolish it."

15/12 *But thus he said: "Leave one of its roots in the earth,*
**so that it may graze on grass like an ox in the mountains with the
beasts of the earth,**

16/13 **and from the dew of heaven its body may be changed,**
and for seven years it may be pastured with them,

17/14 **until it knows that the Lord of Heaven has authority over all
things in heaven and on earth,**
and whatever he wills, he does to them.

14a *Before me it was cut down in one day,*
and it was destroyed in one hour of the day.

---

[84] The sources are indicated as follows:
Standard type = Condemning Dream Source (Dream A);
Bold italic = Less Condemning Alterations of Dream (Dream B);
Bold = Redactor of Whole Chapter;
SMALL CAPS = Nebuchadnezzar's Sojourn as a Bull; and
Italic = Wall Pronouncement Story.

The branches were spread to all the winds,
and it was dragged off and thrown away.
And it ate grass with the beasts of the earth
and was taken under guard,
and was bound by them in shackles and bronze manacles.
I was awestruck by all this,
but then the dream disappeared from before my eyes.

18/15 And when I arose early from my bed,
I summoned Daniel,
the leader of the sages
and the head of those who interpret dreams.
I described the dream to him,
and he showed me the entire interpretation of it.

19/16 **Daniel was greatly amazed,**
and dark forebodings gripped him,
and he grew frightened and began to tremble,
and his appearance changed,
and his head bobbed up and down for an hour,
and awestruck, he answered me in a soft voice:
O King, may this dream be for those who hate you,
and may its interpretation come upon your enemies.

20/17 The tree which grew up in the earth,
whose appearance was great,
is you, O King.

21/18 *And all the birds of heaven which were nesting in it,*
they are the greatness of the land and of the nations
and of all the tongues to the ends of the earth
and all the regions which serve you.

22/19 And that the tree rose up and approached heaven
and the foliage of it touched the clouds:
you, O King, were raised up over all the people
who are on the face of the whole earth,
your heart was raised up in arrogance and might
through all the acts against the holy one and his angels.
Your deeds were seen, in that you made desolate the house
of the living God on account of the sins of the sanctified people.

23/20 And the vision, which you saw,
that an angel was sent with all authority from the Lord and
that he said to pull out the tree and cut it down:
The prophetic word of the Great God will come upon you,

24/21 and the Most High and his angels are pursuing you.

25/22 *They will take you under guard*
and will send you away to a deserted place.

26/23 *And the root of the tree which was left,*
since it was not thrown away:

The place of your throne will be safeguarded for you
for a time and an hour.
Indeed they are preparing themselves against you
and will whip you
and will bring on the things judged against you.

27/24 The lord lives in heaven,
and his authority is over all the earth.
Pray to him concerning your sins
that in his mercy he may pardon all your wickedness,
in order that it may go easily for you
and you remain on the throne of your kingdom for many years,
and not be destroyed.
Heed these words,
for my accounting is accurate,
and your time is at hand.

28/25 *And at the conclusion of these words,*
Nebuchadnezzar, when he heard the interpretation of the vision,
took these words to heart.

29/26 **And after twelve months**
The king was strolling about on the walls of his city in all his glory,
and on the towers of the city he walked.

30/27 *And he said: "Is not this Babylon great, which I have built,*
and the house of my kingdom which is in my firm control shall redound to
my glory."

31/28 *And when he finished speaking he heard a voice from heaven:*
"Take heed, King Nebuchadnezzar,
the kingdom of Babylon has been taken away from you and given to
another,
a man hated in your house.
Now I will set him upon your throne,
and he will receive your authority and your glory and your riches,
so that you will know that the God of heaven has authority in the
human realm,
and he will give it to whomever he wills,
By morning another king will reside contentedly in your house
and will take control of your glory and your might and your authority.

32/29 **And the angels will pursue you for seven years,**
and you will not be seen nor will you speak with anyone,
and you will be fed grass like a bull,
and your portion shall be from the grass of the earth.
And, indeed, instead of receiving glory, you will be bound,
and the house of your riches and your kingdom another will have.

33/30 *By morning all these things will be visited upon you,*
Nebuchadnezzar, king of Babylon,
and not one of all these things will be lacking.

33a/30a I, NEBUCHADNEZZAR, KING OF BABYLON, WAS SHACKLED FOR SEVEN YEARS.
I WAS FED GRASS LIKE A BULL,
AND FROM THE FIELDS OF THE EARTH I ATE.
AND AFTER SEVEN YEARS I DEVOTED MY SOUL TO PRAYER
AND MADE SUPPLICATION CONCERNING MY SINS BEFORE THE LORD GOD OF
  HEAVEN,
and concerning my transgressions I prayed to the Great God of Gods.

33b/30b **And my hair became like the feathers of a bird**
and my nails like a lion's.
My flesh and my heart were changed,
and I walked about naked with the beasts of the earth.
I saw a dream, and dark forebodings came over me,
and eventually a great sleep overcame me
and a drowsiness fell upon me.

34/30c **And at the end of the seven years, the time of my redemption came,**
and (the expiation of) my sins and my transgressions was fulfilled
  before the God of heaven.
I PRAYED CONCERNING MY TRANSGRESSIONS TO THE GREAT GOD OF GODS,
WHEN AN ANGEL CALLED TO ME FROM HEAVEN AND SAID,
"NEBUCHADNEZZAR, SERVE THE HOLY GOD OF HEAVEN
AND GIVE GLORY TO THE MOST HIGH.
THE PALACE OF YOUR PEOPLE IS RETURNED TO YOU.

36/33 AT THAT TIME MY KINGDOM WAS RETURNED TO ME,
AND MY GLORY WAS GIVEN BACK TO ME.

37/34 **I give praise to the Most high**
and praise the one who created the heaven and the earth and the seas
  and the rivers and everything in them.
I confess him and praise him,
because he is the God of gods and Lord of lords and king of kings,
because he makes signs and wonders
and changes times and seasons,
taking away a kingdom from kings
and establishing others instead of them.

37a/34a **From now on I will worship him,**
and out of fear of him a trembling has overtaken me,
and all his holy ones I praise;
For the gods of the nations do not have strength in themselves to take
  away a kingdom from one king and give it to another,
and kill and make alive and do signs and great marvels and fearful
  things and to alter the course of events,
as the God of heaven did to me
and altered great events with me.
I will bring forth a sacrificial offering to the Most High
each day of my rule for the sake of my soul,
as a pleasant smell for the Lord,

and I shall do what is pleasing to him,
I and my people, my nation and the regions which are under my authority.
And anyone who speaks against the God of Heaven,
and anyone who, having spoken thus, is convicted,
I will condemn to death.

37b/34b Then King Nebuchadnezzar wrote a circular letter to all the nations in every place and to all the regions and all the tongues which reside in all the regions for generation after generation:
Give praise to the Lord God of Heaven
and bring forth a sacrifice and an offering to him openly.
I, KING OF KINGS PUBLICLY GIVE THANKS TO HIM, BECAUSE HE DEALT WITH ME THUS:
ON THE SAME DAY HE RETURNED ME TO MY THRONE,
AND I REGAINED CONTROL OF MY AUTHORITY AND MY KINGDOM AMONG MY PEOPLE,
AND MY MAJESTY WAS RETURNED TO ME.

37c/34c KING NEBUCHADNEZZAR, TO ALL THE NATIONS AND ALL THE REGIONS
AND TO ALL THOSE WHO RESIDE IN THEM:
MAY PEACE BE MULTIPLIED TO YOU FOR ALL TIME.
AND NOW I SHALL RECOUNT TO YOU THE MIGHTY ACTS
WHICH THE GREAT GOD WORKED WITH ME.
HE CONSIDERED ME WORTHY TO SHOW TO YOU AND TO YOUR SAGES
THAT HE IS GOD (VAR.: GOD IS ONE), AND HIS MARVELS ARE GREAT,
HIS PALACE IS A PALACE FOREVER,
HIS AUTHORITY IS FROM GENERATION TO GENERATION.''
AND HE SENT LETTERS CONCERNING EVERYTHING THAT HAD HAPPENED TO HIM
IN HIS RULE TO ALL THE NATIONS WHICH ARE UNDER HIS RULE.

Here the material assigned to the three reconstructed sources is gathered and presented separately. The less-condemning alterations of the dream source (Dream B) and the passages assigned to the redactor of the chapter as a whole are omitted.

Condemning Dream Source (Dream A):

In the eighteenth year of his rule, Nebuchadnezzar said:
"I was happily residing in my house
and resting contentedly on my throne.
I saw a dream and was dumbfounded,
and fear seized me.
I was sleeping, when before me there appeared an exceedingly tall tree growing up out of the earth.
And the appearance of it was great.
The foliage of it reached to heaven

and the shade-area up to the clouds,
filling the whole area under heaven,
and the sun and the moon dwelt in it
and illuminated the whole earth.
I was watching this dream before my eyes,
when, suddenly, an angel was sent with all authority from heaven
and he called and said concerning it, "Cut it down and destroy it,
for it has been decreed by the Most High to uproot it and demolish it."
Before me it was cut down in one day,
and it was destroyed in one hour of the day.
The branches were spread to all the winds,
and it was dragged off and thrown away.
I was awestruck by all this,
but then the dream disappeared from before my eyes.
And when I arose early from my bed,
I summoned Daniel,
the leader of the sages
and the head of those who interpret dreams.
I described the dream to him,
and he showed me the entire interpretation of it.
The tree which grew up in the earth,
whose appearance was great,
is you, O King.
And that the tree rose up and approached heaven
and the foliage of it touched the clouds:
you, O King, were raised up over all the people
who are on the face of the whole earth,
your heart was raised up in arrogance and might
through all the acts against the holy one and his angels.
Your deeds were seen, in that you made desolate the house
of the living God on account of the sins of the sanctified people.
And the vision, which you saw,
that an angel was sent with all authority from the lord and
that he said to pull out the tree and cut it down:
The prophetic word of the Great God will come upon you,
and the Most High and his angels are pursuing you.
Indeed they are preparing themselves against you
and will whip you
and will bring on the things judged against you.
The Lord lives in heaven,
and his authority is over all the earth.
Heed these words,
for my accounting is accurate,
and your time is at hand.

Bull Sojourn:

> I, Nebuchadnezzar, king of Babylon, was shackled for seven years.
> I was fed grass like a bull,
> and from the fields of the earth I ate.
> And after seven years I devoted my soul to prayer
> and made supplication concerning my sins before the Lord God of heaven,
> I prayed concerning my transgressions to the Great God of gods,
> when an angel called to me from heaven and said,
> "Nebuchadnezzar, serve the Holy God of Heaven
> and give glory to the Most High.
> The palace of your people is returned to you.
> At that time my kingdom was returned to me,
> and my glory was given back to me.
> I, King of Kings publicly give thanks to him, because he dealt with me thus:
> On the same day he returned me to my throne,
> and I regained conrol of my authority and my kingdom among my people,
> and my majesty was returned to me.
> King Nebuchadnezzar, to all the nations and all the regions
> and to all those who reside in them:
> May peace be multiplied to you for all time.
> And now I shall recount to you the mighty acts
> which the Great God worked with me.
> He considered me worthy to show to you and to your sages
> that he is God (var.: God is one), and his marvels are great,
> his palace is a palace forever,
> his authority is from generation to generation."
> And he sent letters concerning everything that had happened to him
> in his rule to all the nations which are under his rule.

Wall Pronouncement Story:

> The king was strolling about on the walls of his city in all his glory,
> and on the towers of the city he walked.
> And he said: "Is not this Babylon great, which I have built,
> and the house of my kingdom which is in my firm control shall redound to my
>   glory."
> And when he finished speaking he heard a voice from heaven:
> "Take heed, King Nebuchadnezzar,
> the kingdom of Babylon has been taken away from you and given to another,
> a man hated in your house.
> Now I will set him upon your throne,
> and he will receive your authority and your glory and your riches,
> By morning another king will reside contentedly in your house
> and will take control of your glory and your might and your authority.
> and you will not be seen nor will you speak with anyone,

And, indeed, instead of receiving glory, you will be bound,
and the house of your riches and your kingdom another will have.
By morning all these things will be visited upon you,
Nebuchadnezzar, king of Babylon,
and not one of all these things will be lacking.

Daniel 5

This court contest is based on Daniel's ability to interpret mysterious words inscribed on the wall of the palace by an unearthly hand. As in Daniel 2, a contradiction arises between the severity of the judgment pronounced against the king by Daniel and the king's joyous bestowal of reward upon him. Haag's source analysis accounts for this tension here by positing an older prophecy against the king as the source for this chapter.[85]

Haag's reconstruction of Daniel 5 follows:

1 King Belshazzar made a great feast for one thousand of his lords, and before these thousand he drank wine. 2 While he was tasting the wine, Belshazzar ordered that the gold and silver vessels be brought which his father Nebuchadnezzar had taken out of the temple in Jerusalem. 4 They drank wine and praised the gods of gold and silver, bronze, iron, wood and stone. 5 At the same time fingers appeared of a man's hand, and wrote on the plaster of the wall of the king's palace opposite the lampstand. 9 Then the king was very alarmed, his appearance changed, and his lords were perplexed. 25 And the writing that was inscribed was this: *mene' tekel uparsin*. 30 On that same night the king of the Chaldaeans was killed.

It is striking that at this point Haag ignored the OG version; it is composed of two conflated accounts, one of which is very similar to this reconstruction. The OG begins with a short preamble, which is a doublet of vss 1–5 OG, and it is likely a key to the source of the chapter.[86] The proem, with a literal translation, reads:

Baltasar the king gave a great reception on the festival day of the consecration of his palace, and of his chief people he invited 2000 men. On that day

---

[85] Haag, *Errettung*, 56–61. A similar story is found in Numbers 22–24, regarding Balaam. This account parallels Daniel 5 in some respects: it is a court legend of sorts, culminating in a prophecy against the king. In the Balaam story, however, the prophecies dominate the story, while in Daniel 5 the contest elements come to hold center stage, although the source of Daniel 5 may be more similar.

[86] Although Charles and Jahn preferred some of the OG readings of Daniel 5 (see the discussion above on pp. 87–88), they ignore the short preamble of OG.

Baltasar was puffed up with arrogance from the wine, and haughtily praised all the gods of the nations made of molten metal or carved by hand which were in his palace, but he did not give praise to the God Most High. In that night appeared fingers like a person's and they inscribed in the plaster of the wall opposite the lampstand, *"Mane phares thekel."* The interpretation of these words is *mane*, numbered, *phares*, taken away, *thekel*, placed.[87]

The proem thus forms a doublet with vss 1 – 5 OG, but several details of narrative color are presented here which are not found elsewhere: the reception was at the time of the consecration festival, and there were 2000 leaders present, not 1000 as in MT and Th. The proem, then, does not simply summarize the rest of the chapter. Many problems of Daniel 5 can, in fact, only be remedied by assuming that the proem of the OG version is based on an older *Vorlage* than the rest of the OG narrative (vss 1 – 5) or the MT. This will partially corroborate the outlines of Haag's reconstruction of the source, but an investigation of the slight differences between his reconstruction and the OG proem will show that the latter is closer to the original source.

The first problem of Daniel 5 to be alleviated by this hypothesis is that in MT there are two somewhat confused sins of Belshazzar (Baltasar in OG) for which he incurs divine punishment: drinking from the hallowed vessels taken from the Jerusalem temple (MT vs 3), and praising the gods of gold, silver, bronze, iron, wood, and stone (MT vs 4; cf. above on *Prayer of Nabonidus*). These are not identical sins, although the later redactor of Daniel 5 would see them as related. In the proem of the OG, however, the statement of the dramatic problem is much simpler. There is only one sin of Baltasar, which is to praise "all the gods of the nations made from molten metal or carved by hand," while at the same time *neglecting* to praise the God Most High *in addition*. This is quite a different matter. The desecration of the Jerusalem temple vessels is not mentioned, as it is in the longer version of the OG and in MT, and the focus seems unmistakably on the *omission* of the God of the Jews in the toast, rather than the *commission* of praise to idols.[88] One is reminded of the reliefs on the Persepolis palace, in which all the major nations of the Persian Empire are depicted bearing tribute to the king, but Jews were not included because they were too insignificant. Here is the Jews' chance to assert their worth, even if the fictitious setting is the Babylonian and not the Persian court.

The redactional stance toward the king's sin can be seen to shift in a fascinating way. In the OG proem the sin of the king is the omission of any

---

[87] I.e., "placed" on a scale. Cf. ἐστάθη ἐν ζυγῷ at Dan 5:27 Th.

[88] In *Prayer of Nabonidus* the king is ignorant of the God Most High, but is not guilty of blasphemy, as is also the case in the similar Bull Sojourn source.

praise to God, and to a lesser extent, the praise of idols. In the rest of the OG
version of Daniel 5, it is the desecration of the Jerusalem temple vessels
(mentioned first), the commission of idolatry in praising the idols made with
hands (τὰ εἴδωλα τὰ χειροποίητα), and last, the omission of praise to the
"God of eternity." In MT/Th, the desecration of the temple vessels is first,
the idols are now listed in detail (gold, silver, etc.), but the omission of praise
to God is not mentioned. The despoiling of the Jerusalem temple, present in
both the long OG version and in the MT, was also noted in Daniel 4 OG as
part of the anti-Babylonian Dream Interpretation story. The belittling of the
idols by listing the materials of which they are composed is a commonplace
of post-exilic Jewish propaganda, which presupposes a strict monotheism and
contempt for representations of other gods. In this context it would have
been demeaning to mention the pique caused by the omission of God from
the drunken toast, since for God to be included in such a debauched
ceremony would have been sacrilegious; thus no reference of this is made in
the MT/Th version. The OG proem does end on a confusing note regarding
the writing on the wall, and it is most likely this fact which has caused it to be
viewed in such a negative light.[89]

Aspects of this fictitious setting may be more precisely drawn in the OG
proem than in the MT. The vague "great feast" (לחם רב) in MT occurs at a
very specific time in the OG proem: "in the day of the consecration festival
of his palace" (ἐν ἡμέρᾳ ἐθκαινισμοῦ τῶν βασιλείων), most likely the day
of the New Year (akîtu) Festival.[90] We see in the Wadi Brissa inscription
mentioned above in regard to Daniel 4,[91] that in the very context of the
renewal of the palace there is a description of the New Year Festival and of

---

[89] The three words are in a different order from MT/Th, i.e., *mane phares thekel*, instead of
mane thekel phares. At this point the words are interpreted, not to the king, but for the reader, as
meaning ἠρίθμηται, ἐξῆρται, ἔστασαι, perhaps something like "numbered, taken away, placed
(or established)," and are mentioned again later in OG with various Greek words (vss 17,
26–28). It is difficult to see how these permutations could be faithful to the Aramaic play on
words that is used in the MT/Th, i.e., the similarity between the coins mina, shekel, and parsin
(two half-minas) and the verbs for numbered, weighed, and divided. The OG then seems to have
lost some of the sense of the Aramaic text, and this is certainly evidence that *in regard to these
words*, it is inferior to MT/Th.

[90] Cf. 1 Kgdms 11:14 ἐγκαινίσωμεν τὴν βασιλείαν, translating Hebrew ונחדש המלוכה. An
alternative reading, βασιλειῶν (feminine plural, kingdoms) for βασιλείων (neuter plural,
"palaces"), would only strengthen the allusion to the New Year's Festival, although the plural
would be unusual. The plural neuter for "palace" is common. Mathias Delcor (*Le livre de
Daniel* [Paris: Gabalda, 1971] 126) opposes the connection of this feast with the New Year celebration, but ignores the OG evidence. He is followed by Haag, *Errettung*, 56.

[91] Stephen Langdon, *Building Inscriptions of the Neo-Babylonian Empire* (Part I; Paris:
Leroux, 1905) Col. VII, lines 1–31, p. 169.

the magnificent feast which Nebuchadnezzar set out for his honored guests. Corresponding to this setting in the OG proem is the way the gods are presented. The long OG version and the MT both demean the gods as mere material idols, but the OG proem, while being critical, recognizes their position and significance in the king's palace: "all the gods of the nations molten and carved which were in his palace." A theological critique is not yet articulated in this source. This presentation of the gods also reflects an allusion to the Babylonian New Year festival, where gods of all the cities would be paraded through Babylon. Although their final destination is the *bit akîtu* outside of Babylon and not the palace, in the popular Jewish conception this would be a minor misunderstanding.

A chart at this point would make the relationship among the three versions clearer:

OG Proem	OG Body	MT/Th
New Year's Feast	great feast	great feast
	desecration of temple vessels	desecration of temple vessels
praised all gods made of metal or carved	praised idols made with hands	praised idols made of various materials
did not praise God Most High	did not praise God of Eternity	

It appears, then, that the notion of the sin of Baltasar in the OG proem is an older one, that is, not reckoning with the power of Yahweh among the gods, while in MT we find a later aversion to all idols as insults to the one true God. These two views could have existed contemporaneously for hundreds of years, but I would suggest that this at least counts as evidence for the priority of OG. This by itself cannot prove that the OG proem existed prior to the rest of Daniel 5 OG or the MT version, but if we were to take the position that the proem is merely a summary of the rest of the chapter, as most scholars have, we would also be forced to conclude that the editor:

1) eliminated the theme of the theft and desecration of the temple vessels;
2) replaced the up-to-date Hellenistic term εἴδωλα χειροποίητα[92] with the older standard term θεοὺς χωνευτοὺς καὶ γλυπτούς[93];

[92] This term is used also at Bel 5 Th, Dan 5:23 and 6:27 Th, but nowhere else in the Greek Bible, including the NT. It is likely a redactional theme of the editors of the Daniel corpus.

[93] The LXX translation of the Pentateuch uses this often, e.g., Exod 34:17; Lev 19:4; Num 33:52; Deut 9:12, 16, and 27:15. It is also found elsewhere in the older books of the Bible, but never in the Apocrypha or late books.

3) shifted the weight of the king's sin from the praising of idols to the omission of God from the toast—a step back from monotheism and toward an
older, seemingly polytheistic conception.

It is hard to accept that a redactor, no matter how inept or "traditional,"
would have made these changes. To postulate the changes in the opposite
direction is, however, quite plausible. Although I do not wish to presume
that a shorter, simpler version of a story is necessarily prior, here it seems to
be the more likely alternative.

Another doublet can be discerned in Daniel 5 OG which indicates the
conflation of two different accounts, but it may be impossible to match these
with the two different introductions postulated above. Verses 7a and 7b–8
OG can be easily separated into two different ways of relating the same
event. In vs 7a the king first *calls* (ἐφώνησε φωνῇ μεγάλῃ καλέσαι) for the
"enchanters, magicians, Chaldeans, and soothsayers" to decipher the
inscription, which they are unable to do. Verses 7b–8 show this process
repeated, but here the king *publishes an edict* (ἐξέθηκε πρόσταγμα) promising reward to whoever can interpret it, but the "seers, magicians, and soothsayers"[94] are again reported to be unable to interpret it. A nearly identical
account is thus repeated, giving the impression that the same diviners bump
into each other coming in and out the door, although a kind reader might
allow that the two events would not necessarily occur on the same day.

The fact remains, however, that two accounts of essentially the same event
are described. It is likely that this is what the redactor of the MT found, and
edited these two descriptions into one, using elements from both. The king
calls and pronounces an edict at the same time: "The king cried out to bring
in the magicians, Chaldeans, and soothsayers and said to the wise men of
Babylon, 'Whoever reads the writing. . . .' " The *lectio difficilior* in this
case is the doublet of the OG version, and it should be preferred as the older,
for it is easier to imagine an editor combining and smoothing out the doublet
than creating it from a single coherent account.[95]

Another major difference between the MT and OG versions of Daniel 5
may now be seen in a new light, if it is granted that the OG is the older of the

---

[94] 7a: ἐπαοιδοὺς καὶ φαρμακοὺς καὶ Χαλδαίους καὶ γαζαρηνούς / 8a: ἐπαοιδοὶ καὶ φαρ-
μακοὶ καὶ γαζαρηνοί.

[95] Charles (*Daniel*, 119–25) reconstructs a hypothetical earlier text based on OG and
Josephus, which in some respects agrees with mine. Although the MT has been smoothed over
and made more concise, it likely still harbors a trace of the former doublet: in vs 8 the wise men
are said to come in when they were already addressed in the previous verse. One might allow
that they were brought into a separate room in vs 8 to see the writing, but the text never implies
this. Montgomery (*Daniel*, 254) suggests weakly that the courtiers filed in more or less continu-
ously during "these ominous hours."

two. The queen-mother's account of Daniel's abilities and his deeds under
the previous king, Nebuchadnezzar, is very short and summary in OG vss
11 – 12, while in MT the description of Daniel is quite full, and the entirety of
Daniel 4 is recounted. The repetition of the events in chapter 4 which occurs
at 5:18 – 22 serves to increase the connections between originally independent legends and to give the appearance of a unified whole to chapters 1 – 6.[96]
The longer description in MT of Daniel's abilities, however, may also reflect
a development in the view of the nature of Daniel's wisdom. In OG, as in
MT, Daniel's status is based on his mantic wisdom, but this is stated quickly
and Daniel is brought before the king:

> (The queen-mother) said to the king, "The man (Daniel) was knowledgeable
> and wise (ἐπιστήμων καὶ σοφός) and exceeded all the wise men of Babylon,
> and a holy spirit is in him, and in the days of your father, the king, he inter-
> preted great signs."

The MT likewise attributes mantic wisdom to Daniel, but it is emphasized
at length and repeated. The queen-mother says (vss 11a, 12a):

> There is a man in your kingdom in whom is the spirit of the holy gods, and in
> the days of your father illumination and understanding and wisdom
> (נהירו ושכלתנו וחכמה), like the wisdom of the gods was found in him . . . ; an
> excellent spirit, knowledge, understanding, interpreting of dreams, revealing
> enigmas, and "dissolving of knots" were found in Daniel (רוח יתירא ומנדע
> . . . .(ושכלתנו מפשר חלמין ואחוית אחידן ומשרא קטרין

Nearly the same words are used again in vss 14 and 16, when the king
addresses Daniel. The fuller description in MT could be seen as merely the
hyperbolic flourish of the editor, but it also represents a greater interest in the
nature of mantic wisdom and in the fuller attribution of it to Daniel. The
queen-mother's recommendation of Daniel and the king's repetition of it
enlarge this section of MT to twice the size of the equivalent section of OG.
This emphasis on the "vertical" nature of Daniel's wisdom, that is, direct
revelation from God, was also found above in Daniel 2. While it is possible
that the shorter OG may reflect an attempt by a merciful redactor to edit out
the queen-mother's and king's repetitions of chapter 4, they are better
explained as expansions in the MT over and above the OG, since they tie the

---

[96] The addition of a queen-mother who has a preference for one of the courtiers is a trait of the
"harem intrigues" of Xenophon, Ctesias, and Herodotus; these will be introduced into the discussion of Esther.

chapters closer together and show the same emphasis on mantic wisdom as in Daniel 2.

In respect to Haag's theory of the source of Daniel 5, then, we see that his reconstruction is very close to the OG proem, which is our best guide to the original form of the narrative. But following the MT, he incorrectly retains elements of both of Belshazzar's sins—defiling the temple vessels and praising the idols. In light of what has been said here, the proem is to be preferred for the body of the account. Haag also postulates that this story, like the Dream story, ended quite abruptly with the writing of the letters and the death of the king.[97] This is possible, but it is more likely that the original ending can still be discerned in the present OG text at vs 30: "And the interpretation (which was briefly stated at the end of the proem) came upon Baltasar the king, and the palace was taken away from the Chaldaeans and given to the Medes and Persians." What is still lacking, however, is a Jewish interpreter of the writing, which was probably part of the original account. For this, the longer version of Daniel 5 OG (that is, not the proem) may be the best source. It seems clear, though, as Haag shows, that the original oracle is thoroughly condemning and the role of Daniel, or at least his positive relation with Belshazzar, are secondary.

English Translation of
the Old Greek of Daniel 5

(Proem) Baltasar the king gave a great reception on the festival day of the consecration of his palace, and of his leading citizens he invited 2000 men. On that day Baltasar became inflated with arrogance from the wine, and haughtily praised all the gods of the nations made of molten metal or carved by hand which were in his palace, but he did not give praise to the God Most High. During that same night there appeared fingers like human fingers, and they inscribed in the plaster of the palace wall opposite the lampstand, "*Mane phares thekel.*" The interpretation of these words is *mane*, numbered, *phares*, taken away, *thekel*, placed.[98]

(1) Baltasar the king gave a great feast for his friends. (2) He drank wine and his heart became inflated with arrogance, and he commanded that the gold and silver vessels from the house of God be brought, which Nebuchadnezzar his father brought from Jerusalem, and that they be used to serve wine to his friends. (3) They were then brought, and they drank from them (4) and blessed their idols made with hands, but they did not bless the eternal God who has

---

[97] Haag, *Errettung*, 56.

[98] The exact translation of ἕσταται is difficult, but vss 26–28 Th have ἐστάθη ἐν ζυγῷ at this point, which is likely the implication here as well.

charge of their spirit. (5) In that same hour fingers as of a human hand appeared and wrote on the palace wall in the plaster opposite the lampstand, in the presence of King Baltasar, and he watched the hand as it wrote. (6) His appearance was changed, and fears and dark forebodings gripped him. Jumping up, the king looked at the writing, while his friends circled in a hubbub[99] around him.

(7) Then the king called out loudly to summon the enchanters, magicians, Chaldaeans, and soothsayers so that they might declare the interpretation of the writing. They entered to examine the writing, but were unable to interpret the writing for the king. Then the king proclaimed an edict saying, "Whoever declares the interpretation of the writing will be robed in purple and a gold necklace will be placed upon his neck, and control of one third of the kingdom will be given to him." (8) The enchanters, magicians, and soothsayers entered, but none of them could declare the interpretation of the writing.

(9) Then the king called in the queen-mother and showed her how great the sign was, and told her how no one could interpret it to the king. (10) The queen-mother then recounted to him about Daniel, one of the exiles from Judaea. (11) She told the king, "This man was learned and wise, excelling all the sages of Babylon, (12) and a holy spirit is in him, for in the days of your father the king he interpreted great prophecies to Nebuchadnezzar your father. (13) Then Daniel was brought in before the king, and the king said to him, (16) "Daniel, are you able to declare to me the interpretation of this writing? If so, I shall place a purple robe upon you and put a gold necklace upon your neck, and you will have control of one-third of my kingdom."

(17) Then Daniel stood before the writing and read it, and then answered the king, "This is the writing: numbered, weighed, taken away. And after the hand wrote it, it ascended.[100] Here is the interpretation of it: (23) King, you gave a great feast for your friends and you drank wine, and the vessels were brought to you from the house of the living God, and you drank from them, both you and your leading citizens, and you praised all your peoples' idols made with hands, but you did not bless the living God, even though your spirit is in his hands. He is the one who gave you your palace, yet you have neither blessed nor praised him. (26) Here is the interpretation of the writing: The days of your rule are numbered, your rule will cease, it has been cut short and brought to an end, and your kingdom is given to the Medes and Persians."

(29) Then Baltasar the King clothed Daniel in purple and placed a gold necklace upon his neck and gave him control of one-third of his kingdom. (30) This prophetic oracle came upon Baltasar the king; the palace was taken away from the Chaldaeans and given to the Medes and Persians. (6:1a) Artaxerxes of the Medes then came to power.

---

[99] Reading with the conjecture reported in Joseph Ziegler, *Susanna, Daniel, Bel et Draco* (Septuaginta, Vetus Testamentum Graecum 16:2; Göttingen: Vandenhoeck & Ruprecht, 1954) ad loc.: ἐξεκέχυντο for ἐκαυχῶντο. Cf. Odyssey 8.515; Iliad 16.259; and Herodotus 3.13.

[100] The Greek has ἔστην, the meaning of which in this context is unclear.

Daniel 6 and Bel and the Dragon: Introduction

Bel and the Dragon and Daniel 6 are often considered variants of the same story, because in each Daniel is thrown into a lions' den and escapes unharmed.[101] The mutual sympathy between Daniel and the king, found nowhere else in the Danielic corpus, or in any other court legend to this extent, also indicates a close relation between the two stories. Other similarities bring us to the same conclusion, as we shall see below. To discuss the two together, however, Bel and the Dragon must be analyzed first, and only then compared with Daniel 6.

Bel and the Dragon can be divided into two separate stories, even though they may have been composed as a unit. They have also come down to us in two subtly, but significantly different forms, the OG version and the Th recension. Whether the difference reflects two different Semitic sources, or resulted from the translation process, is not clear, but for our purposes we can proceed without deciding the issue. The more familiar Th version of Bel begins: "And the king Astyages was gathered to his fathers and was succeeded as king by Cyrus the Persian. And Daniel was confidant of the king, and the most honored of all his friends." The OG translation, on the other hand, has been assimilated to the Habbakuk corpus: "From the prophecy of Habbukuk, the son of Joshua, of the tribe of Levi. There was a certain man who was a priest by the name of Daniel, son of Abal, confidant of the king of Babylon." In addition to the surprising ascription to the Habbakuk corpus,[102] there are several other important differences as well. The information concerning Daniel here (priest, son of Abal) does not correspond with other traditions about Daniel, although Ezra 8:2 mentions a Daniel who was evidently a priest.[103] The discrepancy with the rest of the Daniel tradition is

---

[101] Collins (*Vision*, 4, 53) allows that Daniel 6 and Bel are variant accounts of the same tradition about Daniel in the lions' den, but does not make a judgment about which attests an older *Vorlage*; Montgomery (*Daniel*, 270) suggests that Bel is an "earlier, popular form of the story." Hartman and Di Lella (*Daniel*, 21,197) see a relation between the two, but believe that Daniel 6 influenced Bel. Moore (*Additions*, 147–49) and Augustinus Kurt Fenz ("Ein Drache in Babel. Exegetische Skizze über Daniel 14, 23–42," *SEÅ* 35 [1970] 5–16) insist that there is nothing more than a vague and distant kernel of tradition in common between the two stories. Some scholars would associate the reverence for a snake with Egypt (Wofgang Roth, " 'For Life, He Appeals to Death' (Wis 13:18): A Study of Old Testament Idol Parodies," *CBQ* 37 (1975) 43; and *APOT*, 1. 653–54), but it is more likely a mythological dragon parodied here.

[102] The OG version is presented as a prophet legend more than a court legend, regardless of which class the legend may have belonged to originally. In the Dragon story, this impression is strengthened by the use of the prophetic form "Thus says the Lord" (vs 34), which is missing in Th. The attempt to turn this court legend into a prophet legend can be detected only in those sections which deal with Habbakuk, and may not be original to the text.

[103] Haag (*Errettung*, 127–32) and Gammie ("Intention," 285) are at pains to associate some

striking. Also, in the OG story as we have it the king is said to be Babylonian, but is not named. The hero or heroes of the story were considered of primary importance. The lack of a named king and the fact that the character Daniel must be introduced indicate that the legend probably circulated independently.[104] The Th version adds a chronicles-style introduction, that is, dating by the year in the reign of the king, which was mentioned above in regard to Daniel 4, and a named king (now Persian). These differences between the two texts are best explained by presuming that the Th has reworked the OG: the unnamed king is given an identity, the dating is specified, and the legend is removed from the Habbakuk tradition and placed in the Danielic. These changes probably resulted from the incorporation of the legend into a collection of stories concerning Daniel.

In addition to these major differences between the two versions, there are also some lesser variations, which nevertheless give an intriguing view of the redactional developments in this popular literary tradition. For instance, when Daniel is asked by the king why he refuses to worship Bel, he replies in the OG version: "I worship no one (οὐδένα) except the Lord God (κύριον τὸν θεόν) who created heaven and earth, and who has lordship over all flesh." In the Th version, on the other hand, he replies, "I do not worship idols made with hands (εἴδωλα χειροποίητα), but the living God (ζῶντα θεόν) who created heaven and earth, and who has lordship over all flesh." The theological language has been brought up to date; the theologically ambiguous οὐδένα has been replaced by an epithet for idols, εἴδωλα χειροποίητα, which in the Greek Bible is used only in Daniel. Also, κύριον τὸν θεόν, the standard OG translation of יהוה אלהים, is replaced by the common title for God in Hellenistic pagan and Jewish monotheism, ζῶντα θεόν.[105] In the OG version Daniel also swears by the Lord God of gods (vs 7), which is not found in Th. The implication of polytheism inherent in that title may have been a problem for the redactor of Bel Th. It is also possible, however, that the prohibition of swearing attested elsewhere in this period may have influenced this omission by Th.[106] The OG version further notes that one of the results of Daniel's being thrown into the lions' den is that

---

part of the redaction of the Daniel legends with priestly circles, yet have missed this somewhat ambiguous clue in Bel and the Dragon OG.

[104] This latter point is made by Moore (*Additions*, 133).

[105] Cf. Tob 13:1; Bel 24; and 1 Thes 1:9; but also note Deut 4:33, 5:26 MT. On the term "living god" see Edward Everding, "The Living God" (Th.D. dissertation, Harvard University,1968).

[106] Cf. Matt 5:33–37; and Josephus *Bell.* 2.8.6 § 135 on the Essenes. See also BAG, under ὀμνύω, for important information on pagan scruples regarding swearing since the fifth century BCE.

there will be no body left for burial. This issue, which is paralleled in Tobit 1–2, is lacking in Th, and instead we find a melodramatic heightening of the threat of the lions: contrary to the normal feeding practices, the daily ration of meat for the lions had been withheld to make them even more voracious (vs 32).

Another redactional shift in the later document may be indicated at several points. In OG, when the king becomes aware of the angry crowd, he orders that Daniel be killed (vs 30). The Th translation at this point, however, depicts the king as very reluctant to give Daniel over,[107] and the crowd holds Daniel responsible not just for the destruction of the dragon, but for the execution of the implicated priests of Bel as well. The priests are seen as a competing group over against Daniel,[108] and the deaths of the guilty priests are evidently seen by the crowd as a mere political execution. The angry mob's threats against the king are made much more explicit: "Give us Daniel or we will kill you and your whole household!" These changes may have been made purely in the interest of adventurous storytelling—this would correspond to what happens in the Th version of Susanna—but it is also interesting that the resentment of the people for the execution of their priests is emphasized, which perhaps reflects a heightened expression of ethnic competition and defensiveness. As will be seen in Chapter 4 of this thesis, this is evident in the later stages in the composition of MT Esther.

The relation of Bel and the Dragon to the Jewish "idol parodies" has been noted by Roth.[109] The poetic denunciation of foreign idols and the fashioners of idols became formalized in a genre which can be detected in the prophetic works of Deutero-Isaiah, Jeremiah, Habbakuk, and also in other works, such as Psalms 115:4–8, 135:15–18, and Epistle of Jeremiah. Roth rightly notes that Bel and the Dragon is a prose example story which gives expression to the same ideas as the other poetic examples: the idols worshipped by the nations are nothing but clay or flesh-and-blood animals. Whereas I would agree with his findings, in regard to the Danielic corpus I would add some more detailed observations.

Since in the Daniel stories we are dealing with narrative, rather than poetic fragments, we should compare other narratives in which a Jew confronts foreigners with their gods. Two stories which can be compared are those of

---

[107] The king does so "under compulsion" (ἀναγκασθείς). Both versions do, however, show the king mourning after Daniel is thrown into the den, vs 40.

[108] Unlike the situation in Esther, the plight of Daniel does not include other Jews. Is the interest of the author or editor of these stories in all Jews or just those Jews who are righteous, such as the *maskilim*? In an idol parody narrative only one Jew is necessary for the plot, but the omission of other Jews in the court legends is striking.

[109] "Idol Parodies," 21–47.

Moses and the Pharaoh in Exodus (esp. 7:8 – 13) and of Elijah and the priests
of Baal in 1 Kings 18. In the Moses story God exercises power over the
Egyptians, and is, as he is generally presented in the Hebrew Bible, the Lord
of history. There is, nonetheless, no attempt to prove that other *gods* do not
exist, and herein we have one of the ironies of pre-exilic Hebrew faith: other
gods are not denied, they are simply ignored. The Elijah legend perhaps
comes closer to denying the existence, or at least the efficacy, of other gods,
when Elijah defeats the priests of Baal in a fire-starting contest. This story
should perhaps be considered transitional to the later idol parodies.

The later idol parody narratives, however, must show the idol to be not
just a vanquished or otiose god, but thoroughly without substance, and must
rub the pagans' noses in it. In the post-exilic parodies this is usually effected
not by God, but by a mortal, who uncovers the idols for all to see. This is
clearly seen in the idol parody narrative attributed by Josephus to Hecataeus
of Abdera concerning the Jewish archer Mosollamus (*Contra Ap.*
1.22.201 – 4), who shoots a bird which pagan soldiers were watching closely
to see if their military campaign would be auspicious. They protest in anger
at the shooting of this divine messenger, but Mosollamus responds that if the
bird had been capable of foresight into divine matters, it would not have been
at that spot at that time to be shot by Mosollamus the archer. Idol parody
narratives presume a naturalistic world and monotheism, while the older
wizardry contests implied polytheism or, at best, henotheism, and a god-
inhabited world.

Bel and the Dragon, then, differs from Daniel 1 – 6 in regard to this question of the nature of the anti-idol polemic. Although other gods are not mentioned in Daniel 1 – 6, still the Jewish heroes do not explicitly *uncover* idols
and show them to be baseless, but vanquish them with the protection and
intervention of the God of the Jews. While it is true that the comparison of
the foreign gods with pieces of wood or stone lies at times just beneath the
surface in Daniel 1 – 6 (esp. in Daniel 3 and 5), the MT Daniel retains—even
insists upon—one aspect of the older contest view of the relation of the Jewish God to other gods, which is that the issue is settled through God's intervention, not through a naturalistic and scientific exposé of the mundane
nature of idols. But although Bel and the Dragon is built upon two idol-
parody narrative episodes, the ending (Daniel's lions' den ordeal) does
involve God's direct intervention. This suggests the mixing of two genres in
the composition of the story.

Two other differences between Bel and the Dragon and Daniel 1 – 6 are
noted by Roth.[110] First, Daniel 3 and 6, the two court conflicts in the MT

[110] "Idol Parodies," 42.

Daniel, depict Daniel's crises as thrust upon him, while the additions show him precipitating the problem through his own actions, and in one case, solving them as well. The story of Mosollamus the archer is similar in this regard, and we should connect this aspect to a general characteristic of legends which was noted in chapter one. The protagaonists of legends are often portrayed as invulnerable to the "buffeting" of the dramatic situations. Although this is true of contests, conflicts, and idol parody narratives, this invulnerability is expressed in a passive way in the conflicts, while in the contests the hero is active, and in the idol parody narratives, even brazen.

Second, Roth states that Daniel 1–6 have as their principal issue the incompatibility of obedience to king with the worship of God, while in the additions obedience to the king is quite compatible with Jewish identity, although it is threatened by the demands—or enticements—of foreign religions. This last difference is overstated by Roth, however, since Collins has shown that, contrary to the general scholarly view, the legends of Daniel 1–6 vary in regard to the view of the king and the possibility of obedience. Daniel 4 and 5 are quite condemning of the king, but chapters 1–3 and 6 hold out the possibility of living in harmony with the imperial authorities.[111]

Several comparisons of Bel and the Dragon with Daniel 1–6 would give the impression that they have very little in common until they are artificially placed together in the Danielic corpus. The righteous sage of the MT chapters who relies solely on the intervention of God can be contrasted in the additions to a cunning, even brazen, hero who succeeds by his wits alone. This hero has some of the traits of the rogue mentioned in Chapter 1 of this thesis. This distinction is seen in even greater relief, if we assume that the older idol parody narratives of Daniel exposing the priests of Bel and destroying the Dragon were only later concluded with the conflict ending of Daniel in the lion's den. To be sure, in the present state of the additions to Daniel there are some examples of God's direct intervention—at Susanna 45, for instance, God inspires the young Daniel to protest, and in Bel and the Dragon God has a direct role in saving Daniel—but in general the whole tone of the additions reflects a much less "interventionist" theology. From what has been said here, then, we can summarize several important differences in theological outlook between Daniel 1–6 and the additions:

1) Daniel 1–6 emphasize an interventionist theology while the additions do not to the same extent;

2) Daniel 1–6 are in general more negative toward the king than the additions, although variations within the legends can be found from very negative (chaps. 4, 5), to "critical distance" (chaps. 1–3) to positive (chap. 6);

---

[111] Collins, "Court-Tales," 27–65, esp. 47.

3) the crisis in Daniel 1–6 is not intentionally initiated by the heroes, as it is in Bel and the Dragon;

4) in Daniel 1–6 the heroes maintain their observances, while in Bel and the Dragon they destroy others'; and

5) there is no reductionistic explanation of idols in Daniel 1–6, as there is in Bel and the Dragon.

Bel and the Dragon and Daniel 6 Compared

The differences between Bel and the Dragon and Daniel 1–6 should not detract us from the consideration of the similarities between the former and Daniel 6. In both Daniel is thrown into the lions' den and survives, a motif that is very rare indeed,[112] and they are also alike in being much more positive toward the pagan king than Daniel 1–5 are. The view that the stories are not even doublets of each other, but developed quite separately, should be rejected, since several motifs are quite close, and indicate a more involved relationship between the stories.[113] What I would like to show here, however, is not just that Bel and the Dragon and Daniel 6 are similar and variants of the same story, but also that the story now attested only in the Greek Bible is an *older* version of the one in the MT.

Although the two stories in Bel and the Dragon were at one time probably independent,[114] they have now been tied together by several literary devices: their common introduction (vs 2) and the similar declarations of the king, "Great is Bel, and there is no guile in him!" (vs 18), and "Great is the Lord God, and there is no other beside him!" (vs 41). It is the last half of this story complex, the ordeal in the lions' den, which is a close parallel to the last half of Daniel 6, and as we have seen, this punishment scene is not common enough to ascribe the similarity to the coincidence of folklore motifs. The first half of each story, the setting up of the predicament, is quite different, however. Daniel 6 begins by focusing on Darius and his reorganization of the Persian Empire into satrapies; his name is used several times in that section, but in the last half, the section that is parallel to Bel and the Dragon, it is used only once in the OG translation (vs 20), and not at all in MT or Th. The

---

[112] Hartman and Di Lella, *Daniel*, 199. The motif of Androcles and the lion is really quite different, since it involves recognition and personification of the lion.

[113] The structural integrity which Fenz finds in Bel and the Dragon, and which is lacking in Daniel 6, merely illustrates the adaptation of the former, probably oral, source, in the literary redaction of the latter.

[114] Carey A. Moore, *Daniel, Esther, and Jeremiah: The Additions* (AB; Garden City: Doubleday, 1977) 119.

insertion of this royal personage and the focus upon satrapies is likely a redactional motif in Daniel 6, and the first half of the chapter has probably been thoroughly rewritten. The intention of such a redaction is not to locate the story in the historical period of Darius the Mede's reign—this figure did not exist—but to recreate the setting of the empire-wide reorganization into satrapies, which was associated with the name of Darius (king of Persia). The positive ethos of the imperial organization is reflected in the redactor's point of view, a further extension of the positive view of the unnamed king in Bel and the Dragon OG.

More important, however, in Daniel 6 we find two motifs—the use of the king's ring as a seal and the execution of the priests' families along with the priests—that are paralleled not in the story about the destruction of the Dragon, where the lions' den figures, but in the story of the exposé of the priests of Bel. There are three possibilities of how this correspondence of motifs could come about:

1) Daniel 6 has borrowed motifs from both parts of Bel and the Dragon to make one story (my view);
2) Bel and the Dragon have split up motifs from Daniel 6 and placed them in two related stories; or
3) the two works coincidentally made use of the same common folk motifs.

Option 3 cannot be discounted, although the coincidence of motifs in the same overall plot device of the lions' den makes this unlikely. The two motifs at issue—sealing with the king's ring and punishment of the families of the malefactors—are, after all, not so common as to make the "coincidence" theory seem plausible.[115]

Numbers one and two would seem at first to have equal claim to acceptance, but the two motifs fit much more logically in the Bel and Dragon story, and are artificially intruded into the MT version. First, the king and his most honored subjects use their rings to place a seal on the doors of the Bel temple in Bel and the Dragon, but in Daniel 6 they place a seal over the rock covering the lions' den. The former, sealing a door, is a logical and certainly believable occurrence which plays a crucial role in this story of detection,

---

[115] The tale type being discussed here is attested elsewhere, however. A rogue tale in Herodotus 2.121 is very similar to the Bel story, except that the robbers—here treasury robbers—are seen as folk heroes. Both motifs mentioned above find their equivalent in this tale: unbroken seals on the treasury doors, and the fact that it is a family affair (a father and two sons). According to Thompson (*Folktale*, 171–72), this story is widely attested in folklore, given the type no. 950, but this still does not greatly increase the chance that both Daniel 6 and Bel and the Dragon took these motifs from a common oral tradition. The stories are found together in the Danielic cycle of stories, with many similarities of plot and theme.

while the latter—placing a seal on a stone over a pit *with a ring*—is not only unheard of elsewhere to my knowledge,[116] but is practically impossible! Montgomery merely ascribes this problem to the fact that the author had no idea what a lion pit looked like,[117] but it is more likely that it has been added to Daniel 6 to heighten the drama, borrowed from the context where it did make sense, in the Dragon story. Second, the persecutors of Daniel in Daniel 6 are put to death, *together with their wives and children*. These poor innocent people are first heard of in this story at their execution, which is not impossible, but in Bel they have a very logical and entertaining role: the families sneak into the temple through the secret door with the priests, and suffer the same fate as a result of their complicity.

In both cases it is easier to imagine a scenario in which a story motif which has a logical role in one narrative was selected out and expanded into a digression in another narrative, than the opposite scenario, in which illogical motifs are selected out of a narrative, and allowed to generate their own narratives in which the motifs now have a logical home. It is unlikely that a redactor would conclude that the sealing of the stone on a lions' den with a ring was illogical, and thereupon decide to take that one motif and construct an entire story which would contain that motif in a logical way. The analogy of *lectio difficilior est preferenda* from text criticism should not be applied here, for it is not the case that the OG version is "smoothing over" difficulties by such a complicated method. Individual motifs can certainly be used to generate narratives, but here they are too insignificant to justify the wholesale transformation of the story line. The formal, almost poetic structure which Augustinus Kurt Fenz discerns in the dragon episode[118] and the unstructured, prosaic style of Daniel 6 MT can best be explained as an adaptation of an oral legend into a written one, and that corroborates the argument given here. In the following discussion, other arguments will also be given to strengthen this position.

Bel and the Dragon can be divided into two idol parody narratives that are given a more serious tone by the presence of the episode at the end, in which Daniel must witness to his Jewish identity, nearly to the point of death. It is still quite possible that the same person composed the whole, even if common folk motifs were being used. It is certainly true, however, that idol parodies have different moral and metaphysical presumptions from the

---

[116] Sealing a tomb in Matt 27:66 is not the same thing; there is no indication that any kind of ring or similar device is used, but only that the stone is secured and guarded.

[117] Montgomery, *Daniel*, 276.

[118] Fenz, "Ein Drache in Babel. Exegetische Skizze über Daniel 14, 23–42," *SEÅ* 35 (1970) 10–16.

"witnessing" legends and court conflicts. Whether or not the witnessing aspect was part of the original idol parody narrative of Bel and the Dragon, the redaction of that story into Daniel 6 clearly heightens the sense that the bureaucratic organization represents a threat to the Jews. The increased emphasis on the hostility of the majority ethnic group can be seen in four steps, from Bel and the Dragon OG to Bel and the Dragon Th to Daniel 6 OG to Daniel 6 MT.[119] Bel and the Dragon Th already increases the violent opposition of the people over OG: "If you do not hand over Daniel, we will kill you and your whole household!" (vs 29). The opponents in Daniel 6 are no longer priests or the masses,[120] but court counselors and satraps, which corresponds to the change in genre from the more general setting of the idol parody narrative to the court legend, and also to the focus on satrapies. Their conspiracy against Daniel out of jealousy, using Jewish law as a pretext (Dan 6:5–6 MT; not present in OG), reflects a clear development from Bel and the Dragon, where it was Daniel himself who provoked a reaction.

Here again, if the old OG text of Daniel 6 is compared with the MT, we find in the former a more muddled, but probably older version of the story, reflecting an intermediate point of development between Bel and the Dragon and MT Daniel 6. A seam can be detected in Dan 6 OG between the middle of vs 4 and the beginning of vs 5. Verse 4: "At that time the king decided to appoint Daniel over all of his kingdom (τότε ὁ βασιλεὺς ἐβουλεύσατο καταστῆσαι τὸν Δανιηλ ἐπι πάσης τῆς βασιλείας αὐτοῦ), and vs 5: "When the king decided to appoint Daniel over all of his kingdom . . . (ὅτε δὲ ἐβουλεύσατο ὁ βασιλεὺς καταστῆσαι τὸν Δανιηλ ἐπὶ πάσης τῆς βασιλείας αὐτοῦ). The material between contains an awkward reference to the 127 satraps (but does not mention their complicity), and the story runs much smoother without it. It is quite possible that this was lacking in the story of Daniel and a Median king,[121] although we would also have to excise

---

[119] Although it is not certain that this was the exact order of the tradition, this seems to correspond to a clear trajectory. There were likely other variant versions circulating as well.

[120] Bel and the Dragon OG calls the opponents in the lions' den scene "the people of the land" (ὁ ὄχλος τῆς χώρας, vs 30), while in Th they are called "the Babylonians" (vs 28).

[121] Originally perhaps Astyages. Darius is introduced incorrectly here because he is associated with the division of the empire into satrapies. Note that Bel and the Dragon Th begins with "King Astyages was taken to his fathers, and Cyrus the Persian received the kingdom" (cf. 6:29 OG). This is the correct Mede for the succession of kingdoms. Daniel 6:1 OG now has "Artaxerxes of the Medes" after Belshazzar, which is incorrect, but a possible scribal error for "Astyages of the Medes." In support of this, note also the almost identical phrases used in 6:1, 29 OG and Bel and the Dragon Th vs 1. Compared with Bel OG, Bel Th has been assimilated to the court legend introductions of the other Daniel chapters, and at one time may have stood in the place of Daniel 6 in the corpus, beginning with a reference to Astyages the Mede and ending, as Daniel 6 OG does now, with a formula for succession to Cyrus. The story was perhaps changed to the present Daniel 6, Darius was substituted for Astyages when satraps were added, and Bel

it at the very beginning—a reasonable emendation, but not marked by any literary clues. Whether the satraps are originally mentioned or not, in the OG only the two coregents of Daniel conspire, and the issue of "the laws of Daniel's god" is not explicitly brought in.[122] Thus, in this line of development from Bel and the Dragon OG through Daniel 6 MT can be detected an increase in the ubiquitousness of the threat, the injustice of it (that is, it is not provoked), and the belief that the threat is somehow related to Jewish *observance*, and not to Jewish ethnic identity per se.[123]

English Translation of the Old Greek of Daniel 6

(1b) Darius was advanced in age and noble in years. (2/1) He appointed 127 satraps over all of his kingdom, (3/2) and over these he set three governors; Daniel was one of these three men (4/3) and had authority over everyone in the kingdom. Daniel was robed in purple and was powerful and influential with Darius the king, because he was great, learned, and wise, and a holy spirit was in him, and he was very successful in administering all the affairs of the king which he undertook. As a result, the king decided to place Daniel over his whole kingdom and over the two other governors, whom he had previously appointed with him, and over the 127 satraps. (5/4) When the king decided to place Daniel over his whole kingdom, the two other men formed a pact between them, but since they could find no evidence of any sin or oversight in Daniel concerning which they could condemn him to the king, (6/5) they said: "Let us proceed ourselves to establish an edict that no person is allowed to make a petition or a prayer to any god for thirty days, except to Darius the king. Further, the person who does so will die." This they did in order to ruin Daniel in the king's eyes, and so that he would be thrown into the lions' den. For they knew that Daniel prayed and made petitions to his Lord God three times a day.

(7/6) These men then entered in before the king and said to him: (8/7) "We have established an edict and order that any person who makes a prayer or any

---

and the Dragon Th was eventually shifted to the end of the corpus, where the succession to Cyrus was necessarily moved to the beginning of the story—as it now stands—to agree with the chronology.

[122] Note that by including all the satraps in the conspiracy, MT/Th is caught in an absurdity: as in OG, all the conspirators are thrown in the lions' den, together with wives and children, but whereas in OG this amounts to only two villains and their families, in MT/Th it is 122 conspirators and all of their loved ones. Surely they died of suffocation and not from the hungry lions.

[123] Contrast Esther, where it is ethnic identity and not observance that is at issue, since Esther marries a Gentile and eats nonkosher food. Only her secret ethnic identity provides dramatic tension, and ethnic identity and not God is the focus of the hope for deliverance: 4:3, 13, 16; 6:13. The "help from another quarter" passage (4:14) is perhaps an exception.

petition to any god except Darius the king for a period of thirty days will be thrown into the lions' den.'' (9/8) And they petitioned the king to establish the edict and not alter it, because they knew that Daniel prayed and made petitions three times a day, and thus he would be ruined by the king himself and thrown into the lions' den. (10/9) And so it happened that King Darius declared it and established it as law. (11/10) When Daniel learned of the decree which had been declared against him, he opened the windows of his upper room toward Jerusalem and prostrated himself three times a day, just as he had done previously, and he prayed. (12/11) They watched Daniel and caught him praying three times a day every day. (13/12) These men then charged him before the king and said, ''King Darius, have you not established a decree that no one is allowed to pray or make a petition to any god for thirty days except to you, O King, and if anyone does, that person will be thrown into the lions' den?'' The king answered them, ''What you say is true, and the decree stands.'' (13a/12a) They said to him, ''We adjure you by the laws of the Medes and Persians, that you not alter the edict nor show any favoritism, nor lessen the severity of the imposed sentences when you punish the person who did not abide by this decree.'' And he said, ''I shall do exactly as you have said, and I shall stand by this decree.'' (14/13) And they said, ''Indeed, we have found Daniel, your friend, praying and making petitions before his god three times a day.'' (15/14) And although he was grieved to hear this, the king commanded to have Daniel thrown into the lions' den, according to the decree which he had declared against him.

The king was extremely grieved for Daniel and tried[124] to save him from the hands of the satraps until sundown, (16/15) but he was not able to save him from them. (17/16) But Darius the king cried out and said to Daniel, ''Your god, whom you worship three times a day, day in and day out, will save you from the lions. Have courage until morning!'' (18/17) Daniel was then thrown into the lions' den, and a stone was brought and placed over the mouth of the pit, and the king set his seal on it with his own ring, as well as with the rings of the other officials, so that Daniel could not be taken up by them nor the king be able to pull him up out of the pit. (19/18) Then the king returned to his palace and passed the night fasting and grieving for Daniel. The God of Daniel, however, foresaw Daniel's need and closed the mouths of the lions, and they did not harm Daniel at all.

(20/19) King Darius arose early and, taking the satraps with him, proceeded to the mouth of the lions' den and stood beside it. (21/20) The king called out to Daniel loudly and with much wailing and said, ''O, Daniel, are you still alive, and has your god, whom you worship constantly, saved you from the lions, and kept them from destroying you? (22/21) When Daniel heard the loud cry he said, (23/22) ''O King, I am still alive, and God has saved me from the lions, because I was found to be righteous before him; and before you as well,

---

[124] So 88-Syh.

O, King, I was found to be innocent of any sin or misdeed. But you have listened to men who lead kings astray, and have thrown me into the lions' den to be destroyed. (24/23) Then all the leaders were gathered so that they could see that the lions had not touched Daniel. (25/24) But the two men who had testified against Daniel, they and their wives and children, were all thrown to the lions, and the lions killed them and crushed their bones.

(26/25) Then Darius wrote to all the peoples, regions, and tongues, to all those living in his whole kingdom, saying, (27/26) "Let all the people who live in my kingdom come forward to kneel and worship the God of Daniel, for he is the God who abides always and lives from generation to generation forever. (28/27) I, Darius, shall worship and serve him all my days. The idols made with hands do not have the power within them to save in the same way that the god of Daniel rescued Daniel." (29/28) King Darius was gathered to his ancestors and Daniel was appointed over the kingdom of Darius. Soon thereafter Cyrus the Persian received his kingdom.

English Translation of
the Old Greek of Bel and the Dragon

From the prophecies of Habbakuk, son of Joshua, of the tribe of Levi

(2) There was a certain man who was a priest, by the name of Daniel, son of Abal, who was a confidant of the king of Babylon. (3) There was also an idol, Bel, whom the Babylonians worshipped. Each day, he was provided with twelve bushels of fine flour, four sheep and six measures of oil. (4) The king worshipped him also, and the king went each day to kneel before him. Daniel, on the other hand, prayed to the Lord. (5) The king said to Daniel, "Why do you not worship Bel?" Daniel replied to the king, "I worship no one except the Lord God who made heaven and earth, and has authority over all flesh." (6) The king then said to him, "But is this not a god? Do you not see how many offerings are placed before him each day?" (7) But Daniel replied, "That is totally wrong! Do not let anyone lead you astray, for he is clay on the inside, bronze on the outside. I swear to you by the Lord God of gods, that he has never eaten anything." (8) Enraged, the king called for the chief priests of the temple and said to them, "Show me the one who eats the things offered to Bel. If you do not, you will die, (9) but if you do, Daniel, who says that these things are not eaten by him, will die." They replied, "Bel himself is the one who eats these things." But Daniel said to the king, "Let it stand this way: If I cannot prove that Bel does not eat these things, let me die, along with all my friends and associates."

(10) Now there were seventy priests of Bel, not counting wives and children. They led the king to the temple, (11) and the food was placed there in the presence of the king and of Daniel, and mixed wine was brought in and placed before Bel. Daniel said, "See yourself, O King, how these things are arranged; when the temple is closed, place a seal on the locks of the temple."

This idea pleased the king. (14) But Daniel commanded his friends to lead everyone outside the temple, and then to cover the whole temple with ashes without letting anyone outside see them. Then he commanded that the temple be sealed with the ring of the king and with the rings of some of the chief priests, and this was done.

(15–17) On the next day they returned to the temple. The priests of Bel had entered through hidden trap doors and eaten all the food set out for Bel and drunk all the wine. Daniel said, "You priests, examine your seals to see if they are still intact. And you also, O King, check to see if everything is in order." They found the seals intact, and they broke them open. (18) When they opened the doors they saw that all the food that had been set out was consumed, and the tables were empty. The king rejoiced and said to Daniel, "Great is Bel, and in him there is no guile!" (19) But Daniel laughed loudly and said to the king, "Come, then, and look at the guile of the priests." Then Daniel said, "King, whose footprints are these?" (20) The king responded, "The footprints of men, women, and children."

(21) He then proceeded to the house where the priests resided and found the food and wine that had been offered to Bel. Daniel then pointed out to the king the trapdoors, through which the priests entered and consumed the offerings to Bel. (22) The king brought the priests out of the temple of Bel and handed them over to Daniel, and in addition gave Daniel the food which had been offered, and destroyed the temple of Bel.

(23) There was also a dragon in the same place, which the Babylonians worshipped. (24) The king said to Daniel, "Will you also say that this one is bronze? Indeed he lives and eats and drinks, so worship him." (25) Daniel replied, "King, give me the authority, and I will destroy the dragon without sword or staff." (26) The king consented and said to him, "It is granted to you." (27) So Daniel took thirty minas of pitch, mixed it with fat and hair, boiled them together and made them into a cake, and threw this into the mouth of the dragon. When the dragon swallowed it, he swelled up and burst. Daniel showed him to the king and said, "Do you worship such things as this, O King?"

(28) All the people of the countryside rose up in protest on account of Daniel and said, "The king has become a Jew! First he destroyed Bel, then he killed the dragon!" (30) When the king saw that the people from the countryside had risen up against him, he called for his counselors and said, "I hand Daniel over to you to be executed." (31–32) Now there was a pit in which seven lions were kept, in which conspirators against the king were thrown; every day the lions fed on the bodies of two people condemned to death. The people threw Daniel into the pit, so that he would be totally devoured and there would be nothing left for a burial. Daniel remained in the lions' den six days.

(33) And on the sixth day Habbakuk was walking, carrying stew in a bowl, mixed with bread, and wine in a jar, on his way to the field to give it to the harvesters. (34) But an angel of the Lord said to Habbakuk, "Thus says the Lord God: 'Take the dinner which you have and give it to Daniel in the lions' den in

Babylon.' " (35) But Habbakuk said, "Lord God, I have never seen Babylon and I do not know where the lions' den is." (36) The angel of the Lord then picked Habbakuk up by the hair of his head and put him down beside the lions' den in Babylon. (37) Habbakuk said to Daniel, "Eat this dinner which the Lord God sent to you." (38) Daniel said, "The Lord God, who does not forsake those who love him, has remembered me." (39) While Daniel ate, the angel of the Lord on the same day placed Habbakuk back at the spot from which he had taken him. For the Lord God remembered Daniel.

(40) After these things, the king went out mourning Daniel, but when he looked into the lions' den, he saw Daniel sitting there. (41) The king cried out and said, "Great is the Lord God, and there is no other beside him." (42) The king then pulled Daniel up out of the lions' den, but those who were responsible for his execution he threw into the pit in Daniel's presence, and they were devoured.

Analysis of Daniel 6

With this comparison of Daniel 6 and Bel and the Dragon complete, it is possible to introduce Haag's proposed reconstruction of this chapter:

6:4 Daniel rose to a high position among the ministers, because an excellent spirit was in him. The king thought it appropriate, therefore, to set him over the entire kingdom. 5 The ministers, however, sought to find some grounds for complaint against Daniel concerning the kingdom, but they could not find any grounds for complaint, because he was faithful.

7 The ministers stormed in before the king, and asked that he make an order and establish an edict, that anyone who makes a prayer within the next thirty days, shall be thrown into the lions' den. 10 The king signed the edict and the prohibition. 11 Daniel, however, went into his house and prayed and gave thanks before his God, as he had done before. 15 The king was very distressed; his thoughts were with Daniel, and he labored till the setting of the sun to deliver Daniel.

17 Then the king gave the order, and they led Daniel away and threw him into the lions' den. 19 Thereupon the king went to his palace and passed the night with fasting. He allowed no food to be brought to him, and sleep did not come to him. 20 When morning finally came, he proceeded to the lions' den. 21 As he approached the lions' den, he wailed with a loud voice. 22 Then Daniel spoke to the king. 24 The king was overjoyed, and commanded that Daniel be pulled up out of the lions' den. It was found that there was not the least sign of injury on him.

26 Therefore the king wrote to all peoples, nations, and languages, which reside in the whole world: May you have peace! 27 A decree goes out from me, that in every dominion of my kingdom, everyone tremble and fear before the God of Daniel.

Haag gives a plausible earlier version of Daniel 6, but if my argument above is correct, it is not the original source—Bel and the Dragon is. Still, his reconstruction could be considered as the midpoint between Bel and the Dragon and the present Daniel 6, that is, the first version which reflects the metamorphosis of the story from the idol parody narrative to the court conflict concerning Darius the Mede. Even here, though, beginning with the OG of Daniel 6 would have required fewer excisions for Haag. The law as a pretext for executing Daniel, omitted from Haag's hypothetical source, is not found in Daniel 6 OG.[125]

The similarity of Daniel 3 and 6 has of course been noted by scholars, as these are both conflicts, as opposed to the contests of chapters 2, 4, and 5. However, the similarity goes beyond this generic similarity, and indicates that these two conflicts were edited at the same time by the same redactor. Above it was noted that Daniel 3 was a well-constructed oral composition, which had received only a few editorial glosses. Here I will compare the plot outlines of chapter 3 without these glosses with chapter 6.

Daniel 3	Daniel 6
Introduction:	Introduction:
	Darius establishes satrapies
	Daniel preferred over satraps
Neb. makes gold image	
Neb. gathers all officers, by list	(MT: all officers gather, by list)
	two satraps conspire
edict proclaimed:	edict proclaimed:
must worship image	cannot pray except to king
punishment for violation:	punishment for violation:
fiery furnace	lion's den
	king signs edict
all worshipped image	
Body:	Body:
violation: Jews ignore edict	violation: Daniel ignores edict,
(implied)	prays
mighty men accuse Jews	satraps accuse Daniel
	Darius resists
	Darius compelled by edict
Jews brought to Neb.	Daniel brought forward

---

[125] The OG is fuller in vss 11–14 than Haag's source, but the latter seems too economical, and his reasoning at this point (*Errettung*, 38–39), while plausible, is not compelling.

king's discourse with accused:	king's discourse with accused:
theological theme:	theological theme:
God will deliver	God will deliver
king and courtiers attempt	king and courtiers attempt
to execute three	to execute Daniel
Resolution:	Resolution:
	Darius sleepless
	Darius comes to den
antagonists slain by own device	
king's witness:	king's witness:
sees Jews in fire	hears Daniel's voice
	commands Daniel taken up
	antagonists slain by own device
witness of all	
Neb.'s doxology	
king's new decree:	king's new decree:
glorify God of three	glorify God of Daniel
good rewarded:	good rewarded:
Jews promoted	Daniel serves Darius and Cyrus

Daniel 6 probably resulted from a long editing process, while Daniel 3 is a barely retouched oral legend. The similarities between them, therefore, must have resulted from the editing of Daniel 6 with Daniel 3 as a model. This editing of Daniel 6 could only come about when the corpus of Daniel 4–6 was combined with Daniel 3. It is possible, therefore, that Bel and the Dragon stood in place of Daniel 6 in the corpus of Daniel 4–6 before this change took place.

The Evolution of Daniel 4, 5, and 6

Daniel 4, 5, and 6 must be considered separately from the other legends in Daniel because of the great differences between the MT and the OG text for these chapters. Although this difference has generally been attributed to the inferiority of the OG recension, here I have taken up the view of Charles, Jahn, and others that the OG attests an older version of the legends. I have given evidence that the OG version of Daniel 4, 5, and 6 in each case reflects an older *Vorlage* than does the MT. The evidence in each case was different, and although there is no reason to presume that the same judgment of priority must be made in all three cases—they may have had three quite different text histories—the fact that only these chapters reflect a separate recension indicates that they may very well have circulated together before being combined first with chapters 1–3 and then with 7–12 and the additions.

An evolution of each chapter of Daniel 4–6 was postulated above based on a comparison between the variants of the stories, and we find similar redactional motifs in each case. A theory based on the possibility that the three chapters circulated as a corpus is thus strengthened by the parallel developments in each, and by the fact that the theory can give a meaningful explanation of why the evolution took place. When considered together, the following redactional traits can be detected in the evolution of these chapters:

1. Competition or explicit threat from other courtiers is increased; social setting more narrowly focused on court;
   a. angel in "Bull Sojourn" may become unnamed seer in 4QOrNab;
   b. Dan 4 OG as a whole names courtier and emphasizes his status;
   c. Dan 4 MT adds explicit contest elements to Dan 4 OG;
   d. Bel OG country folk become "Babylonians" in Bel Th, and threaten king with death;
   e. Bel political organization changed to satraps with courtiers in Dan 6 OG, two of whom conspire against Daniel;
   f. two conspirators in Dan 6 OG become 122 in Dan 6 MT;

2. Theological language and epithets for idols are updated; henotheistic conceptions give way to monotheism;
   a. Dan 5 OG proem "gods of nations molten and carved" becomes "idols made with hands" in Dan 5 OG long version;
   b. sin of praising gods of nations, while ignoring Jewish God in Dan 5 OG proem, has added to it desecration of temple vessels in Dan 5 OG long version;
   c. Dan 5 MT eliminates sin of ignoring Jewish God as one of gods; praising idols and desecrating temple vessels constitute Belshazzar's sin, with monotheism presupposed;
   d. in Bel OG Daniel worshipped "no one except living God," while Bel Th specifies he did not worship "idols made with hands";

3. Incorporation into literary structure of a Danielic corpus is carried forward;
   a. Dan 4 OG conflated "prayers" are shortened in MT and assimilated to other hymnic passages in Daniel;
   b. Dan 5 OG long version only alludes to events of chap. 4, while Dan 5 MT includes a complete retelling;
   c. Bel OG is given a "Danielic" introduction in Bel Th;
   d. Dan 6 OG shows the succession to a "Median" king;

4. Literary seams and inconcinnities are eliminated;
   a. Dan 4 OG prayers are edited (see 3a above), placed at beginning and end of narrative;
   b. Dan 5 OG long version contains doublets which are eliminated in Dan 5 MT;
   c. Dan 6:4–9 OG shortened, smoothed out in 6:4–9 MT;

5. Character of hero demarcated by Jewish personal piety;
   a. Bel Th depicts Daniel as heroic defender of Jewish monotheistic ideas (in destroying idols), while Dan 6 OG depicts him as righteous and pious; his sin in the latter is to pray to God;
   b. in Dan 6:5 OG, conspirators against Daniel mention no possible pretext by which to accuse him, while in 6:6 MT they give as pretext the "law of his god," (דת אלהה) which is directly contrasted with the "law of the Medes and Persians" (דת־מדי ופרס, vs 9);

6. Daniel's wisdom described in theocentric and mantic terms, not in the general terms of courtly wisdom, and is not available to everyone;
   a. Dan 4 OG depicts Daniel as best of court diviners, while Dan 4 MT says he has the "holy spirit of God";
   b. mantic wisdom in Dan 5 MT described in more depth;

7. Genre at several points shifted toward the court legend;
   a. sources of Daniel 4 OG combined into larger story with Daniel as central character;
   b. Dan 4 MT increases contest element with other courtiers, over and above Dan 4 OG;
   c. Daniel 5 OG long version probably adds to proem version Daniel as interpreter of heavenly inscription;
   d. Daniel 5 MT adds to OG long version queen-mother's retrospective of Daniel 4;
   e. Bel Th changed to typical court conflict in Dan 6 OG; conflation of idol parody narrative and conflict in Bel thus eliminated; and

8. Political organization explicitly emphasized, especially in regard to satrapies;
   a. Bel Th and OG merely call Daniel συμβιωτής of king, while Dan 6 OG makes him one of three vice-regents;
   b. figure of 127 satraps is added to Dan 6 OG.

These redactional tendencies, then, can be detected in the evolution of Daniel 4–6, although not every redactional trait can be found in the evolutionary stages of each chapter. Several of the traits mentioned above should not surprise us after a study of the use of the court legend in the ancient near east; they reflect an adaptation of various kinds of materials—fictitious royal testimony of *Prayer of Nabonidus*, prophecy against the king of Daniel 5 and the Wall story of Daniel 4, idol parody narrative of Bel and the Dragon—to the court legend genre and a focus on the social setting of that genre, the royal court. There is an awareness of the worldwide imperial political structures which came to dominate Jewish social life, such as satrapies and the imperial court. Some redactional traits above reflect an attempt to incorporate the individual legends into the corpus of Daniel 4–6 as a collected whole, and this same process is carried forward with the incorporation into

Daniel 1–6, for instance, where lists of officers from Daniel 3 appear in Daniel 6. Other traits, however, demonstrate a consciousness of the threat to Jews which is not focused on Jewish identity per se, as it is in Esther, Judith, and Tobit, but more on Jewish righteousness.[126]

The emphasis on witnessing to Jewish *observance*, and not merely national or ethnic identity, seems as well to go hand in hand with a greater emphasis on the vertical nature of revealed, mantic wisdom as God's reward to the righteous, a source of wisdom not available to everyone.

When these traits of Daniel 4–6, arrived at through source- and redaction-critical analysis, are compared with the redactional traits postulated above for Daniel 1–3, we find a great deal of agreement. Since comparisons between MT and OG are not as significant in Daniel 1–3, an *increase* in the tendencies in Daniel 1–3 is generally impossible to demonstrate; still the *presence* of some of those traits shown to be redactional in Daniel 4–6 can be found in 1–3 as well. I will list here the redactional traits of chaps. 4–6 outlined above, noting the evidences for their presence in Daniel 1–3:

1. Competition or threat from other courtiers increased;
   a. In Dan 3 Jews are accused of noncompliance by Chaldaean courtiers (perhaps originally "strong men of army");
   b. Dan 1: Daniel and friends ten times better than other court sages;
   c. Dan 2: Daniel does what pagan courtiers assert only the gods can do;[127]

2. Theological language updated;
   (No evidence of this is found in Daniel 1–3.)

3. Incorporation into the literary structure of corpus;
   a. References to temple vessels and mantic wisdom probably added to source of Dan 1;
   b. References to three companions added to Dan 2; last verse introduces situation of Dan 3;

4. Literary seams and inconcinnities eliminated;
   (Without comparisons, this is impossible to identify in chaps. 1–3)

5. Character of hero demarcated by Jewish personal piety;
   a. Dan 1 *maskilim* are select group of Jews, of whom Daniel and the three companions are a select group of *maskilim*; their theocentric wisdom is superior to the Babylonian sages;

---

[126] In MT Esther Jewish observance is nowhere to be found. In Judith and Tobit observance and ethnic identity are more closely merged, but it is significant that Tobit gets into trouble for burying the bodies of Jews, and not for praying at a window.

[127] However, Daniel 1 and 2 show a cooperative attitude toward other courtiers, and the king does not threaten Jews in particular, so much as exercise a capricious power over everyone.

    b. addition of vss 17–23 to Dan 2 focuses on deliverance of Daniel, et al., on basis of piety, without mentioning danger to or deliverance of other Jews;

6. Daniel's wisdom theocentric and mantic, not general courtly wisdom;
    a. verses 17, 20 probably added to Dan 1 in regard to Daniel's ability to interpret dreams;
    b. addition of vss 18–23, 29–30 to Dan 2 emphasizes "vertical" revelation;

7. Genre shifted toward court legend:
    (There is no evidence in chaps. 1–3 of a shift in genre, but court elements are quite strong and belong to the earliest levels); and

8. Political organization emphasized, especially in regard to satrapies;
    a. Dan 3 lists every major political officer, including satraps.

These traits, where they are attested both in the redaction of Daniel 4–6 and 1–3, may be taken to indicate the tendencies that were operative in the growth of the whole corpus, even though Daniel 4–6 may very well have grown as a separate corpus before the addition of 1–3. In looking at the two groups of legends, however, we should also note that certain of the tendencies mentioned above are peculiar to the contests on one hand or the conflicts on the other, whether they are in chapters 1–3 or 4–6. In the two conflict legends, chapters 3 and 6, it is the political titles of the threatening officials which are emphasized (MT 3:2–3, 6:5–8),[128] while in the contests the role of competitor is assigned to the practitioners of mantic wisdom, that is, the magicians, astrologers, Chaldeans (in the mantic, not ethnic sense).[129] Corresponding to this distinction, we note that the conflicts have a definite witness aspect: the trouble for Daniel and his companions begins when they are forced to witness to Jewish law. The contests of chapters 2, 4, and 5 lack this element.

In regard to these distinctions Daniel 1 does not fit neatly into either category. The hypothetical source of the chapter, isolated tentatively above,

---

[128] But cf. 3:8, "Chaldaeans." This term can denote the ethnic identity of courtiers, or refer more generally to the mantic practitioners in the court. In Daniel it is used in the ethnic sense at 1:4 and probably also in 2:4 and 3:8 (where it was added for ethnic, not mantic, interests). Elsewhere in chaps. 2, 4, and 5 it is used synonymously with other terms for practitioners of mantic wisdom. See Montgomery, *Daniel*, 120–21, 143–44, on the use of the term.

[129] F. F. Bruce ("The Book of Daniel and the Qumran Community," in E. Earle Ellis and Max Wilcox, eds., *Neotestamentica et Semitica: Studies in Honor of Matthew Black* [Edinburgh: T. & T. Clark, 1969] 225) has pointed out that the words *rāz* and *pešer* occur several times in Daniel; the distribution of these words, however, is instructive: 2:18, 2:24, 4:6, 4:15, and 5:26—all contests! (Also attested at 7:16.)

more closely approximates the contest in respect to genre, but it emphasized courtly wisdom and included a witness aspect, and in these respects is more similar to the conflicts. However, it is only in vss 17 and 20—probably insertions—that mantic wisdom is an issue. There is, then, a strong correlation in Daniel 1–6 between the witness aspect and courtly wisdom, found in the conflicts of chapters 3 and 6 and in the possible source of chapter 1, and at the same time mantic wisdom is found in the contests, where there is no witness element, and has evidently been added to chapter 1 at vss 17 and 20.

It may be possible as a result of this analysis to give the layers of redaction a relative dating. If it is granted that Daniel 4–6 did circulate independently, then the strong element of mantic wisdom found in the redactional level of chapters one and two indicates that the editing of Daniel 1–6 as a whole was governed by this same interest. Daniel 3 and 6, the two conflicts, were obviously to the liking of the editor of 1–6, but neither were reworked with the idea of mantic wisdom in mind. It was stated above that the transformation of Daniel 6 from an idol parody narrative into a conflict with a satrapy setting and a focus on witnessing evidently occurred when 4–6 were combined with chapter 3, although there was no indication above as to what other chapters may have been added at that time. Now, however, it would seem that, since the mantic interests of chapters one and two are not found in chapter 3, the former were added at a later time than chapter 3. Note that in the OG, Daniel 3 has its own chronicles-style dating, which would have been appropriate for the introductory chapter of a collection.[130] At any rate, the interests associated with the conflicts—witness motif, political officials as competitors instead of mantic sages—were probably secondary interests for the redactor of Daniel 1–6 as a whole. The independent stories in chapters 3 and 6 are also negative toward the courtiers, but we should be careful to note that some of these characteristics may simply result from the different premises of the two subgenres, contests and conflicts. Contests in general presume a more amicable relationship among the courtiers, even if the Jewish courtier is shown to be the wisest and ablest, while the court conflict must take as its dramatic problem the persecution of the hero by his or her equals, and a reinstatement before the king.

Collins proposes that the redaction of 1–6 as a whole is toward a more negative and condemning view of the king. He notes especially that the oracle in Daniel 2, which condemns the ruling kingdom, is more important in the literary structure of 1–6 than the story outline itself, which concludes on a positive note regarding the relation between Daniel and the king.[131] The

---

[130] Whether chapter 7 entered the corpus before chapter 1, to form a corpus of 2–7 (the Aramaic corpus), will not be addressed here.

[131] Collins, "Court-Tales," 229.

older, independent story was not negative toward the king. Collins may very well be right, but the difficulty comes in matching redactional layers of the various legends and discerning the *Tendenz* of any part of the growing corpus. Daniel 4, for instance, in the Dream Interpretation story, moves from a source which condemns Babylon, to a more positive redaction which allows for Nebuchadnezzar's potential to repent. Daniel 5 begins with a totally condemning political oracle against Belshazzar, and this is changed by representing him as friendly toward Daniel.

The conclusions from Chapter 2 of this thesis concerning the use of the court legend in the ancient Near East can now be applied to the corpus of stories about Daniel. The case of the legends from Herodotus concerning the fallen Croesus in the court of the Persian kings is very instructive for our purposes. There court legends about Croesus could be isolated which fit the genre quite closely, affirmed the wisdom and perhaps even the righteousness of the fallen Croesus as a courtier, and championed his ability in the court of the greatest kings in the world. What is most important here is not simply that parallels can be drawn between the depiction of Croesus and Daniel, but that there was more than one legend of this sort concerning Croesus, indicating that a cycle of such legends existed, perhaps even collected into a corpus of legends concerning this cultural hero. In addition, I tried to demonstrate in Chapter 2 that the court legend was generally used as a propaganda device to assert ethnic identity, whether from the point of view of the ruling ethnic group or of the ruled ethnic group. The hypothetical corpus of legends about Croesus was very likely composed and circulated by Lydians to affirm their role in Persian social and political life. If this reconstruction of the use of court legends by the Lydians is correct, then it is very close to the way that the Daniel corpus was used: a corpus of legends about a cultural hero of a ruled minority is transmitted which affirms the role of that minority in the ruling empire, even though the identity of the empire is in flux in the Daniel legends. Not only was the individual court legend a common genre, but the collection of legends into a larger book may have also been a common enterprise. This step perhaps presumes a scribal process and a broader degree of literacy, which goes well beyond that required for the oral or written transmission of the individual legends. For this, a "Danielic school" can be posited, which passed on both narratives and visionary materials. As Lebram has pointed out, many of the activities and ideals mentioned in Daniel 2–7 are reflected also in Ben Sira's paean to the scribe (39:1–11).[132] The OG version of Susanna also ends with an appeal to recognize the role of youth, which appears to be an affirmation of education in Jewish wisdom. It is

---

[132] Lebram, *Buch Daniel*, 19–20.

incorporated into the larger design of the Danielic corpus, but the affirmation of the role of the wise seems to be retained throughout.

When making this comparison between the Daniel cycle of legends and those concerning Croesus, it is necessary to keep in mind, however, the distinctions I have drawn between the early stages of a Danielic corpus and the process which leads up to the MT text. The early forms of the Danielic corpus probably served to affirm the ethnic identity of the Jews, just as other Jewish court legends had. The direction of development in the Danielic corpus, however, is toward a focusing on the issue of righteousness and obedience to the laws of God, and not Jewish ethnic identity, as it was in Esther. In this way the Danielic corpus leaves behind the normal application of the court legend genre, and becomes an instrument of a scribal group of devout Jews. It is Collins's contention that Daniel 1–6 seemed amenable to the Hasidim or *maskilim* who compiled Daniel as a whole; they wanted to connect Daniel the court sage with Daniel the visionary. It is possible to go further, however, and say that several tendencies can be observed in the redaction of Daniel 1–6 which are already moving in the direction of a strict Jewish personal piety.[133] It is in Daniel 1–6 that we can best see the radicalization of wisdom genres that might have been a parallel development to the renaissance of apocalypticism in the third and second centuries.

Corresponding to this we can also detect in Daniel 1–6 a new focus which is not found in the earlier apocalyptic writings (that is, Ezekial, Haggai, Zechariah 9–14, Isaiah 24–27 and Second and Third Isaiah). The focus of righteousness on all Israel has given way to a focus on those few who are truly righteous before God. Other writings roughly contemporary with Daniel keep a broader, pan-Jewish perspective, for example, Esther, Judith, even Susanna, but Daniel 1–6 begins the process of narrowing the parameters of those who are deemed righteous. If the above analysis is correct, this can be seen in two parts, perhaps in two successive steps. First is the growing emphasis in Daniel 3 and 6 on the ''witness'' ideal, the threat of the non-Jewish courtiers, and physical deliverance by God, and the second, especially to be noted in the contests, is direct revelation by God. Daniel 1–6 is not as radical as the contemporary apocalypses, which condemn both the Gentile nations and unrighteous Jews, but it does stand in an intermediate position between the bourgeois novellas—including the other court legends—and the

---

[133] So also Blenkinsopp, *Wisdom*, 125, 152. Lebram (*Buch Daniel*, 81) asserts something like this for Daniel 6, i.e., a Jew's relation to God is for the first time based on individual piety and not on the land, communal group, or temple; so also a personal communication from John Collins. A parallel development can perhaps be traced in the Enoch literature, especially in relation to the speculations of a scribal group, but here I am primarily interested in what a scribal group may have been doing to court legends in particular.

pious protests of the apocalypses: the "ruled ethnic perspective" for Daniel 1–6 is not that of "Jews" but of "righteous Jews." What is lacking in a comparison with the later Jewish apocalyptic writings is any accounting for unrighteous Jews. Jews, in general, are simply not mentioned.

4

Esther: From Court Legend to Novella

A New Approach to Sources in Esther

Although the Book of Esther is often justifiably compared with other Jewish court legends, it is in many ways more complex in its literary structure, and a thorough examination of its place in the history of the genre must take full regard of these complexities. Many of the basic elements of the court legend can be easily discerned here—the setting in the royal court, the wise hero (and in this case a heroine as well) who represents a ruled ethnic group, the dramatic testing of the protagonists, and their ultimate success—but, just as the Joseph story in Genesis and the later redactions of *Ahikar* display expanded and episodic versions of the basic court conflict plot line, Esther does also. We briefly note, for instance, that an entire subplot concerning the king's first wife Vashti is used to introduce the story, that the main body of the work proceeds by moving back and forth from Mordecai to Esther, and that the resolution of Mordecai's predicament in the capital of Susa is followed by a long description of the Jews' revenge on their would-be tormentors in the provinces and the celebration of the success.

Lewis Bayles Paton could say in his ICC commentary of 1908, "The Book of Esther presents no complicated problems of documentary analysis, such as are found in most of the other historical books of the Old Testament ... its unity is recognized by all schools of criticism."[1] This is no longer the

---

[1] Paton, *A Critical and Exegetical Commentary on the Book of Esther* (ICC; Edinburgh: T. & T. Clark, 1908) v.

case. It is now often presumed, in fact, that the MT version of the story is based on other sources, which have been conflated and expanded into our present story of the heroic role of Esther and Mordecai in saving the Jewish people of Persia. For instance, it has been suggested that the separate incidents of Vashti, Mordecai, and Esther represent the kernels of older stories.[2] Although these separate subplots are successfully interwoven in the present version, the fact that Mordecai and Haman are often presented separately, without any mention of the character Esther, has given rise to this common view. The use of common folk motifs and parallels with other writings certainly suggests that some of the plot elements are common and that the storyline is borrowed from popular traditions. The Vashti segment of chapter 1, for example, has often been compared with other folk traditions, notably the story of Gyges and the wife of Candaules in Herodotus 1.8 – 13. The closest literary parallel to the story as a whole, however, is the story of the Magophonia, or revenge on the Magi, in Herodotus 3.61 – 79.[3] Many of the same scholars, however, who have suggested that Esther is composed of several stories edited together, have also asserted that the sources are now so intertwined that they are ultimately irrecoverable, and that we must be content with generalizations about the background of the scroll.[4]

Some have nevertheless tried to deal more specifically with the question of the nature of the sources and the process by which they were edited. Paul Haupt made many conjectural emendations of the text and rejected many readings as glosses, although his method was quite eclectic and he ultimately only pared down the text somewhat to a more logical and economic narrative.[5] Others have applied more ambitious programs of isolating earlier sources of the scroll, which, though comprehensive, applied a clear, simple set of criteria, rather than an eclectic combination. Henri Cazelles postulated two sources of different genres: on the one hand a non-Jewish liturgical source originating from a pagan ritual in the provinces, which revolved around the figure of Esther, and on the other hand a narrative source

---

[2] Max Haller, *Das Judentum* (Die Schriften des Alten Testaments; Göttingen: Vandenhoeck & Ruprecht, 1914) 2/3, 277; Hans Bardtke, *Das Buch Esther* (KAT; Gütersloh: Mohn, 1963) 249 – 51; Helmer Ringgren, *Das Buch Esther*, (Das Alte Testament Deutsch XVI; Göttingen: Vandenhoeck & Ruprecht, 1958) 114 – 15; Georg Fohrer, *Introduction to the Old Testament* (Nashville/New York: Abingdon, 1968) 254 – 55; Nickelsburg, *Resurrection*, 50 – 51; and a helpful review of literature in Carey A. Moore, *Esther* (AB; Garden City: Doubleday, 1971) L – LIII.

[3] Hermann Gunkel, *Esther* (Tübingen: Mohr, 1916) 115; Arnaldo Momigliano, "Fattori orientali della storiografia ebraica post-esilica e della storiografia greca," *Revista storia italiana* 77 (1965) 457; and Roland de Vaux, *Ancient Israel* (New York: McGraw-Hill, 1961) 516.

[4] Ringgren, *Esther*, 114; Bardtke, *Esther*, 250.

[5] Haupt, "Critical Notes on Esther," *AJSL* 24 (1907 – 8) 97 – 186, reprinted in Moore, *Studies*.

concerning the persecution of Jews in the capital of Susa, revolving around Mordecai.[6] The many duplications of feasts, officials, events, and petitions, among other things, suggested this analysis to Cazelles. According to him, the combined version functioned to justify the observance by Jews of an originally pagan ritual. Lebram concentrated on the Mordecai sections of the story only, and produced a somewhat more detailed version of the verses which make up this part of the scroll.[7]

Charles C. Torrey, approaching the matter through a comparison of the Masoretic Text with one of the Greek versions, the so-called Greek A text, suggested that the original story of Esther ended at 8:17 in Greek A (7:17 in the Göttingen edition), approximately equal to MT 8:2.[8] From this point on the versions diverge a great deal, and it seemed quite plausible to Torrey that the body of an earlier edition ended here. The book was extended by the addition of the revenge of the Jews on their would-be assailants, and by the institution of Purim (8:3–9:32). Torrey's analysis made no attempt to isolate an earlier version which focused on either Esther or Mordecai separately, as the other scholars mentioned hypothesized, but he attempted to demonstrate instead an earlier stage involving both of the main characters. Recently Clines has retraced Torrey's steps in greater detail, at many points strengthening the argument,[9] and his improvements resulted in much more convincing conclusions and greater progress in the details of the analysis.

Here a new source analysis will be proposed, which will use different methods and criteria for isolating sources from those previously used. Although I follow Clines (and Torrey before him) in his assessment that the Greek A text (hereafter Gk A), minus the LXX additions, in general attests an earlier Vorlage than MT, I will propose an earlier layer to that, a shorter and more economical narrative about Esther and Mordecai. In a separate analysis, I will also propose that within this source a short court legend can be isolated which takes Mordecai alone as the protagonist. The results will still at many points corroborate Clines' conclusions, although some aspects of his reconstruction will here be modified as a result. Since Clines' theory—the most recent of those above—makes full and profitable use of Cazelles's and Torrey's work, I will make closest reference to his.

I isolate the older source of Esther by two means. First, using literary-critical methods, one might be led to hypothesize that certain passages are

[6] Cazelles, "Note sur la composition du rouleau d'Esther," in H. Gross and F. Mussner, eds., *Lex tua veritas: Festschrift für Hubert Junker* (Trier: Paulinus, 1961) 17–29; reprinted in Moore, *Studies.*

[7] Lebram, "Purimfest und Estherbuch," *VT* 22 (1972) 208–22; reprinted in Moore, *Studies.*

[8] Torrey, "The Oldest Book of Esther," *HTR* 37 (1944) 1–40; reprinted in Moore, *Studies.*

[9] Clines, *Esther.*

glosses or expansions of what was once a more economical and straightforward story. The first nine verses, for instance, can be summarized in five words: "King Ahasuerus gave a banquet." The extra words could be considered a general introduction and a generous setting of the scene, but they could at the same time be omitted with no loss to the basic story line. Is there any justification for omitting them? Let us proceed with this experimental procedure. We also see that in 1:10 and 1:14 two lists of seven eunuchs are found, with no names in common,[10] but with the second list intruding into the smooth flow of the story:

> Then the king said to the wise men who knew the times—for this was the king's procedure toward all who were versed in law and judgment, the men next to him being Carshena, Shethar, Admatha, Tarshish, Meres, Marsena, and Memucan, the seven princes of Persia and Media, who saw the king's face, and sat first in the kingdom—"According to the law, what is to be done to Queen Vashti . . . ?"

How much simpler to leave out vss 13b–14 altogether: "Then the king said to the wise men who knew the times, 'According to the law, what is to be done to Queen Vashti . . . ?'" Even more surprising, however, is that it requires twelve verses, down to 2:4, for the question to be finally answered. It would have been more easily accomplished if we had only 2:2–4 as the response: "Then the king's servants who attended him said, "Let beautiful young women be sought out for the king....And let the maiden who pleases the king be queen instead of Vashti."

This radical editing of the text may seem arbitrary or even destructive of the literary artfulness of the Scroll of Esther, but when this process is carried through the entire scroll, we find that the shorter version which results is written in a Hebrew style markedly different from those sections considered here to be expansions. Thus a weighty amount of linguistic evidence (examined below) corroborates the resulting economical source. Further, a comparison with the shorter Greek A text which Clines depended on for his reconstruction also gives partial confirmation, since at many points the verses subtracted in my analysis are also lacking in that text. Some scholars who have examined the style of Esther closely, such as Hans Striedl and Robert Polzin,[11] considered the Hebrew of the Scroll to represent a combination of

[10] Several of the names are, however, similar, although the order of the similar names is strangely reversed; see J. Duchesne-Guillemin, "Les noms des eunuques d'Assuérus," *Muséon* 66 (1953), 105–8; reprinted in Moore, *Studies.*

[11] Striedl, "Untersuchung zur Syntax und Stilistik des hebräischen Buches Esther," *ZAW* 55 (1937) 73–108; and Polzin, *Late Biblical Hebrew: Toward an Historic Typology of Biblical Hebrew Prose* (HSM 12; Missoula: Scholars Press, 1976) 74–75.

classical and late elements which resulted from a late writer's partially successful attempt to mimic the patriarchal stories. But what we actually find here are two different stages of late biblical Hebrew in Esther. One reflects a style which is in most respects closer to classical Hebrew, corresponding to an economically written source, and the other, in the more verbose expansions, a style which evidences further development in the evolution of late biblical Hebrew. As a result, the syntactic analysis and dating of each should be carried on separately.

The most important syntactical observation to be made is that the source story of Esther and Mordecai (abbreviated "S" for source) uses converted verbs 126 out of 135 times (93%), the redactional sections (abbreviated "R") use converted verbs 23 out of 71 times (32%), while those sections which are difficult to assign (abbreviated "I" for indefinite) use converted verbs 9 out of 14 times (64%).[12] This observation in itself is strong evidence of literary stages in the composition of Esther, but in addition there are other linguistic criteria which corroborate this division of the text:[13]

1) When S uses infinitive construct + *bĕ* or *kĕ*, it is generally introduced by *wayhî*: 1:2, 2:8, and 5:2. In R the same temporal construction is introduced without *wayhî*: 1:4, 5, 10, 17; 2:1, 7, 12, 15, 19, 20, and 9:25. 3:4 and 5:9 follow this latter pattern, and are presently in I.

2) Every instance but one of repeated nouns in a distributive sense (for example, *yôm wayôm* = each day) is in R: 1:8, 22 (3x); 2:11, 12; 3:12 (6x), 14; 4:3, 8:9 (3x), 11, 13, 17 (2x); 9:21, 27, 28 (3x). The single exception is 3:4, presently in I.

3) Most instances of subject-verb word order are in R: 1:9, 12, 20; 2:10, 13, 14 (2x), 20; 3:15 (4x); 4:3, 14; 6:4, 12, 14; 7:6, 7 (2x), 8, 10; 8:1, 15; 9:16, 32. It is found in S only at 4:1. In all, 26 out of 27 instances are in R.

4) Infinitives absolute fall into both S and R, depending on how they are used: a) with cognate finite verb, they are found in R (6:13) and I (4:14); b) in place of a jussive or imperative, in S (6:9) and I (2:3); c) in place of a finite verb, all in R (3:13; 8:8; 9:1, 6, 12, 16 (3x), 17 (2x), 18 (2x). These

---

[12] I counted those converted and unconverted verbs in positions where a free choice between the two was possible; e.g., I did not count jussives or verbs after *ăsher*, *kî*, *'im* or *lo'*. It should also be noted that the indefinite sections are relatively small, and so however these are construed, there is still a very significant discrepancy between S and R in the use of converted verbs.

[13] The literary indicators used here have been isolated by Polzin (*Hebrew*, passim), but similar approaches to a dating of Hebrew syntactical features can be seen in Avi Hurvitz, "The Date of the Prose-Tale of Job Linguistically Considered," *HTR* 67 (1974) 17–34; and Andrew Wilson and Lawrence Wills, "Literary Sources of the Temple Scroll," *HTR* 75 (1982) 275–88.

last references (9:16–18) may be part of a separate Purim correction redaction.

5) Pronominal suffixes on infinitives and participles are found in both S and R, but object suffixes on finite verbs are almost exclusively in S (2:17; 3:1, 10; 4:5, 7; 5:11 (2x); 6:9, 11; 7:9; 8:2; 10:2). Two other attestations are now in I (2:7, 4:10), and another is in R (6:13), but the latter is likely the redactor's duplication of 4:7.

Indicators 1–3 would, taken separately, indicate that the source S used an older form of biblical Hebrew, which is precisely what we might expect. However, indicator 4 shows that R uses an early element which S does not, infinitive absolute for a finite verb, while indicator 5 shows that S uses a late element which R does not, object suffixes on verbs.[14] Both S and R, then, use late biblical Hebrew, S utilizing a style which is *in general* closer to classical Hebrew, while R *in general* reflects a style which betrays more elements of late usage.

Of course, it could be argued, and indeed has, that these variations in certain syntactical features reflect the attempts of one author to give shades of expression to the narrative. Werner Dommershausen, for instance, produced a major monograph which analyzes every odd syntactical arrangement as an intended nuance of the author.[15] For example, he accounts for sentences with subject-verb word order (which by necessity use unconverted verbs) in this way. His premise and method are so totally at odds with mine that it would not be helpful to comment on our opposite construal of each verb. Our two approaches must be judged on the probability of the overall conclusions and the soundness of the method, and not on a debate over each detail.

In the following excursus I will present the reconstruction of Esth S, although it must be admitted that in many individual details some doubt remains. The linguistic evidence points clearly and unequicocally in the direction of two or more levels in the Esther scroll, but it does not necessarily provide the criteria to judge every individual line. The overall outlines of Esth S are discernible, but some of the individual phrases, as well as some key issues, are still to be finally decided.

---

[14] See Polzin, *Hebrew*, 43–44, for infinitive absolute as an indicator, and pp. 28–31 for verbal siffixes. Note that the infinitives absolute are difficult to discern if the pointings are discounted; I have chosen to follow Masoretic pointings for the sake of discussion. At any rate, this indicator is probably the least significant of the five for my argument.

[15] Dommershausen, *Die Estherrolle: Stil und Ziel einer alttestamentlichen Schrift* (Stuttgart: Katholisches Bibelwerk, 1968). Berg (*Esther*, 15–16) distinguishes her literary-critical approach from Dommershausen's in her excellent study. She analyzes the larger structural patterns of the MT version, rather than the individual words and phrases.

Reconstruction of Esth S

The reconstructed version of the source of Esther (Esth S) is given below in sections, with comments following. Those passages which are indefinite in the analysis are placed in parentheses. The comments often refer to the R sections, which are not included here; the reader will thus have to compare this reconstruction side-by-side with the MT version.

(1:2) In the days when King Ahasuerus sat on the throne of his kingdom, which was in Susa the capital, (3) he made a banquet for all his princes and ministers. (10) When the king was feeling merry with wine, he commanded the courtiers who served before him, (11) to bring Vashti the queen in to the king, wearing her royal crown, to show the people and the princes her beauty, for she was very beautiful. (12) But Queen Vashti refused to come at the king's command which came by way of the courtiers, and the king became very angry. (13) Then the king said to the wise men who knew the times: (15) (According to law,) what should be done to Queen Vashti, since she did not obey the command of King Ahasuerus which came by way of the courtiers.

For the introduction of Esth S, cf. Ruth 1:1, Jonah 1:1, Josh 1:1, Judg 1:1, and 1 and 2 Sam 1:1. The repetition of "in the days" at the beginning of vss 1 and 2 indicates that a seam has resulted from the insertion of the intervening digression about Ahasuerus. Gk A differs somewhat here, but since it contains a separate introductory chapter, the verses in question here no longer stand at the beginning and have likely been altered in that text. The chronicles-style dating, "In the third year of his reign" is now lacking at this point in Gk A, but was likely moved to the new beginning of the text, before Mordecai's dream (Gk A 1:1), now used in a typical fashion to introduce dream and vision reports (cf. Dan 7:1, 8:1, 10:1, etc.). "Persia and Media," in this order, are mentioned four times in Esther (1:3,14,18,19), all likely in R. At 10:2 we find instead "Media and Persia," and this is likely S.

The list of courtiers in vs 14 contains names similar to those in the first list of vs 10, but in reverse order; surely two different traditions are represented. Each list is presented in a similar way: the first group is (a) the seven courtiers who (b) serve in the presence of the king, and are (c) wise men who know the times (vss 10, 13a); the second are (a) the seven princes who (b) see the king's face and (c) know law and judgment (vss 13b-14). Gk A lacks both lists, but instead the king calls his "servants" (παῖσιν). For this reason, and because vss 10–11 are very long and cumbersome, I have suggested that neither list is part of S.

The courtier's fear that all women will be insolent because of Vashti is likely an addition to Esth S. MT 2:2 flows better as the response to the king's problem, following immediately after 1:15 MT/ 2:13 Gk A. There is also some linguistic evidence to exclude the anti-feminist policy meeting of 1:16–22 from the source: vs 22 attests the distributive x wĕ-x, typical of R, and although vss 21–22 use several converted verbs, they only do so in stereotyped phrases found elsewhere in S. The strongest argument, however, is that although the two sessions would seem to be closely related in terms of the search for a replacement for Vashti, the second is not only the simpler and more direct of the two, it also reflects no awareness of the first. The first, which is actually a total digression from the plot, is much longer than the second, which is absolutely essential. The transition between them, 2:1, is also very unsatisfactory and betrays a secondary hand. The listing of Persians and Medes in that order is associated with R.

The kĕdāt of vs 15 is here placed in the indefinite category, since it is possibly introduced with the second list of courtiers of Esth R. The whole issue of irrevocable edicts is expanded in R, but whether this particular phrase, vague as it is, is part of that tendency is uncertain.

(2:2) Then said the king's ministers who served him, "Let beautiful young women be sought for the king, (3) (and let the king appoint officers in all the provinces of his kingdom, so that they may gather all the beautiful young women to Susa the the capital,) to the harem into the custody of Hege, the king's courtier who watches over the women, (4) and let the young woman who pleases the king be queen instead of Vashti. This plan pleased the king, and he followed it.

(5) There was a certain Jew in Susa the capital, whose name was Mordecai, (son of Jair, the son of Shim'i, son of Kish, a Benjaminite,) (7) and he brought up Hadassah, that is, Esther, his uncle's daughter, for she had neither father nor mother. This young woman was very beautiful, (and at the death of her father and mother Mordecai adopted her as his daughter.) (8) And so it happened that when the king's command was heard and many young women were gathered at Susa the capital, (into the custody of Hegai,) Esther was also taken to the king's palace, into the custody of Hegai, the custodian of the women. (9) The young woman pleased him, and won his favor, and he readily gave to her ointments and her portion of food, and seven select maids-in-waiting from the king's palace, and he advanced her and her maids to the best position in the harem.

Part of the response to the king's problem is here placed in the indefinite category because it is repetitious and lacking in Gk A. The granting of ointment by Hege is also lacking in Gk A. Hegai (spelled differently) is mentioned again in vs 8, as if for the first time, giving rise to the possibility that it is in this latter reference where he was originally introduced into the story. The mentioning of the provinces in this verse, however, is done in the manner typical of S, and not in the manner typical of R (cf. 3:8, 9:20 S, 3:14 R). Mordecai's genealogy, to be compared to Haman's below at 3:1, is accompanied in MT by a note about the exiles; these may both be a secondary identification of the hero. However, Gk A contains the genealogy but no mention of the exiles.

The introduction of Esther in 2:8 is clouded by two duplications: her name is given in two forms, and the double mention of the death of her parents seems unnecessarily repetitive. (She is also reintroduced at vs 15; see below) There may be two versions of the story conflated at this point, and the establishment of S becomes difficult. The second reference to the death of her parents is here placed in I. Gk A lacks it, but that could result from an editorial attempt to smooth over a clumsy duplication. Gk A also lacks the reference to the king's command, but that command uses converted verbs and *wayhî* + *bĕ* + infinitive construct, both typical of S.

> (2:16) So Esther was taken into the royal palace of King Ahasuerus, (17) and the king loved Esther more than all the women, and she won his favor more than all the young women, so that he set the royal crown on her head and made her queen instead of Vashti. (18) And the king gave a great feast for all his princes and ministers, and gave gifts according to the royal practice. (20) (Esther had not revealed her kindred nor her people, according as Mordecai commanded her.)

These lines from the source exhibit a striking parrallelism of members, which is not present anywhere else in S or R. Verses 11–14, concerning the elaborate organization of the harem, use various verbal forms, but no converted sequences; they are purely a digression to the essential plotline and are excluded from S. Verses 7–9 (in S above) also have many elements repeated in vs 15, which suggests that vs 15 was added:

2:7	Esther's relation to Mordecai	2:15	Esther's relation to Mordecai
2:8	Esther's turn with king		Esther's turn with king
2:9	Hegai gives ointments		Hegai gives ointments
	Esther preferred by Hegai		Esther preferred by all
		2:16	Esther goes in with king
		2:17	king makes Esther queen
		2:18	king makes feast, gifts
		2:19	Mordecai sits in king's gate
2:10	Esther doesn't tell kindred	2:20	Esther doesn't tell kindred

What I have chosen for S is the account of these events in vss 7–9, along with the unparalleled events of vss 16–18. These verses correspond in large measure to Gk A, use converted verbs, and tell a coherent story without unnecessary duplication. The digression of vss 11–14 concerning the elaborate preparations for the harem was probably added to the narrative, and a seam has resulted where the narrative is resumed in 2:15.

Verse 20a is more likely in S than is its duplicate in vs 10, since the latter uses *'ăsher* for *kî*, which is late. Verse 20b is syntactically muddled, revealing late elements.

Part of vs 18 is retained in S, and part excluded. The phrase "for all his princes and ministers" לכל־שריו ועבדיו of vs 18a is identical to 1:3 (also S). The feast of Esther is excised as a redactional trait of R which balances the feast of Vashti at 1:9. The "release of the provinces" focuses on the provinces and uses an unconverted verb, both characteristic of R. The bestowal of gifts in general, however, would be the stereotyped practice of the Persian kings since Cyrus, and is evidently the image taken up by S; a converted verb is used. The tribute which Ahasuerus grants at 10:1 (S) is similar, in that it emphasizes the world-wide Persian empire, including the coastlands.

(2:21) In those days, while Mordecai sat in the king's gate, Bigtan and Teresh, two of the king's courtiers who guarded the door, became angry and conspired to make an attempt on the life of the king. (22) This plan was made known to Mordecai, and he informed Esther about it, who in turn informed the king on Mordecai's behalf. (23) The matter was investigated and found to be so, and so they were both hanged on a gallows. And it was recorded in the book of the chronicles in the king's presence. (3:1) After these things King Ahasuerus promoted Haman (the son of Hammedata the Agagite), and placed his seat above all the other princes that were of the same rank. (2) And all the king's servants who were in the king's gate bowed and did obeisance to Haman, for the king had commanded it. But Mordecai did not bow nor do obeisance to him. (3) (And the servants of the king who were in the king's gate asked Mordecai, "Why do you disobey the king's command?" (4) When they said this to him each day and he did not listen to them, they told Haman to see if Mordecai's practices would prevail. For he had told them he was a Jew.)

Verses 19 and 21 contain identical notations of Mordecai returning to the king's gate ומרדכי ישב בשער־המלך, which likely result from the interweaving of source and redaction. I have included vs 21 in S, which leads smoothly into the next plot development.

In this section the princes are mentioned first, then the servants, in two groups; it is the same two groups which have been used most often in S for the administrative officers of the kingdom. Verses 3–4 are here retained in the indefinite category. They are not necessary to the story, since in vs 6 it is stated that Haman learned that Mordecai was a Jew. These verses only serve to heighten the tension of Mordecai's rebellion, and to emphasize that it is the king's law that is being violated (see also vs 2). The servants in vs 3 are also introduced with the same long phrase that is used in vs 2. The linguistic information is mixed, however: the phrase *yôm wayôm* in vs 4 pushes somewhat in the direction of R, but *wayhî* + *bĕ* + infinitive construct is characteristic of S.

(3:5) When Haman saw that Mordecai neither bowed nor did obeisance to him, Haman was filled with fury. (6) But he disdained to make an attempt on the life of Mordecai alone, for he had been shown who Mordecai's people were, and so Haman sought instead to destroy all the Jews who were in the whole kingdom of Ahasuerus, the people of Mordecai. (8) Haman said to King Ahasuerus, "There is a certain group of people scattered about and dispersed among the peoples in every province of your kingdom, and their laws are different from those of every other people. Further, they do not observe the laws of the king. There is no advantage gained by tolerating them. (9) If it please the king, let it be written that they may be destroyed, and I will pay ten thousand talents of silver into the hands of the treasurers, to place it in the king's treasury. (10) So the king took his ring from his hand and gave it to Haman (son of Hammedata the Agagite), the enemy of the Jews. (11) And the king said to Haman, "The silver is given to you, and the people too, to do with as you see fit." (12) Then the king's scribes were called, and it was written according to all that Haman commanded.

(4:1) When Mordecai saw everything that was done, he tore his clothes and put on sackcloth and ashes, and went out into the middle of the city and wailed a loud and bitter cry. (2) Then he came up to the opening of the king's gate, for no one could enter the king's gate clothed in sackcloth. (4) So Esther's maids and her courtiers came and told her, and the queen was very grieved, and she sent clothes with which to dress Mordecai, so that the sackcloth could be taken off of him, but he would not take them.

The Purim references of vs 7, which use an unconverted verb, are omitted, and part of the account which follows. From vs 12b to 15, unconverted verbs are used in the elaborations of the plot, and there are three motifs associated with R: Purim, emphasis on the provinces, and a written decree.

Verse 3 is a good example of a shift of focus on the part of R. Verse 2 describes Mordecai's dress and wailing, and vs 4 details Esther's reaction to *Mordecai's* situation. Verse 3, inserted between these, abruptly broadens the perspective to the wailing of all the Jews of the empire, told in a melodramatic fashion. Verse 4 knows nothing of this situation. Note also that vs 3 uses מדינה ומדינה, typical of R.

(4:5) Then Esther called for Hatach, one of the king's courtiers, whom he had appointed to serve her, and she commanded him to go to Mordecai and find out what the problem was and why it had come about. (6) So Hatach went to Mordecai in the street of the city which was in front of the king's gate, (7) and Mordecai told him everything that had happened to him, and the amount of silver which Haman had said that he would pay into the king's treasuries to destroy the Jews. (8) (And Mordecai charged Esther to go into the king, to try to gain his favor, and to make a supplication before him on behalf of her people.) (9) Hatach then came and reported everything that Mordecai had said to Esther. (10) (And Esther spoke to Hatach and gave him a command for Mordecai: (11) "All the king's servants know that for any man or any woman who comes before the king in the inner court who has not been called, there is but one law for that person, and that is to be put to death, except for that person alone to whom the king extends the golden scepter, that he or she may live. I, however, have not been called to come before the king for thirty days." (12) And Mordecai was told the words of Esther. (13) Then Mordecai commanded that a resoponse be given to Esther: "Do not think that you can save yourself in the king's house any more than all the other Jews. (14) For if you remain completely silent at this time, help and deliverance will arise for the Jews from someplace else, but you and your father's house will be destroyed. Besides, who knows whether you have come to the throne precisely for a situation such as this?") (15) Then Esther commanded him to return this answer to Mordecai: (16) "Go and gather all the Jews residing in Susa and fast for me; neither eat nor drink for three days, night and day. Then I will go into the king. (17) So Mordecai left and did everything that Esther commanded him.

The reconstruction of Esth S runs into more difficulties here than elsewhere, resulting in a large indefinite section. There is no clear linguistic separation between S and R, nor is the resulting sense of the narrative significantly improved, nor any seams or literary problems explained by the stratification of layers. The Gk A text differs somewhat from MT both in content and in order, but not in a way that would either confirm or refute this reconstruction.

Above we noted that the Magophonia in Herodotus bore many similarities to Esther, but in the analysis here presented, these similarities all fall into R or the indefinite sections. Esth S, R and Magophonia all have a dialogue between a woman within the harem and her father or uncle outside the court, but the closer parallels between Esther and the Magophonia are here limited to the R sections: vss 8 (command to woman in harem), 11 (danger involved, harem restrictions), 13 (appeal to ethnic/family background), and 16b (woman's resolve, to point of death). This closer similarity between the Magophonia and the R layer could suggest that the Magophonia narrative, or something like it, has influenced Esth R, but it could also suggest that the S and R levels belonged together in the first place, producing a more rounded parallel story to the Magophonia.

Most troubling, however, is that much of the literary integrity of this central scene in the narrative would be lost by removing these verses. The dialogue in MT reflects much more tension between the protagonists, as Esther is compelled to make a decision, and the danger in approaching the king unsummoned would remain only implicit in my reconstruction of S. The very drama and artistry of this passage would have to be attributed to a later stage only.[16] These controversial sections of chapter 4 are thus retained as indefinite.

Still, it is worth considering that S contained a simpler dialogue between Mordecai and Esther, which is only partially recoverable. If the indefinite verses here were placed in the later layer, what would be the nature of Mordecai's and Esther's dialogue? Mordecai would refuse clothes, Esther (through Hatach) would ask what the matter was, Mordecai would explain the danger, Esther would counsel a joint Jewish observance and promise to go to the king. Esther's donning royal garb would then stand in close and direct contrast to Mordecai's sackcloth. The initiative for the action would shift under this theory from Mordecai (who is even more emphasized in Gk A) to Esther.

(5:1) On the third day Esther dressed in her royal apparel and stood in the court of the king's palace, facing the king's palace. The king was sitting on his royal throne in his palace, facing the door of his palace. (2) When the king saw Esther the queen standing in the court, the king extended the golden scepter to Esther which was in his hand, and Esther approached and touched the top of the scepter. (3) The king said to her, "What do you want, Queen Esther? What is your request? It shall be given to you, up to half of my kingdom." (7) Esther answered and said, "My petition and my request is: (8) If I have found favor in the sight of the king, and if it pleases the king to grant my petition and perform my request, let the king come with Haman to the banquet which I shall prepare for them, and tomorrow I will do as the king has said." (9) Then Haman went out that day happy and light-hearted, (but when Haman saw Mordecai in the king's gate, neither rising nor bowing before him, Haman was filled with fury against Mordecai. (10) Nevertheless, Haman restrained himself) and went to his house, where he sent and called for his friends and Zeresh, his wife. (11) Haman recounted to them the greatness of his riches, and the number of his children, and every way in which the king had advanced his position, and how he had promoted him above the other princes and servants of the king. (12) And Haman added, "And indeed Esther the queen did not invite anyone with the king to the banquet which she is giving except for me, (13) yet all this is of no advantage to me as long as I see Mordecai the Jew sitting at the king's gate." (14) Then Zeresh his wife and all his friends said to him, "Have a gallows made, fifty cubits high, and in the morning speak to the king so that Mordecai may be hanged on it. Then you can go happily with the king into the banquet." And Haman was pleased with this idea and he had the gallows made.

[16] Cf. Clines, *Esther*, 137–38.

Verses 4–6 are likely R, but this can only be argued on the basis of economy. There are few linguistic indicators to separate it out, since it copies the language of the previous verses, but the extension of the narrative by duplication is typical of R.

S reads more smoothly at this point if vss 9b-10a are omitted, and there is also found there the use of *kě* + infinitive construct without *wayhî*, a trait uncharacteristic of S. Verse 9b is a doublet of 3:5, however—"Haman was full of anger (at Mordecai)" (וימלא המן (על־מרדכי) חמה)—and may indicate a seam where an even earlier source of Esther (which will be proposed in the section below) was expanded into Esth S. We shall see that what follows, 10a, is likely also from this earlier source, and therefore *ex hypothesi* must be in S as well. Further consideration of this must then await the presentation of this source behind Esth S. These verses are here retained as indefinite.

Since the first banquet of 5:4–6 has been omitted here, the reference in vs 12 to it has been altered to reflect only one. This creates a slight difficulty in vs 9, where Haman knows of his supposedly good fortune without the audience being told how. Although it is possible that the first banquet was in S, it is more likely that some connective in the original Esth S has been omitted. It would, however, hardly be necessary to the flow of the plot as here reconstructed.

(6:1) On that night the king could not sleep, and he commanded to have the book of the chronicles brought, and they were read before the king. (2) It was found written there that Mordecai had informed against Bigtana and Teresh, the two courtiers of the king who guarded the door and sought to kill King Ahasuerus. (3) The king then said, "What honor and reward has been bestowed upon Mordecai on account of this?" The servants of the king who ministered to him responded, "Nothing has been done for him." (4) Just then the king said, "Who is in the court?" (5) The king's servants replied to him, "Indeed it appears that Haman is standing in the court." So the king said, "Let him come in." (6) Haman entered, and the king said to him, "What is to be done to the man whom the king desires to honor?" Haman said to himself, "Whom would the king desire to honor more than me?" (7) So Haman said to the king, "For the man whom the king desires to honor, (8) let the royal robes be brought which the king wears, and the horse which the king rode when the royal crown was placed upon his head, (9) and let the robes and the horse be given to one of the king's most noble princes, that the man may be thus arrayed whom the king desires to honor, and that he may be ridden on the horse in the street of the city, and proclaim before him, 'Thus shall it be done to the man whom the king desires to honor!'" (10) And the king said to Haman, "Go quickly, take the robes and the horse just as you said and do exactly that for Mordecai the Jew who sits in the king's gate. Omit nothing from what you suggested." (11) So Haman took the robes and the horse and arrayed Mordecai, and rode him around in the street of the city, proclaiming before him, "Thus shall it be done to the man whom the king desires to honor."

Verse 4b is excised from S; it is unnecessary to the narrative and uses subject-verb word order with an unconverted verb. Verses 12b-13 are also a clumsy digression within the story, since a change of setting is required which must be undone in vs 14, and the fact that Mordecai was a Jew was not only already known, but treated before only as grounds for scorn. The pious acclamation by the villain's family and friends has a role in the narrative of R, by making the inevitability of the Jews' salvation explicit. (It is more logically expressed in Gk A, where Zeresh tells Haman that "God is with them.") This is all corroborated by the subject-verb word order of the first clause, vs 12b, and by the fact that only here are Haman's "wise men" introduced. Other than vs 12b, the other verbs of this R section are converted where possible, but this is probably so because they duplicate the previous family council of Haman at 5:10–14, attributed to S.

(6:12) Afterward Mordecai returned to the king's gate, (7:1) and the king and Haman came to celebrate with Esther the queen, (2) and the king said to Esther, "What is your petition, Queen Esther, for it shall be given to you, and what is your request, for it shall be done, up to half of the kingdom." (3) Esther the queen answered and said, "If I have found favor in your sight, O King, and if it seems good, let my life be granted as my petition, and my people as my request. (4) For we are sold, I and my people, to be destroyed, to be slain, to die! If we had been sold as slaves, both men and women, I would have remained silent, but as it is the gain cannot be compared to the king's loss." (5) Then King Ahasuerus said to Esther the queen, "Who is this person, and where is he, who would presume to do such a thing?" (6) Esther said, "Here is the foe and enemy, this wicked Haman!" (9) Just then Harbonah, one of the courtiers, said to the king, "Indeed it appears that the gallows which Haman made for Mordecai, who spoke up on behalf of the king, is standing in Haman's house, fifty cubits high!" The king said, "Hang him on that!" (10) So Haman was hanged on the gallows which he made for Mordecai.

Verses 6b–8 are preposterous from the narrative point of view—perfectly in keeping with the style of R—and with one exception (8b) each clause uses subject-verb word order and unconverted verbs. Only the stomping and howling of a Purim celebration could cover up the ludicrousness of this turn of events, but it is quite significant that it only exists in R. Without these verses, the story succeeds in giving a measured release of the dramatic tension.

Verse 10b is lacking in Gk A, and uses subject-verb word order and an unconverted verb. It balances a similar statement at 2:1 concerning Vashti, and like that one, achieves a temporary release of tension in the long R version.

> (8:2) Then the king took off his ring, which he had taken from Haman, and he gave it to Mordecai, and set Mordecai over the house of Haman. (3) Esther spoke once again to the king, and falling down at his feet she wept and besought him to avert the evil design of Haman the Agagite and the plan which he had devised against the Jews. (4) The king extended the golden scepter to Esther, and Esther arose and stood before the king. (5) She said, "If it seems good to the king and if I have found favor in his sight, and this thing seems right to the king, and I am pleasing in your eyes, let it be written to recall the letters devised by Haman son of Hammedata the Agagite which he wrote to destroy the Jews. (6) For how could I stand by and watch the destruction of my kinfolk?" (7) King Ahasuerus replied to Esther the queen and to Mordecai the Jew, "(Already I have given Esther the house of Haman, and he has been hanged on the gallows because he sought to destroy the Jews.) (8) Write also on behalf of the Jews whatever seems good to you."

These verses in the MT are in general written in the style of S, but the parallel section of Gk A is much shorter. It is therefore possible that Gk A, rather than the proposed reconstruction here, is closer to Esth S. At one point, however, Gk A corroborates the reconstruction here, since 8:1 MT, which uses unconverted verbs and is excised here, has no equivalent in Gk A. Gk A also has Ahasuerus, not Esther, give Haman's house to Mordecai, and in light of the excision of 8:1 MT, I follow Gk A here as well.

In Gk A Mordecai asks for the letters of Haman to be rescinded, while Esther asks permission to institute a revenge. In MT chapter 8 Esther initiates both requests, although Mordecai takes a greater role in the sending of the letters. Although Gk A is shorter here, the contents of MT at this point are also found later in Gk A, at 8:45–46. Esth R likely moved this material in expanding this whole section, and MT reflects a duplicated revenge motif not present in Gk A. All of this is probably lacking in Esth S, where we find no revenge motif at all—the only act is to undo the treachery put into motion by Haman, by having his letters rescinded.

The writing in the name of the king and sealing with the king's ring appears to be throughout a trait of R; certainly the irrevocability of the king's decrees is, since it does not appear in Gk A.[17]

> (8:9) Then the king's scribes were called and it was written according to all that Mordecai commanded to the Jews. (10) He wrote in the name of King

---

[17] See Clines, *Esther*, 151.

Ahasuerus and sealed it with the king's ring, (9:20) sending letters to all the Jews in all the provinces of King Ahasuerus, both near and far, (30) in words of peace and truth. (10:1) King Ahasuerus then laid a tribute on the land and the coastlands of the sea. (2) And all the great and wonderful deeds, and the proclamation of the authority of Mordecai to which the king promoted him, are they not written in the book of the chronicles of the kings of Media and Persia? (3) For Mordecai the Jew was next in rank to King Ahasuerus, received great honor from the Jews, and was very popular among them, seeking the welfare of his people and speaking words of peace to all his kin.

There are two possibilities for the ending of Esth S: as here, where there is no revenge motif, but only the cessation of hostilities, or a restrained revenge motif, which would include 8:13, 9:5, parts of 9:11–15, and perhaps other verses as well. The former reconstruction offers the possibility of a more coherently balanced moral resolution, where Haman is executed and his order is stopped. The Jewish reverse pogrom is not present, but the place of the Jews in Persian society is assured. The revenge motif seems to enter in only when Purim is added to the story, and the narrative takes on an unreal quality. Note that the phrases of the ending chosen here all use converted verbs. The second alternative, the restrained revenge motif, could conceivably be stitched together from the various phrases in chaps. 8 and 9 listed here which use converted verbs, but this confusing interplay of petitions, letters, massacres, and romantically intoned festal inaugurations seems to emanate from R.

Gk A reflects a limited revenge motif (relative to the excesses of MT) at 8:18–21, and also a resolution without revenge at 8:33–42. Dividing Gk A into possible source divisions, we note: Mordecai's audience with the king (no revenge, 8:15–17), Esther's audience (revenge, 8:18–21), and Mordecai's decree (no revenge, 8:33–42).[18] Mordecai's decree could follow very smoothly on Mordecai's audience with the king, and the intervening Esther/revenge material can be seen as secondary. The Mordecai material corresponds approximately to Esth S. Although I have in general isolated Esth S based on the MT, using the linguistic propensities discernible in that text, it is interesting that Gk A gives important supporting evidence.

Part of the ending constructed here is based on the similarity of 9:20 and 30. They suggest a seam, between which a whole addition has been inserted dealing with Purim. The two verses:

9:20	וישלח ספרים אל־כל־היהודים
9:30	וישלח ספרים אל־כל־היהודים

---

[18] Clines (ibid., 64–68) takes this to be the original ending.

9:20	אשר בכל־מדינות המלך אחשורוש
9:30	אל־שבע ועשרים ומאה מדינה מלכות אחשורוש
9:20	הקרובים והרחוקים
9:30	דברי שלום ואמת

The peculiarity of the verses beginning with 9:20 has long been noted: they summarize the story, but only mention the execution of Haman and his sons as the revenge motif, and do not mention the king's knowledge and assent to the plan, nor Esther's part in the intrigue, for she only enters at the end.[19] However, the peculiarity does not extend to the end of Esther as Paton[20] contends, but only to 9:32. This addition was perhaps added to Esth S to turn it into a Purim writing. It is not part of Esth S, where there is no Purim motif, nor is it necessarily part of the larger part of Esth R, where there is an exaggerated revenge motif. They probably reflect an independent account of the events, and were perhaps the first addition to Esth S, inserted before the further changes of Esth R. The small bit of 9:30 retained in S, ''words of peace and truth,'' finds an echo in 10:3, also S.

Retaining 10:1 – 3 as the original ending is strongly opposed by Clines.[21] Only here do Media and Persia appear in this order, but the other instances noted above, in the opposite order, are assigned to R. These verses are, contra Clines, a plausible ending to an earlier version, and use a converted verb and a verbal pronominal suffix, characteristics of S. They do not bear any obvious stamp of Esth S concerns, but neither do they reflect Esth R; they are taken here to be a likely ending of Esth S.

Differences Between Esth S and MT Esther

With Esth S in view, we may note some of the important differences between it and the MT scroll. First and most important is the absence of Purim from the source document. Not only is this element usually deemed characteristic of the scroll, it has even been considered constitutive of it and its *raison d'être*. Based on this source analysis, however, this cannot be the case. The narrative possessed a life of its own before it took on this association. It also appears that R as a whole puts Esther's role on a par with Mordecai, while in S (and possibly in the separate addition of 9:20 – 32), Mordecai takes more of the authority of the single ethnarch. A further surprise is the lack of any

[19] Lewis Paton, *A Critical and Exegetical Commentary on the Book of Esther* (ICC; Edinburgh: T. & T. Clark, 1908) 295 – 96.
[20] Ibid., 57 – 60.
[21] *Esther*, 57 – 60.

revenge motif, beyond the execution of Haman on his own contrivance. Finally, another difference between Esth S and R, not to be passed over lightly, is the florid elaborations of the narrative found in the latter. The descriptions of the feasts in chapter one, the preparation of the members of the harem in chapter two, the verbiage deemed necessary just to get an edict circulated in 3:12–15 and 8:9,13–14—these and many other details of the narrative find fuller expression in R.

In Esther MT, there are several climaxes to the story, beginning with chap. 6 as the first release of tension from the threat to Mordecai and the Jews. Other climaxes and releases of tension come in chapters 7 and 8–9. In Esth S, however, the climax is much more coherent, moving from the elevation of Mordecai in chap. 6 to the execution of Haman in chap. 7, to the recognition scenes and conclusion in just a few verses taken from chaps. 8–10.

These expansions are not introduced, however, in the interest of a finer sensibility of artistic expression, but in the service of the farcical turn of the narrative in the later layer. As mentioned in the commentary on the analysis above, Haman's urgent petition at Esther's knees (7:7), and even more, Ahasuerus' response (7:8), reflect a total abandonment both of verisimilitude and a measured release of narrative tension. Considering the way that Ahasuerus is portrayed, we have here nothing short of flagrant disrespect for Persian royalty (or royalty in general). We note further in R the improbabilities of the Jewish reverse-pogrom and the anti-feminist decree of 1:16–22, to the effect that important business (of the narrative, at any rate) should stop, so that all women can be cautioned to obey their husbands. I quote approvingly the words of Glendon E. Bryce: "...does (Esther) contain a kind of comic charity, a promiscuous celebration of right over wrong that is unsuited to the serious attacks of sober critics?"[22] I wonder whether he does not go far enough, however. "Comic" might describe earlier stages of Esther—Esth S or the *Vorlage* of Gk A—but the MT has passed over into farce. Finally, there is in R the move to an empire-wide focus, with a coordinated account of Purim celebration in Susa and in the Persian provinces. These, then, are

---

[22] Bryce, Review of Berg, *Esther*, in *JBL* 100 (1981) 276–77. Despite many good contributions to the study of Esther, Berg (*Esther*, 178–84) and Clines (*Esther*, 152–58) still lean too heavily on a theologically "serious" interpretation. Clines' view may be defended somewhat, however, by the fact that he is not talking about MT, but about an earlier layer of Esther, which was certainly less farcical, and may have even contained references to God. I have profited from conversations with Professor James Kugel of Harvard on the comical aspects of Esther. See also Bruce William Jones, "Two Misconceptions about the Book of Esther," *CBQ* 39 (1977) 171–81 (reprinted in Moore, *Studies*); and Theodor H. Gaster, "Esther 1:22," *JBL* 69 (1950) 381.

the main redactional tendencies in R: Purim, revenge, farce, and an empire-wide focus.

Reference has been made at many points to Gk A as a way of helping to establish Esth S. It was reasoned that if those passages not considered part of S according to my criteria were also lacking in Gk A, this would be taken as additional evidence for their assignment to R. The converse of this, however, was not a helpful criterion for establishing S: the presence of a passage in Gk A was not corroborating evidence for inclusion in S, since Gk A likely attests a stage in Esther after Esth S. The other implication of this is that Gk A can be seen as an intermediate stage in the expansion of Esther between Esth S and MT. Clines' identification of Gk A as a representative of an earlier Vorlage than MT[23] still stands, in my view, but before Gk A I have attempted to identify yet an earlier level. In my nomenclature, Gk A can be considered a first step beyond Esth S toward MT, and therefore its pluses as compared with Esth S usually constitute a subset of Esth R. We cannot think of these steps in a rigidly linear way, however, since parallel versions of the story could have existed at every level.

The Mordecai/Haman Source

Now that an earlier version of the story of Mordecai and Esther has been isolated, we can turn our attention to the possibility of yet earlier sources, which have more often preoccupied scholars. It has often been suggested that the Book of Esther was ultimately based on a story in which Mordecai alone was the hero, but this earlier version is not usually reconstructed in detail. Cazelles's theory gives broad outlines of a Mordecai story and an Esther story, but not isolated as independent narratives. Only Lebram, to my knowledge, actually ventures a detailed description of the Mordecai source.[24] Here I will follow his suggestion with one important difference: whereas he sees the Mordecai/Haman traditions as an addition to the skeleton of the Esther story, I believe that the verses which relate the conflict between Mordecai and Haman, with no reference to Esther, constitute the original core of the narrative which was expanded first to Esth S and then, by the addition of Esth R material, to the present MT. It is possible hypothetically to reconstruct this Mordecai story, simply by isolating those elements which deal

---

[23] Clines, *Esther*, 139–74, with a diagram on p. 140.

[24] Lebram, "Purimfest und Estherbuch," *VT* 22 (1972) 214–15. 214–15. He emphasizes that the process of introducing the Mordecai material into the Esther story is "not a literary adaptation, but an interlarding of traditions" (216–17). Clines (*Esther*, 115–43), though skeptical, outlines a hypothetical Mordecai source.

with the court conflict of Mordecai and Haman, and eliminating those sections which do not. As arbitrary as this may seem at first, the integrity of the resulting narrative makes a quite credible case for this reconstruction, especially considering that several difficulties in the present story are eliminated in the process. When this step is taken, the evidence is seen to justify the hypothesis. To reconstruct the original story I must perform radical surgery in steps, shedding layers that do not focus on Mordecai and Haman alone, even though the full justification for this can only come when the process is done.

First, 8:3 – 9:32, which can be eliminated as a detailed description of the revenge of the Jews on those who would do them harm, also serves as a further etiolological explanation of the origins of Purim. Both of these lie outside of the interests of the original court legend.[25] Likewise chapter 1, the Vashti incident, can be set aside as an imaginative introduction which also lies outside of the basic drama between Mordecai and Haman. Further, this Vashti episode is only required as a way of introducing Esther into the royal harem, and it is likely that even Esther must go. Esther does not serve to save Mordecai from the gallows, but only to approach the king to rescind Haman's letter condemning all Jews. Although the two threats—against Mordecai and against all Jews —have been woven together in the MT version, they are easily separable issues, as will become more evident below. What this also means is that, if Esther is added secondarily to the text, so, very likely, is her main function, the saving of all the Jews of Persia from slaughter. The problem of how to save the Jews of Persia, not explicitly present in Moredecai's dealings with Haman, may have been inserted into our present text, along with the role of Esther as the solution to that problem. Note that Haman's plot against the Jews (3:6b – 15) is concocted before his plot against Mordecai (5:14), although his attempt to destroy the Jews results from his hatred of Mordecai.[26]

Thus if we eliminate these large blocks of material and retain only those sections which deal with the court conflict between Mordecai and Haman, we find that we are left with a short but well-wrought story that fits the pattern of the court legend genre nicely. This in itself would not warrant the conclusion that this shorter story existed and was the basis for the longer version.[27] The

---

[25] It is this section that Charles C. Torrey ("The Older Book of Esther," *HTR* 37 [1944] 14 – 19) would eliminate, based on a comparison with the Gk A text, but he makes no reference to the court legend genre.

[26] In the literary structure of MT Esther, a chiastic order obtains: threat to Jews, threat to Mordecai/saving of Mordecai, saving of Jews. See Berg, *Esther*, 107 – 9; and Yehudah T. Radday, "Chiasm in Joshua, Judges, and Others," *Linguistica Biblica* 3 (1973) 6 – 13.

[27] This would especially be the case if the stories were orally recounted and passed on, since folklorists rightly have rejected the notion that the shorter and simpler version of a story is neces-

real evidence for the assertion that an older Mordecai/Haman source existed comes from (1) the consistency of style in the Mordecai/Haman sections in comparison to the writing as a whole, and (2) the elimination of certain difficulties in the present text as a result of this process. A proposed reconstruction of the earlier Mordecai/Haman story can be so easily isolated from MT Esther that the constituent parts can be cut out of the present text and placed end to end, without so much as a transitional addition being necessary.

Excursus on the Reconstruction of the M/H Source

The proposed Mordecai/Haman source (M/H) is here reconstructed, with less certain sections placed in parentheses. Explanatory notes following each section.

> (2:5a) There was a Jewish man in Susa the capital whose name was Mordecai. (2:21–22a) In those days, as Mordecai was sitting at the king's gate, Bigthan and Teresh, two of the king's eunuchs who guarded the threshold, became angry and sought to lay hands on King Ahasuerus. This came to the knowledge of Mordecai, and he told the king. (2:23–3:2) When the affair was investigated and found to be so, the men were both hanged on the gallows, and it was recorded in the Book of the Chronicles in the presence of the king.

This opening phrase makes a fine beginning for a Hebrew narrative; it is exactly parallel to Job 1:1: אִישׁ הָיָה בְאֶרֶץ־עוּץ אִיּוֹב שְׁמוֹ. Contrast Esth 1:1, which, like Jonah and Ruth, begins with וַיְהִי[28]. The beginning of this verse may have been altered, with the original conjunction now missing. The syntax of the remainder of the verse is troubled, both in Esther and in this reconstructed source.

> (3:1–2a) After these things King Ahasuerus promoted Haman (the Agagite, the son of Hammedatha), and advanced him and set his seat above all the princes who were of the same rank. All the king's servants who were at the king's gate bowed down and did obeisance to Haman. (3:5) But when Haman saw that Mordecai did not bow nor do obeisance to him, Haman was filled with fury.

Haman's identification as "son of Hammedatha, the Agagite" appears to be of little consequence here, but if the full identification of Mordecai as a Jew and a Benjaminite is part of this source, then the same opposition of forebears would apply: Mordecai is descended from Saul (Shim'i) ben Kish,

---

sarily the older. By-forms of various lengths are equally likely possibilities.

[28] See Hurvitz, "Job," 28–29.

who overthrew Agag, king of Amalek (1 Sam 15:7 – 8).[29] The version reconstructed here is a very economical telling of the story at this point; other versions are possible, which might include other lines from vss 2 – 5. For example, it is possible that vs 2b (bowing to Haman as a command of the king) is part of the source, although it detracts from the Haman/Mordecai focus, and introduces further the role of the king and the relation of Mordecai to the king's rule, a redactional trait of the Esther layer. Parts of vss 3 – 4 may also derive from the source, but this is not likely. Aside from the literary judgments given here, vs 2c uses subject-verb word order and vs 4 uses the x *wĕ*-x construction common in Esth R. However, these verses were also judged problematic in the separation of S and R above. Verse 5b is almost identical with 5:9c, and reflects the seam created when the narrative was resumed at the latter point; everything between these two verses is from the Esther layers.

(5:10 – 12a) Nevertheless Haman restrained himself, and went home; and he sent and fetched his friends and his wife Zeresh. And Haman recounted to them the greatness of his riches, the number of his sons, all the ways in which the king had promoted him, and how he had promoted him above the princes and the servants of the king. But Haman added, (5:13 – 14a,c) "Yet all this does me no good, so long as I see Mordecai sitting at the king's gate." Then his wife Zeresh and all his friends said to him, "Let a gallows fifty cubits high be made, and in the morning tell the king to have Mordecai hanged upon it." This counsel leased Haman, and he had the gallows made.

With the insertion of vs 12b into this source, some part of the original was likely disturbed, so that it is not clear how the direct quotation of vs 13 was introduced. I have taken the first words of vs 12 to introduce vs 13.

(6:1 – 4a) On that night the king could not sleep, and so he gave orders to bring the book of the chronicles, and they were read before the king. And it was found written how Mordecai had informed on Bigtana and Teresh, two of the king's courtiers, who guarded the door, and who had sought to kill King Ahasuerus. And the king said, "What honor or reward has been bestowed on Mordecai for this?" The king's servants who attended him said, "Nothing has been done for him." (6:5) And the king said, "Who is in the court?" The king's servants said to him, "Indeed it appears that Haman is standing in the court." And the king said, "Let him come in."

The chronicles are mentioned three times in Esther (2:23, 6:1, 10:2), each time slightly differently. The first two occurrences are definitely from the

[29] See Paton, *Esther*, 194.

Haman/Mordecai source, the third possibly. Certainly the same book is intended here as in 2:23, although we would expect the same name for it. The parenthesis in vs 4b has been deleted here, on the grounds that it is unnecessary, even cumbersome, to the smooth flow of the narrative. The unconverted verb and subject-verb word order could be mentioned as further evidence that this is a later addition, although it could also be argued that these have been used precisely to denote a parenthesis.

> (6:6–9) So Haman came in, and the king said to him, "What shall be done to the man whom the king delights to honor?" And Haman said to himself, "Whom would the king delight to honor more than me?" And Haman said to the king, "For the man whom the king delights to honor, let royal robes be brought, which the king has worn, and the horse which the king has ridden, and on whose head a royal crown is set; and let the robes and the horse be handed over to one of the king's most noble princes; let him array the man whom the king delights to honor, and let him conduct the man on horseback through the open square of the city, proclaiming before him: 'Thus shall be done to the man whom the king delights to honor.' "

The parenthesis in vs 6b has been retained in the source, in apparent contradiction with the excision of vs 4b. Here, however, the parenthesis reflects the attention to Haman's thoughts that is characteristic of the source. Perhaps vs 4b should be included for the same reason, but whereas 6b pauses to allow more omniscient evesdropping into Haman's character, 4b merely provides an unnecessary reminder of why Haman has come. Note that the parenthesis of vs 6b utilizes a converted verb. The spare style of this source is, relatively speaking, expanded at this point into an extended dialogue that is the equivalent length of the entire rest of the story. Even in so short a story, there is a skillful building to a climax, in which the tension of the threat to Mordecai's life is dispelled through the humorous and ironic display of Haman's foolishness.

> (6:10–11) Then the king said to Haman, "Hurry, go take the robes and the horse, as you have said, and do this to Mordecai who sits at the king's gate. Leave out nothing of what you have said." So Haman took the robes and the horse, and he arrayed Mordecai and made him ride through the open square of the city, proclaiming, "Thus shall it be done to the man whom the king desires to honor." (7:9–10) Then said Harbona, one of the courtiers who served before the king, "Indeed, it also appears that the gallows which Haman has prepared for Mordecai, who informed on behalf of the king, is standing in Haman's house, fifty cubits high." And the king said, "Hang him on that." So they hanged Haman on the gallows which he had prepared for Mordecai.

A catharsis is achieved in this resolution, consisting mainly of three elements: humor, irony, and the working out of justice. These three elements do not have to occur one after the other in this well-wrought story, but are simultaneous, wrapped up in the same events. Haman's poorly constructed world simply falls in on him. It is more precisely and humorously drawn in this source than in Esther as a whole, since it is concentrated in one scene. Note especially that the beginning of the climax scene—when Haman enters the court (6:5)—and the ending, when Haman is hanged (7:9), are both introduced in the same way when the courtiers address the king: "Behold, Haman/the gallows is standing ...'' (הנה המן /העץ עמד). In both cases it is then stated: "And the king said, 'Let him come in/Hang him on it'' (ויאמר המלך יבוא /תלהו עליו). In the original these two sets of statement and response would only have been separated by seven verses. A different kind of humor is inserted between these two in Esther MT, a broadside farce of Haman falling on Esther's bed and being accused of making advances toward her.

(8:2) (And the king took off his ring, which he had taken from Haman, and gave it to Mordecai,) and set Mordecai over the house of Haman. (10:1–3) And King Ahasuerus laid a tribute upon the land, and upon the coastlands. And all the acts of his power and of his magesty, and his declaration of the influence of Mordecai, in the manner in which the king promoted him, are they not written in the book of chronicles of the kings of Media and Persia? For Mordecai the Jew was second only to King Ahasuerus, and great among the Jews, and honored by the mass of his kinfolk, seeking the welfare of his people, and speaking peace to all his progeny.

The one problem remaining in isolating this source is the ending. The story could conceivably have ended at 7:10, with Haman's execution, since he has been the focus of the story all along. On the other hand, some part of 8:2 and 10:1–3 more likely concluded this story. The problem here is that the amount of fanfare in 10:1–3 would seem out of place in so short and spare a story. Also, Mordecai is trumpeted so loudly in 10:1–3 that we would have expected more attention to him in a story with that conclusion, as would be the case in Esth S. Nevertheless, the fact that Mordecai alone is mentioned indicates that these lines stood as the ending of a story that treated Mordecai's exploits, but not Esther's.

The Nature of the M/H Source

The original Mordecai/Haman story was probably used, not as a model, nor even as an oral legend, but as an actual written text, although we are left to guess at the language in which it was known. In the original story as spliced together here, we find a coherent and entertaining narrative, which would be quite short for an independently circulating tradition, though not impossible.[30] When we compare the Mordecai/Haman fragments with MT Esther we find several surprising things which argue for the reconstructed text, or something very nearly like it, as the original:

1) In the MT version Mordecai gets himself into trouble (3:1–5) and is extricated from his difficulties (6:1–11) with no involvement of Esther whatsoever. Esther's role is to have the anti-Jewish edict rescinded. The two subplots proceed completely independent of each other for much of MT Esther.
2) The sections which I propose are original constitute a well-structured and complete narrative.
3) These sections have a consistent style which differs from the Esther Scroll. The style is:
   a) compressed and economical, as opposed to expansive (cf. 2:21–3:5 [M/H] with 2:7–20 [Esther], or 5:14 [M/H] with 3:6b-15);[31]
   b) restrained, as opposed to melodramatic (cf. 7:9–10a [M/H] with 7:5–8 [Esther]);
   c) carefully and logically plotted as opposed to haphazard (cf. 6:1–11 [M/H] with 7:5–8 [Esther]).[32]
4) The "Story of Mordecai" is told, surprisingly, from Haman's point of view. The latter's emotions are plumbed (3:1–2, 5, 5:9b-10, 13–14, 6:1–11, and 7:9–10), while Mordecai remains a cipher. The Esther Scroll focuses principally on Esther (esp. 2:12–20, 4:9–17, 5:1–8, and 7:1–8), still with a fair amount of attention placed on Mordecai (2:10–11 and 4:1–end). It is only in the expanded MT version of Mordecai's story that we get any interior view into his thoughts and feelings.[33]

---

[30] Alexander Rofé ("The Classification of the Prophetical Legends," *JBL* 89 [1970] 427–40) suggests in the case of the Elijah/Elisha cycle that short and concise written versions of multiform oral legends were often made, more or less as summaries or records, and it is these which in many cases were written down and preserved. Note also that the length of this reconstruction is about the same as each of the legends of Daniel 1–6, as well as some of the legends in Herodotus.

[31] Only at 6:7–11 does M/H show any expansiveness of the narrative. At this point, however, it becomes very marked, as Haman ironically pulls out all the stops in an orgy of self-congratulation, not knowing that it is his enemy he honors. This is much more powerful in the spare M/H story than it is in Esth S or R, where the expansiveness is more typical.

[32] Comparisons here are between M/H and Esth R, which are more different in style than MT and Esth S. The same distinctions obtain, to a lesser degree, if we compare the following S sections: (a) 2:8–9; (b) 7:3–6; and (c) 8:3–6.

[33] Clines, *Esther*, 149–50.

5) Certain plot difficulties are eliminated. Even though Mordecai provokes Haman, in Esth S and R Haman's elaborate plan to destroy all Jews comes first (3:6b-15), *before* the plan to destroy Mordecai (5:14) has been devised. The plot to hang Mordecai seems trivial compared to Haman's larger designs. Furthermore, there is a complete absence in the second scheme of any mention of the first.[34]

6) Literary seams are eliminated. The similar expression in 3:5 and 5:9b, "Haman was filled with anger (against Mordecai)," indicate that this phrase was repeated when the text was opened up, and the narrative was resumed. The first of these *concludes* a section which deals with Mordecai but not Esther, the second *begins* a section which deals with Mordecai but not Esther, but the intervening material concerns Mordecai and Esther.

7) The M/H narrative adheres closely to a tightly structured timeline, which is as methodical and rigorous as a train schedule, and apparent even in so short a narrative. Other than the description of Mordecai overhearing the plot on Ahasuerus' life, the events are contained within two days.[35] The spatial dimension, however, is quite vague, in that no specifics are given except to say that the action is set in and around Ahasuerus's court. This seems appropriate for a court legend. Esther reverses this, making the temporal scheme incoherent, but focusing the spatial dimension meticulously.

8) The present ending of Esther, 10:1–3, makes no mention of Esther, but heralds Mordecai as a great courtier who was (a) exalted by Ahasuerus and (b) held in high esteem by all the Jews. Note that it does not say that Mordecai *saved* the Jews from destruction, or anything of the sort.[36]

Although Lebram makes note of some of these characteristics of the Mordecai/Haman sections, he comes to the opposite conclusion regarding literary pritority: these traditions have been interwoven into an already existing story about Esther. How is this disagreement to be adjudicated? Lebram's arguments for the priority of Esther hinge on the identification of

---

[34] Various literary explanations are possible, of course, such as that it represents a chiastic arrangement of threat to Jews/threat to Mordecai/deliverance of Mordecai/deliverance of Jews—which is true enough for the later versions—but the two threats are really of two different orders.

[35] Clines (*Esther*, 139–43) does not count Mordecai's discovery of a plot as part of a possible Mordecai source, and wrongly telescopes the timeline even more than it is.

[36] Clines (ibid., 57–60), rejecting it as the original ending, notes that it differs from the style of chapters 1–8. Certainly, it may differ from the bulk of chapters 1–8, probably because it was either originally the conclusion of the M/H source, or it was added to such a source very early on to make it more edifyingly Jewish. Two linguistic aspects would characterize it as the style of M/H or Esth S, but not R: a converted verb and a verbal pronominal suffix. Clines' argument that no other contemporary work ends as this one does is not entirely correct: Susanna is similar.

the Mordecai figure with Palestinian Jewish attempts to bring the Babylonian practices of the Esther narrative in line. Certainly in chapters 8 and 9 there are many passages where Mordecai is associated with Purim "correction" passages, and Mordecai's identification both by genealogy and by his membership in the first group of exiles indicate an attempt to reestablish connections with that normative generation of Jews.[37] However, neither of these aspects of the Mordecai figure are original to the story in my view.

Conversely, is there warrant for positing a separate Esther narrative which was combined with the M/H source? Many scholars have advocated this, but Elias Bickermann has perhaps suggested the most plausible argument for a separate Esther source.[38] Comparing the Esther sections of the narrative with the court intrigues of Ctesias's *Persika*, he proposes that Esther is involved in a tense struggle for power with the Haman figure, much as the queen or queen-mother often is in Ctesias. The issue of her ethnic identity and her intervention for her people may be a Jewish modification of the genre, but the general pattern of similarities holds true.

However, I do not believe that we need to posit an independent Esther narrative which circulated as a court intrigue story. It is difficult to isolate an entire, self-contained Esther story from what we have at hand without bringing in the bulk of the Mordecai/Haman conflict. Bickermann's attempts to compare Haman's plea for protection from Esther at 7:7–8, for instance, with similar pleas in Ctesias are not convincing.[39] It is more likely that there was no independent Esther narrative, but that the influence of the court intrigue stories such as those in Ctesias, Herodotus, and Xenephon is felt only in the expansion of the M/H story, that is, when Esther material is added to an already existing story. The same influence was noted above in the queen-mother's role in Daniel 5. Clines, in discussing the various proposed source theories, is hesitant to assert that there were separate Mordecai and Esther narratives, partially because, as he says, "it is impossible to remove Mordecai from the Esther tradition."[40] I, of course, must agree with him on this point, but would add that it is possible to remove Esther from the Mordecai

[37] Lebram, "Purimfest," 213–14.
[38] Bickermann, *Four Strange Books of the Bible* (New York: Schocken, 1967) 182–84. Cazelles ("Note sur la composition du rouleau d'Esther," in Heinrich Gross and Franz Mussner, eds., *Lex tua veritas: Festschrift für Hubert Junker* [Trier: Paulinus, 1961] 17–29) is another prominent contender for an Esther source.
[39] The distinction in genre between Esther (in any of its stages) and the historians does not prohibit comparison, since it is really the legendary sources behind Ctesias that we are referring to, just as I postulated in Chapter 2 for Herodotus.
[40] Clines, *Esther*, 138.

tradition, and that it is likely that the story of Esther came into existence as an expansion of the original M/H source.

In discussing the Mordecai source, Lebram presumes that it is Jewish, while Bickerman raises the possibility that the original story is non-Jewish.[41] There is little in the proposed narrative to suggest that Mordecai is Jewish— in this respect we may contrast Daniel 1–6—except for the identification of the protagonist as "Mordecai the Jew," and the laudatory conclusion of 10:1–3. Haman's ethnic identity has just as little relation to the plotline as does Mordecai's, and may be secondary. As we have the text, Mordecai is descended from the same tribe as Saul, while Haman is identified as a descendant of Saul's enemy, Agag. Whether the Mordecai of the original story was Jewish is unclear, but several scholars have noted that the characterization of both Mordecai and Haman as *foreign* courtiers may be significant.[42] This is a possibility for even the earliest layer of the story.

The Nature of the Stages of Esther

We now have before us a multi-stage theory of the development of the MT version of Esther, which can be diagrammed thus:

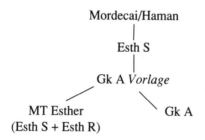

These layers are all argued on independent grounds; none of these proposed sources depends in its argumentation on the others. The M/H source is proposed as the earliest layer on the basis of literary seams and contradictions, and on the fact that the sections which deal only with these two characters can be plausibly connected into a coherent narrative with many generic parallels. The next, Esth S, likewise depends on literary-critical considerations, but here the isolation of a separate layer within the MT text is corroborated by linguistic criteria provided by research into the characteristic

[41] Bickermann, *Strange Books*, 181.

[42] Lebram, "Purimfest," 214; Gillis Gerleman, *Esther* (BKAT 21; Neukirchen-Vluyn: Neukirchener, 1973) 38.

changes in Hebrew in the post-exilic period. The *Vorlage* of Gk A as a layer earlier than MT was argued convincingly by Clines and has been adopted here, with only minor alterations. This diagram is thus not constructed as a house of cards which could tumble if any part were deemed unstable, but it describes a set of hypothetical sources which, although arrived at by separate means, are now judged to be in an interlocking relationship of development. From this point on I will presume the results of this source analysis in order to reconstruct a history of the development of Esther from its origins as a court legend to its present role in the MT.

With this source criticism of Esther in mind, it is also appropriate to bring in two non-Jewish court narratives similar to Esther, which bear not only on the issue of genre, but also on the question of sources. First is the Egyptian *Instruction of Onkhsheshonq*, and second, the account of the Magophonia, or revenge on the Magi, in Herodotus 3.61 – 79. *Onkhsheshonq*, which is dated to the Persian period, concerns a figure from the rural area of Egypt who visits his friend Harsiese, who has become the Pharaoh's chief physician and counselor. Harsiese has initiated a plot against the Pharaoh and informs Onkhsheshonq about it, but the latter, though vocally opposed, does nothing to stop it. Unknown to them, another counselor, Wahibre-makhy, overhears their entire conversation, and that night is called to guard duty outside the Pharaoh's chambers. When the Pharaoh awakes and is unable to return to sleep, he calls to the courtier, who enters and tells him of the plot. The conspirators are executed except for Onkhsheshonq, who is imprisoned and there writes his "instructions," a collection of proverbs, for his son, who will thereby learn to avoid the fate that resulted from his father's foolishness. *Onkhsheshonq* contains several intriguing parallels, not to the Esther story as a whole, but to the M/H core of the scroll. In both narratives conspirators are foiled because they are overheard by a loyal courtier, and in both a sleepless king calls to the courtier to enter from the outer chambers. Further, both *Onkhsheshonq* and M/H have a peculiar perspective—they both focus on the fallen and foolish courtier rather than the wise and loyal one. The world of court wisdom is seen from the perspective of one too obtuse to learn the rules of his environment.

The Magophonia is at first sight only vaguely similar to Esther.[43] While Cambyses is away from his palace, two Magi conspire to usurp his throne. One of them, who had previously lost his ears as a punishment, bears a close resemblence to Cambyses' brother Smerdis, and when he learns that Cambyses has secretly murdered Smerdis, poses as the king's brother, keeping the

---

[43] The parallel account of the Magophonia at Ctesias's *Persika* 10 – 14, for example, is interesting as a harem intrigue, but lacks the close similarities to Esther.

wounds that mark his punishment hidden (presumably by traditional dress). Seven loyal Persians, including Darius, believe that this man is an impostor, and one of them, Otanes, devises a plan to expose him. He sends a message to his daughter, Phaidyme, a member of the harem, and asks her if the man whom she sleeps with is the king's brother or an impostor. Messages go back and forth between these two, as she has no way to tell whether he is a usurper or not. Otanes then tells her to feel for his ears when she is next in bed with him, and this will tell her—and the seven loyal Persian courtiers— whether the man is the true Smerdis or the false. The parallels between this account and Esther are many and indicate some sort of relationship.

First in the comparison is the dialogue section between Otanes and Phaidyme. It is very similar to the dialogue between Mordecai and Esther in Esther 4, both in its external form, and in the content of the words exchanged between the two protagonists. The outline of the two dialogues:

Herodotus	Esther MT:
	Esther sends clothes
	Esther:
	What is going on?
Otanes:	Mordecai:
Is it Smerdis you sleep with?	Beseech king on our behalf
Phaidyme:	
I do not know him.	
Otanes:	
Then ask Atossa, his sister.	
Phaidyme:	Esther:
I cannot, since the harem	If not called I will be killed,
women are separated.	and as harem woman,
	I have not been called
	for thirty days
Otanes:	Mordecai:
You have noble blood. . . .	Do not think you will escape
	more than other Jews
Phaidyme:	Esther:
If caught I would be killed.	Gather Jews and fast,
Nevertheless, I will take risk.	and I will take risk.

The end of the description of Otanes and Phaidyme's dialogue is treated by Herodotus in a short indirect discourse, but the outlines of the interchange can be clearly seen. Some of the elements here are not in the same order in the two stories, but several similarities are clear:

1) an older, male family member takes advantage of his relationship with a young female family member in the harem to carry out an urgent mission;

2) the young woman balks, and invokes the difficulties of the harem organization and the mortal danger as reason for not carrying through the mission; and

3) the older man reminds her of her ethnic or family background, and calls
upon her to push ahead bravely, which she does.

In the source analysis above, all of these elements in Esther were attributed to
the R level, albeit unconfidently. The danger of entering before the king
unbidden is only stated explicitly here in Esther; it may result from the
influence of the Magophonia story or something like it, since in the latter a
very real danger, Phaidyme's searching for Smerdis' ears, is crucial to the
dialogue between father and daughter. In Esther this danger is absent, and so
a somewhat artificial danger is introduced to play the same role.[44]

Other similarities can be detected between the Magophonia and Esther.
The troubling lists of seven courtiers in Esther 1 have a counterpart in the
seven conspirators in the Magophonia. Above it was concluded that neither
of the two lists belongs in Esth S, but they probably reflect two separate traditions which I locate in Esth R, again with some uncertainty as to the first list.
In addition, the false Smerdis proclaims three years' remission from tax and
military service to every nation under his dominion as a way of winning support, which is similar to Esther 2:18b (R) and 10:1 (S).

A point easily passed over in the Magophonia is Darius's promise to
denounce the other conspirators unless they act without delay (3.71). As
brief as this moment of the narrative is, it signifies something crucial for the
worldview of the legend. Specifically, Darius, who the audience already
knows will rule, (1) criticizes Otanes' counsel of prudence and waiting; (2)
suggests that if they wait someone of their number will seek his advantage by
informing; (3) promises that if they do not act immediately he himself will
inform against them, to prevent his being betrayed by someone who acts fas-
ter. This counsel of extreme expedience almost passes too quickly for us to
recognize the moral world from which it springs, but we have seen it before.
Just above, in the discussion of the M/H source, it was noted that the good
sense of Mordecai's having informed against Bigtan and Teresh is what protects him from Haman's ill-conceived attempt to execute him, and likewise
that the character of Onkhsheshonq in the Egyptian story fails to inform the
Pharaoh of a similar attempt and is thrown into prison. The Magophonia
reflects just such a focus on informing immediately against potential
usurpers, although unlike the others, this motif has not been raised to the

---

[44] A similar law prohibiting appearing before the king unless summoned appears just later in
Herodotus 3.117–19.

central point of the story.[45] Other court legends also include the informant motif, but it is only the antagonists who inform or accuse, and only with guile in their hearts—compare *Ahikar*, Daniel 3 and 6, and Bel and the Dragon. The peculiar thing, then, about the Magophonia, *Onkhsheshonq*, and M/H is that the informing is considered a fair or even desirable way to bring justice to light in the king's court.

These three narratives indicate that the informant motif, whether as a positive or a negative act, was broadly attested in the Persian-influenced areas as part of the court legend genre, so that parallels between legends could indicate generic similarities. Beyond the generic similarity, however, in regard to particular motifs and possible literary borrowing, we see that the M/H source is actually the only part of Esther that bears any resemblence to *Onkhsheshonq*, and the parallels between the Magophonia and Esther are more limited to the Esth R section.[46]

Genres of the Individual Narratives

For the larger purposes of this study it is necessary to apply genre categories to the resulting narratives. The Mordecai/Haman source is a wisdom court legend, even though the wisdom of the protagonist is not explicitly mentioned. What we do have is an ironic contrast of two courtiers. Mordecai is fundamentally aligned with the king's interests by saving his life, but in a trivial matter he is disrespectful of the king's prime minister, by refusing to bow to Haman (perhaps breaking an explicit royal command in 3:2). On the other hand, Haman is aligned with the king in the trivial matters of the day-to-day administration of the empire, but fundamentally opposed to the king's interests by ordering the execution of the man who saved the king's life. The ramifications of these two positions are clear in the story, and the typical court legend theme of the court as the highest moral landscape is present.

A sort of fatalism also hangs over this narrative. It is clear that from the moment Haman begins to seeth with hatred for Mordecai, he will be the cause of his own downfall. He heaps up honors on his enemy's head while,

---

[45] Cf. Karl Reinhardt's ("Herodots Persergeschichten," in Walter Marg, ed., *Herodot: Eine Auswahl aus der neueren Forschung* (München: Beck, 1965] 325) characterization of the Persian traditions as concerned with a vassal's loyalty.

[46] Momigliano (*Alien Wisdom* [Cambridge: Cambridge University, 1975] 131) concedes too easily to Alexander Demandt's ("Die Ohren des falschen Smerdis," *Iranica Antiqua* 9 [1972] 94–101) objection that the Magophonia legend must arise in a region where Persians are depicted with their ears covered, i.e. the Greek West, and not Persia. It is most likely Asia Minor where Herodotus heard it.

unknown to him, the gallows he constructed is hanging over his own. This is even more ironic and dramatic in M/H than in Esth S and R, since in the former precisely this issue—and very little else—is played out in the resolution of chapter 6 and the beginning of seven. As noted above, the two scenes where Haman enters the court to have Mordecai executed and where Harbona points out the existence of Haman's gallows are both introduced by the phrase "Behold, Haman/the gallows is standing. . . ." Haman's act of asking for Mordecai's execution is tantamount to asking for his own. To be sure, these elements are also in the redacted versions of Esth S and R, but they have been placed in a different generic context. The M/H narrative is a short, pithy narrative, which is almost as barbed as the fable genre. Clines, in passing, denigrates such a narrative as a "run-of-the-mill court tale,"[47] but he is too enamored of the Esther narrative to appreciate a story which has such different generic conventions.

The comparison of *Onkhsheshonq* with the M/H source of Esther can also be explored further. It was noted that both narratives take the strange perspective of telling the story from the point of view of a foolish, even self-destructive, character who makes a fundamental error in the heady atmosphere of the king's court. In both, the major plot development comes when a sleepless king calls in a courtier and receives news which reveals the true standing of all the characters in the moral arena of the court. Further, both narratives involve the discovery by a principal character of a plot against the king, but in M/H the character, Mordecai, wisely reports it to the king, while in Onkhsheshonq, the witless protagonist strangely keeps silent, to his own destruction. In somewhat different ways, the two principal figures in these stories fatalistically come to their own sad end. Haman's end comes huumorously and with a sense of triumph, while Onkhsheshonq is a more sympathetic—or rather, pathetic—character who, in the received version, passes on his wisdom to his son from prison. *Onkhsheshonq* is a bourgeois tragedy of a feckless protagonist.

The protagonists of reverential legends are not buffeted by worldly events, but are strong enough to withstand them without even flagging. The peculiar silence of this story on Moredecai's character has the effect of making him seem invulnerable to the psychological buffeting that a death sentence would bestow on most people. This might have resulted from the exclusive focus on Haman's state, but it also coincides with the usual depiction of protagonists of reverential legends: they are not normal people.

I have also noted, however, that the wisdom component of wisdom court legends is not necessarily presented directly in the actions of the characters.

---

[47] Clines, *Esther*, 138.

Here also there is no easy "proverbial correlative" to be discerned, since Mordecai's indiscretion of not bowing is what placed him in jeopardy in the first place. However, in narrative it is not the elements or individual motifs that communicate the story's themes, but what actually happens to people. In the M/H story, Mordecai's minor indiscretion must be counterbalanced by Haman's major indiscretion, and we must remember that Haman is the focal character. To a certain extent it does not really matter whether Mordecai is wise or not. Although his actions ultimately placed him in better stead with the king than did Haman's, it is Haman's foolishness that is being narrated, not Mordecai's wisdom. Haman's actions, however, are not foolish in terms of the normal dictates of proverbial wisdom. He does not act rashly or impetuously, but by planning, counsel, and foresight. His foolishness comes to light in a different way: first, Haman is blinded by his hatred for a single person and is driven by it to foolish actions, and second, by the criteria of loyalty and service to the king, Haman is deficient. The king here, unlike in Esth S and R, is not portrayed as the signator of misguided edicts; there is no questioning of the king's authority or his ability to rule well, but on the contrary, he is just and decisive. It should be noted that *Onkhsheshonq* reflects a similar view of the rightful authority of the king and the necessity to identify one's interests with his. The only difference is that in the latter this affirmation is perhaps made a bit more grudgingly.

There are, to be sure, precepts in proverbs collections which apply to M/H, such as that loyalty to the king is a wise course, but the comparison can only be made in the overall intent of the narrative, and not in the details of Mordecai's or Haman's actions, since the actions of both are mixed. Those sections of Proverbs—actually quite small—which touch on the proper posture of a courtier before the king reflect a similar outlook to M/H. This is perhaps the least theological level of Proverbs, affirming as it does the expediency and strategy involved in promoting the king's interests. This motif of a courtier's service to the king, then, is not unknown in wisdom literature, but the theological and class interests of the bulk of the proverbs collections has left this view of M/H behind, a view from which even *Onkhsheshonq* is perhaps beginning to show some alienation.

The categorization of Esth S—assuming the reconstruction here is correct—becomes much more difficult. It has clearly taken quite a step beyond M/H, but still evidently lacked any reference to Purim. Thus any characterization of the document as a festival legend is inappropriate, and all such theories of the origin of Esther must be rethought in terms of the source documents. But the story has changed vis-a-vis M/H. Mordecai and a new character, Esther, become the focus of the narrative instead of Haman, and

Mordecai is no longer impassive, but emotionally engaged[48] and susceptible to the anxieties of the Jewish diaspora worldview. More important, he now has an emotional counterpart in Esther, who actually lives out many of the tensions and decisions of Mordecai's making. As Lebram and Berg have noted, Mordecai's certainty of purpose and identity is contrasted with Esther's "identity crisis," from which she emerges, however, as the active partner who gives orders to Mordecai.[49] According to my source analysis, this is further developed in Esth R, specifically in chapter four, but it is already clear in S that Esther has been introduced into the story as an emotional ally or foil for the *audience's* emotional responses to the position of being in "ethnic jeopardy." The audience—male and female—identifies with her as the one in the throes of a crisis of moral decision, just as it does with several other important women characters of the same period: Susanna, Judith, Asenath, and the martyred mother of 2 Maccabees 7.[50]

The barbed moral lines of the reversal of M/H has become a drama in Esth S, with a shift from the focus on the courtier as courtier, with loyalty as the key, to courtier as dramatic character, with a harem intrigue as the focus. The court setting and the courtier ideal has been shifted subtly to the palace as the setting of a royal family intrigue. The transformation of M/H into Esth S shifts the genre from court legend proper to a new genre, even though all the recoverable elements of the original court legend are still present. The family and ethnic relations are more the center of attention than is the case in M/H with its focus on the courtier *qua* courtier. In the M/H source, the bad advice which surfaced from Haman's family council was contrasted with the king's court as the arena of truth in chapter 6, where records and actions of dispassionate courtiers, bring truth and justice to light. In Esth S, however, the simple lines of a contrast between the Haman family council and the king's court are extended into multiple episodes: the arena of truth is not found only among court counselors in chapter six, but also in Esther's audiences with the king. The relationships of Ahasuerus to Esther and Esther to Mordecai are now paramount to the story.

But if Esth S is no longer a court legend, what is it? The two best analogies which will help define the genre of this stage are the harem intrigues in, for instance, Ctesias's *Persika*, and the much longer (and later) Greek romances. The former were mentioned above, but the latter require some

---

[48] Ibid., 149–50.

[49] Lebram, "Purimfest," 216; and Berg, *Esther*, 121, n. 60.

[50] Nickelsburg ("Genre," 157) isolates "decision" as a common plot element of stories of fall and vindication. Ruth does not apply, not only because the dating is uncertain, but also because she is not a buffeted romantic heroine, but a three-dimensional character rendered realistically in a mundane, everyday context.

explanation. It is not that Esth S or Esth R or even Esther LXX is a full-blown romance, but that many of the motifs of romance are already found budding in such works as Susanna, Tobit, *Joseph and Asenath*, Judith, and short fragments in Josephus and Artapanus. As a genre designation, I would suggest "proto-romance," defined as a popular, written version—which in many cases may derive from an oral source—of an adventure of peril and escape of attractive Jewish protagonists. The setting for these adventure stories is no longer limited to the court, but is usually shifted to a less elevated, even domestic, sphere of activity. Women characters are added in great numbers, and are invested with the main weight of the emotional tribulations, perils, and decisions of the story. The emotional sympathies of the audience are with the woman, even if it is the male protagonist who performs most of the main actions. The main distinction between these proto-romances and romances proper is the number of episodes. Romances are extended proto-romances, expanded for a larger and more literate bourgeois audience, which, in their Greek and Latin forms, developed certain theological motifs, such as the invocation of Tyche/Fortuna.[51]

Several themes are added to the story in Esth S, and are further extended in Esth R, which exemplify this. As noted above, the protagonist of legend—impassive, invulnerable, destined to be vindicated—gives way to protagonists who feel that they are hanging by a thread. The buffeting which they experience is both physical and psychological, and is not necessarily the piling up of threats and perils, but is the sum total of the vicissitudes which appear to be impersonal, controlling forces. For example, Esth 2:8 (from Esth S) states that when the king's decree went out for the gathering of all the young women, Esther was also taken to the palace. Next, she is favored by Hegai, and then by the king, and is crowned queen. These remarkable turns of fortune come about with no active role of Esther whatsoever. In the same way Haman's planned destruction of the Jews is a bizarre overreaction to his hatred for an individual. The fortunes and misfortunes depicted are outside of anyone's control or even involvement, or so it would appear.[52] In reveren-

[51] The famous asseveration of Ben Edwin Perry (*The Ancient Romances* [Berkeley/Los Angeles: University of California, 1967] 12–16) that romances did not evolve but were invented at one point in time by a clever artisan, may be true in a limited sense, speaking of those Greek romances which are modelled on the *Odyssey*. However, the broader phenomenon of the composition of romantic adventures for a literate bourgeois audience must be seen as an older and more evolutionary process—and not just Greek.

[52] Berg (*Esther*, 110) and Clines (*Esther*, 145) correctly note the distinction between Esther's passive period early in the narrative and her active period from chap. 4 on, which is an interesting nuancing and moralizing commentary on the fact that things *appear* to be outside of human control or involvement. In this respect it differs from romance.

tial legends, the protagonist may have personal opposition, as Mordecai does in Haman in M/H, but not impersonal buffeting.

It is not just the actions which are more like a romantic adventure, it is also the psychological suspension of the characters. The buffeting—both psychological and physical—of the protagonists evokes a closer, more emotional response from the audience than is present in other narratives. The identification of the audience with weak, vulnerable, buffeted characters is closer and more direct, and is not mediated to the audience by artistic reflection and abstraction. One example will demonstrate what I mean. When the greater artist of the Succession Narrative wanted to demonstrate David's grief over the death of his son (2 Sam 12:15–23), it was not presented directly, but by an indirect and paradoxical means, not to dampen the effect on the audience, but to mediate it through an "objective correlative." David grieves and fasts while the son is sick, but when he dies, David rises up, bathes and eats. The intensity of the grief which the audience expects is ironically removed, leaving the audience to reflect on the depth of David's emotions, in fact, literally to look around for David's emotions, without seeing them directly. No such distance or reflection is present in romances or proto-romances. People emote directly, and not even their thoughts are kept from us. In M/H we found that there was some artistic distance from Mordecai, but Haman is in part seen as foolish *because* his emotions are presented directly. In the context of the restraint and repression of emotions which courtly wisdom promulgates, it is Haman's lack of restraint and reflection which is examined and condemned.

The view of the king also undergoes some modification in Esth S. The king in M/H is not a very detailed character, precisely because his role and nature are assumed—he is the rightful head of a world-wide authority structure, in whose court all truth ultimately comes to light and is worked out in justice. There is no theological dimension to insure this process. In Esth S, however, the king is not primarily the head of the court, but the head of the palace. Corresponding to all these stylistic changes is a change in one aspect of the *content* of the Esth S expansion as well. It is the broadening of the magnitude of the planned execution from one Jew in M/H to all the Jews of Persia in Esth S. The audiences of M/H and Esth S may have been essentially the same—Jews of Persia. But they are addressed more directly, even threatened directly, in Esth S, with less artistic distance.

In Esth R, whether it is one or more layers of additions, some of the same trends noted above in Esth S are carried forward or modified. Overall, the change in tone is from a fairly realistic Esth S—imaginative to be sure, and possessed of a breezy narration—to a humorous, even broadside farce of an empire-wide intrigue and its exposure and reversal. The "arena of truth" in Esth R, that is, the context in which the truth is ultimately recognized, is no longer the king's court, but Esther's settee, when Haman falls upon it. The sense of progressive revelations that Esth S adds to M/H has been transformed in Esth R to low comedy, with a drunken king holding sway over people's lives. But even this lout of a king can realize that evil is afoot: "What, is Haman assaulting my queen before me in my own house?" (7:8) Only at this point does the king act to hang Haman. To attach a genre to what Esth R has created, that is, the MT version of Esther, is difficult, since the main transformations when compared with Esth S revolve around Purim, farce, and revenge—or at least revenge in some comic dimension. The best genre designation, then, for the ancient MT Scroll of Esther may be the same designation it has today: the reading for a Purim party.

The relationship of M/H to the several redactional layers proposed here has at least one parallel in the ancient world, and this one is close at hand. The version of *Ahikar* found at Elephantine is very spare and typical of the same legendary stage as M/H. The various later versions, however, take on many of the same qualities as Esth S and R, adding episodes of the threats and perils to Ahikar's wife and household servants, as well as a florid emotional directness that is found in the later stages of Esther.[53] As was noted in chapter three concerning the Daniel traditions, court legends are sometimes created out of other genres, and are sometimes altered to be applied in new ways. In the case of Esther, it is only the first recoverable layer, M/H, which is, strictly speaking, a court legend.

---

[53] When the LXX additions to Esther are included in this schema (a task which lies outside of this thesis), then a second editing toward romance must be posited, but the overall picture of the stages remains essentially the same.

Conclusion

The goal of this thesis has been to understand Daniel 1–6 and Esther in the context of their genre. The court legend, to which they are both related, is a popular genre, broadly attested, but not easily defined. Still, the attempt to delineate the nature of the genre and its historical development and demise can be carried out to the extent that it illuminates these Jewish writings, and others as well. Although genre classifications may lie in the mind of the beholder, at every step I have tried to provide as much clarification and empirical evidence as possible, so that the argument will not turn on unspoken presuppositions, but spoken ones. We might wish to believe that literary documents fall of themselves into neat categories, there for us to intuit, but the close study of the individual differences and similarities leads instead to a view of literary works as falling into overlapping sets, depending upon what generic criteria are imposed. The wisdom court legend as a term is one that can easily be abused as a classification, and it is hoped that the method that is employed here is at least clear.

It is appropriate at this point to summarize some of the findings of this thesis, and especially to flesh out the interrelationships among the various court legends studied. The definition of the genre was aided by a comparison with folklore theories about legends cross-culturally. This served most of all to impose precision on the study about what the presuppositions and functions of the narratives might be, suggesting also layers of interpretation that would have otherwise gone unnoticed. The social and historical presuppositions of the court setting were also explored, and the wisdom orientation of the legends was affirmed, albeit not in the rigid way that it has in the past. In regard to wisdom it was noted that in general the court legend, whether

Jewish or non-Jewish, held up a representative of the ethnic or social group as wise, but did not encapsulate the received wisdom tradition in the stories or enact wisdom principles such as courtly behavior, prudence or foresight. Rather, these stories affirm that the person "marked" by wisdom will receive a just end. In this sense, of course, a larger wisdom principle *is* being enacted, which might be compared with Psalm 1.

At some points another connection with wisdom traditions comes to light. It was suggested that the original application of Susanna, reflected in the OG text, was as a sermonic affirmation of Jewish instruction in wisdom. The originally unnamed youth is inspired by God to observe the law of Moses correctly and justly. The context for the observance is a dramatic one—the trial of a beautiful, slandered young woman—but once again, this example is not meant to be the "content" of Jewish law, only a narrative evocation of it.[1] The connection of this legend with the Daniel corpus reflects only one part of the activity of a "Danielic school," which must be seen both in the grouping and adaptation of legends and in the transmission of visionary materials.

We might also ask whether the picture of the genre which emerges outside of Judaism can tell us anything about what the social context of the Jewish stories might have been. First of all, a Persian background for the strong interest in court legends was postulated, based on the coincidence of the attestations with Persian-controlled lands and the traditions about Zoroaster at the court of Vishtaspa. However, although there are some court legends in Persian medieval sources, the lack of preserved writings of any kind from early Persian history leaves this judgment somewhat hypothetical. The non-Jewish legends that do remain can be grouped in several categories: those Ionian and Lydian legends which were used by Herodotus, the two legends which are attested in Egypt from about the fifth century BCE (regardless of their origin), *Onkhsheshonq* and *Ahikar*, and the legends associated with Aesop.

The court legends in Herodotus which were analyzed in Chapter 2 focus on a member of a ruled ethnic group in the court of one of the great eastern monarchs. The king in these legends is not usually viewed negatively, although Cambyses is so characterized in Herodotus. The common thread among them, however, is that a representative of the ruled ethnic group proves himself wise *and valuable* to the eastern rulers—Greeks before Croesus and the fallen Croesus before the Persian kings. It was therefore hypothesized that these narratives arose as popular legends among those

---

[1] D. M. Kay (*APOT*, 1. 638) charmingly but incorrectly says that the point of Susanna is the "value and necessity of cross-examination of witnesses."

groups, and that Herodotus heard them in his travels and researches. These are not likely peasant stories; Herodotus moved most likely in court and entrepreneurial circles. The social class of the legends is likely the cosmopolitan trading and administrative classes of Asia Minor.

Other non-Jewish court legends included *Onkhsheshonq* and *Ahikar*. By placing them in the same category, certain similarities come to light which might have gone unnoticed. To begin with, they are both wisdom court legends which also contain a long sayings section. They are also both attested in Egypt at about the same time, around the fifth-fourth centuries BCE, but because Ahikar was obviously an import, this might be taken to be a mere coincidence. However, this legend was obviously brought to the Jewish military colony of Elephantine because it was considered edifying reading about an admirable—though non-Jewish—hero. The ethnic issue noted above is not in evidence here, but the social class of the readers in this case can be fairly specifically stated, since the colony must have consisted of the military personnel plus the mercantile and administrative class that one would expect in a well-established military colony. It is hard to imagine a highly educated group of courtiers administering the affairs here, although this tells us very little about who might have *composed* the legend.

In the case of *Onkhsheshonq*, a similar picture of the readership, and perhaps the authorship as well, might be inferred from the perspective of the legend. The character of Onkhsheshonq is a member of a rural class of farmers and merchants who visits his friend, a doctor at the Pharaoh's court. He is a sort of country bumpkin in the big city, who becomes inadvertently involved in a conspiracy against the Pharaoh. One is struck by the way in which he *inevitably* runs into trouble and fails, not as if a curse were on his head, but as if this kind could fare no better. The tone is not quite satirical enough to be considered an aristocratic view of the struggling classes, but instead there is a sort of social realism here, and the "wisdom" of the story seems to be in warning the reader not to follow in poor Onkhsheshonq's path.[2] This general appraisal finds some support in the analysis of the sayings section of Onkhsheshonq made by McKane.[3] Comparing this to the other Egyptian "instructions," he finds *Onkhsheshonq* to be much less rigorously developed as a document for the education of an elite class of administrators, but instead it reflects a considerably lower social landscape, not

---

[2] One may contrast in this regard the much older *Story of Sinuhe*, in which a magisterial hero of the inner court is forced into exile and life in the outer rural districts of Egypt—the mirror image of Onkhsheshonq. His triumphant return and defence of the rightful king exhibit a much more romantic view of human potential.

[3] *Proverbs*, 117–21.

incommensurate with a more rural mercantile and farmer class, and a fatalistic and cynical view of what rewards life may have to offer. One of his indicators of a less pretentious educational ideal is the presence of concrete metaphors or images stated in the indicative mood, a proverbial form lacking in most Egyptian "Instructions." Interestingly, he also notes that the sayings section of the Elephantine version of Ahikar is characterized by more indicative proverbs with concrete imagery than do the Egyptian Instructions, indicating again that the social world of the writings is not the highest levels of court education.

The *Life of Aesop* contains a variant of the Ahikar legend as found at Elephantine, and so may very well reflect a similar social world. It has been argued by Perry that it contains an Ionian, anti-Athenian perspective, and whether the *Ahikar*-parallel section does, the *Life* as a whole shows an analogous interest to the ethnically identified court legends of Herodotus. Except for the *Ahikar*-parallel, however, there is not much action set in the court. The conflict is between the lowly born Aesop and his pretentious, pseudo-philosopher master, who seems to represent the entire weight of Athenian control over Asia Minor.

Along with the non-Jewish court legends, in Chapter 2 I also compared the pre-exilic Hebrew legends that could be considered similar. All of them were isolated in the deuteronomistic history, which is often associated with prophet traditions. Whether all the activity of transmitting such stories should be restricted to the central court, as Heaton[4] would have it, or some of the credit should be ascribed to the prophetic guilds, as Cross[5] holds, was not decided. The individual oral legends concerning prophets could certainly have been passed on in prophet guilds, but we do not know whether these guilds committed the oral legends to writing. The composing and redacting of Dtr should rather be ascribed to the scribes at the central court. The level of literary attainment of the court schools in Israel was probably not nearly so high as in the much greater empires of Egypt and Mesopotamia, but the scribes there were nevertheless the most likely locus for such activity.

When we turn to Jewish court legends of the Persian period which constitute our main objects of study—Esther and Daniel 1–6—we find that a source-critical analysis has in both writings necessitated a hypothesis of many writings which, though related to the court, do not fall into the same precise genre classification. In Daniel 1–6 and the LXX additions to Daniel we must distinguish between oral legends, such as the original version of Daniel 3, some of the sources of Daniel 4 and 5, and possibly Susanna and

---

[4] *Solomon's New Men*, 129–61.
[5] *Canaanite*, 223–24.

Bel and the Dragon, and the literary level of the legends as they were collected, first in Daniel 4–6, then, most likely, 1–6 (or possibly 2–7), and ultimately 1–12 and later with the additions. Here we must especially note the scribal interests of the redactors and the affirmation of mantic wisdom. The development of Daniel shows that at some points accounts which were not actually court legends were altered in the direction of this genre, and additions were also made to these, as in Daniel 5, which probably betray the influence of palace intrigues as found in Ctesias, Herodotus, and Xenophon.

Four strata were posited for MT Esther: a court conflict, probably orally composed, concerning Mordecai and Haman, a literary redaction which elaborated many of the dramatic elements and complicated the narrative by adding a subplot concerning the young woman Esther and a threat against all Jews of Persia (Esth S), and two further elaborations of this story which introduce, among other things, the revenge motif and the information concerning the celebration of Purim (Gk A and Esth R). The LXX version of Esther (not analyzed in this thesis) does not extend these comic motifs, but paradoxically attempts to romanticize and rehistoricize the broadside humor of the Esth R level by intimating Mordecai's prophetic dream before the incidents narrated, and by adding the bedroom scenes of Esther and her consideration of her marriage to Ahasuerus. All of these layers beyond the Mordecai/Haman story really lie outside of the definition of court legend proper, and are well on the way to becoming popular romance, or at least "proto-romance." But the Mordecai/Haman story gives us a short, neat court conflict, told effectively, from the villain's point of view.

It is impossible to place all of the post-exilic Jewish court legends, or even the court conflicts, into a single mold, yet within the broader international genre outlined here, we can note some specific nuances of the Jewish "high period" of court legends.

First of all, it is a popular genre, but it probably does not extend to the lower classes. It reflects the orientation of the administrative and entrepreneurial class. The scribal ideals inherent in the stories might restrict this circle somewhat to the extended court circles, for example, to the local administrative courts that might correspond to the training offered by Ben Sira's school. In Daniel 1–6, however, a distinction must be maintained between the various source layers and the redaction, the latter reflecting a more intensely pious outlook.

Second, it promulgates the hero of the ruled ethnic group, and enhances that group's self-esteem in two ways: the ability of the courtier demonstrates the value of that group's wisdom vis-à-vis others'. For the non-Jewish legends above, the wisdom of the protagonist is presented in universal terms, and although different ethnic groups were represented, there was no contest between two different versions of wisdom. In the Jewish examples, however, a shift sometimes occurs toward an affirmation of the superiority of Jewish revealed wisdom. It is less the courtier, or even the ethnic group represented, and more the God that makes the difference. In Daniel 1–6, for example, it is direct revelation from God which outdoes the Chaldaean pretensions of mantic wisdom. Second, the Jewish legends emphasize more strongly the competing courtiers, rather than just the king in his court, and this gives expression to the, at times, uneasy relations and ethnic tensions between, for example, Jews and native Babylonians (that is, "Chaldaeans") in Daniel 1–6. Thus the king can sometimes be good, sometimes arrogant, sometimes neutral—it does not matter, since it is the other courtiers who figure prominently and who are always "other" to the Jews.

The apparent exceptions to this rule about the ethnic-affirmation function of Jewish court legends are not really that different. In the early period the prophetic legends that take place in the king's court, specifically the three "disguised parables" of Nathan's parable of the lamb (2 Samuel 12), the wise woman of Tekoa (2 Samuel 14), and the anonymous prophet before Ahab (1 Kings 20), all likely reflect the traditions of the prophetic guilds. The stories are thus used to promulgate the views of this group within Israel, and there is some consciousness of being a group apart. The healing of Naaman by Elisha (2 Kings 5), also from the prophetic guilds, is similar to the court legends and may reflect, if not a "ruled ethnic perspective," then a "threatened ethnic perspective" of northern Israel vis-a-vis Syria.

Susanna, which reflects the adaptation of the genre to the affirmation of Jewish ideals in a typical diaspora community, also appears to be an exception. The only opposition found here is that between young and old, that is, Daniel and Susanna on one hand and the two wicked elders on the other. But this functions in precisely the same way, since the sermonic application affirms the value of training in wisdom for young people. Exactly parallel to the other court legends, the point is that it is the *youth*, unnamed in the original, who is so wise as to prevent the unjust execution of Susanna.

The court legend, whether Jewish or non-Jewish, as defined here has within it many morphological structures, and the key to genre definition was held to be the court as the setting in which certain issues concerning wisdom could be played out. The value of one's ethnic group could be affirmed, for instance, in the contest, or threatened and vindicated in the conflict, (not to speak of the other related subgenres of disguised parable, royal anecdote, and so on) but these two foci—court and wisdom—remained a dependable guide to the grouping of narratives. A clear social and historical correlation also arose from the discussion, as it became clear that the genre was vastly more popular and developed as a genre in the Persian-ruled lands of the ancient Near East than elsewhere.

One difficulty in studying the court legend is being rigorous in differentiating court legends proper from other writings which may depend on them. A picture of the development of *Ahikar*, Daniel 1 – 6 and the LXX additions, and Esther emerged in this thesis which recognized that new literary demands often changed the original materials, either in the direction of court legends (Daniel 4 – 6), or away from court legends and toward "proto-romances" (later versions of *Ahikar* and Esther). A workable definition of the genre "court legend" was arrived at here, which would allow some discussion of differentiation, at the same time that it established the parameters of the genre. There was also some discussion of whether the exemples of the genre studied were orally composed or written, but this problem was not solved in every case. A closer consideration of this problem, especially in respect to the various layers of the documents, might result in a settlement of this issue.

A search for the contours and use of a genre has led us into the Greek traditions from Asia Minor (Herodotus and *Aesop*), the non-Jewish narratives from the surrounding cultures (*Onkhsheshonq*, *Ahikar*, and Zoroaster legends), older Jewish short legends set in the court (deuteronomistic prophet legends and Solomon legends), and into the parallel developments of other folk traditions. These popular Jewish narratives will perhaps, as a result, be seen in the context of an international folk genre which makes its way into such developed literary adaptations as the Hebrew Scriptures, Herodotus, and the Persian *Shah Nameh*.

Defining possible permutations of the court legend then becomes a way of defining more precisely the genre itself. Beginning with the court conflict, we may note the variations from Müller's broader *Lehrerzählung* category. If we abbreviate Müller's structural diagram, we can compare it to the structure of the court conflicts which were studied here:[6]

Müller's Didactic Narrative	*Court Conflict*
Introduction:	Introduction:
1a) Protagonist's virtue	1a) Protagonist's wisdom
1b) Symbolic deed of virtue	
	1b') Relation to king and courtiers
1c) Antagonists, intermediaries	1c) Antagonists = courtiers
Body:	Body:
2a) Conflict from virtue	2a) Conflict from virtue
2b) Testing, proving of virtue	2b) Testing, proving of virtue

[6] Müller, "Die weistheitliche Lehrerzählung."

Conclusion:	Conclusion:
3a) Punishment of antagonists	3a) Punishment of antagonists
3b) Rewarding of protagonist	3b) Rewarding of protagonist
3c) Miraculous demonstrations	
	3c') New status in court

Beginning with Müller's genre category, it would be possible to include the court legend as an important and fairly consistent variation within it. However, if we arrange our comparison around the common motifs and narrative events of the court legend, it reveals a more pronounced difference. First, in the court legend the court is the moral arena in which the most important issues in the world are decided. Second, the king plays a crucial role as the authority figure who rules over the court, whether he carries out his function brilliantly or not. Third, it is generally the other courtiers who present a threat to the Jews, and carry it out by manipulating the king and his authority by decree.[7]

If we investigate the structure of some of the court legends without reference to Müller's didactic narrative structure, different nuances emerge:

Introduction:

1a) king at head of court of equals
1b) protagonist *or* antagonist ascends within court
    M/H: Haman promoted
    Dan 3: three youths just promoted (end Dan 2; but see 3:12)
    Dan 6: Daniel promoted over all satraps
    Ahi: Ahikar favorite courtier
    Sus: two elders appointed judges

Conflict:

2a) other courtiers conspire or accuse
    M/H: Haman plots in response to Mordecai's refusal to bow
    Dan 3: Chaldaeans/mighty men accuse
    Dan 6: satraps conspire
    Ahi: Nadan plots
    Sus: elders accuse in response to Susanna's spurning them
2b) execution set
    M/H: Haman builds gallows

---

[7] Daniel 3 is an apparent exception, in that it is the king's idea to erect a gold statue and to demand worship of it. However, no sooner is this done than "certain Chaldaeans" (or perhaps "mighty men of the army") come forth to accuse the Jews, which places them among the *dramatis personae.* Only in Croesus before Cambyses do we really see a court legend in which it is the *king* who opposes the protagonist.

Dan 3: fire prepared
Dan 6: Daniel prepared for lions' den
Ahi: Ahikar handed over to executioner
Sus: Susanna condemned to death according to law

Resolution:

3a) execution attempted
  M/H: Haman approaches king
  Dan 3: three thrown in fire
  Dan 6: Daniel thrown in lions' den
  Ahi: Ahikar taken away by executioner
  Sus: Susanna led off to execution
3b) protagonist vindicated
  M/H: chronicles vindicate Mordecai as worthy courtier
  Dan 3: three unharmed by fire
  Dan 6: Daniel unharmed by lions
  Ahi: Ahikar's execution regretted by king
  Sus: Susanna vindicated by Daniel's cross-examination
3c) villain punished by own device
  M/H: Haman hung on own gallows
  Dan 3: mighty men slain by fire
  Dan 6: other courtiers thrown to lions and eaten
  (Ahi: Ahikar "kills" Nadan with parables—not villain's own device)
  Sus: elders executed acording to law
3d) protagonist promoted or confirmed
  M/H: Mordecai second to king, exalted and acclaimed by all
  Dan 3: three promoted in Babylon
  Dan 6: Daniel highest courtier to Darius and Cyrus
  Ahi: Ahikar answers Egyptian demands, is exalted
  Sus: Susanna praised, Daniel exalted by people

The dramatic element overlooked by Müller's structural analysis is the dynamic relationship among the courtiers. They begin as equals, the stability of the court is threatened by a promotion, the other courtiers conspire against the protagonist, he or she is vindicated, the other courtiers are punished, and the protagonist is promoted. The initial promotion advances either the protagonist or the antagonist, but either way, the tensions inherent in the court are aggravated, and the story becomes a model in miniature of a Shakespearean tragedy: order with the possibility of chaos/chaos/true stability. At the end we see the protagonists firmly established in their new positions, even if the editors of Daniel 1–6 have blurred this resolution of the individual narratives by making the process cyclical.

Within this general pattern of the court conflict, several specific nuances can be observed. Daniel 3 and 6 reflect many more similarities than do the others, both following the pattern of the protagonist promoted at the beginning:[8]

Daniel 3	Daniel 6
Introduction:	Introduction:
	1a) king establishes satraps
1b) three promoted (Dan 2)	1b) Daniel promoted
Conflict:	Conflict:
	2a) conspiracy of satraps (in OG?)
2b) king's edict:	2b) courtiers' edict:
worship image	no prayer w/out Darius
2c) (violation presumed)	2c) violation
2d) Chaldaeans accuse	2d) satraps accuse
Resolution:	Resolution:
3a) attempted execution	3a) attempted execution
3c) villains killed by own device	
3b-1) king sees three alive	3b-1) king hears Daniel alive
3b-2) king calls three forth	3b-2) king calls Daniel forth
3b-3) three not singed	3b-3) Daniel not hurt
	3c) villains killed by own device
3d) king's acclamation	3d) king's new decree
and new decree	
3e) three promoted	3e) Daniel continues high office

The main difference between these narrative patterns and the general conflict pattern above is the presence of an edict here, which the protagonists consciously choose to violate. Once that is done, then the accusing of the antagonists follows in a similar way.

The M/H source of Esther and Susanna have the antagonist, not the protagonist, promoted at the beginning, and although Susanna has been altered somewhat for a local court setting, it reflects other nuances which are similar to M/H:

---

[8] *Ahikar* depicts the protagonist as the highest courtier at the beginning, but follows a family conflict and not a true court conflict. Also different here is that Nadan is not executed with his own device. The normal pattern is emphasized by Müller, "Märchen, Legende und Enderwartung: zum Verständnis des Buches Daniel," *VT* 26 (1976) 345–46; and Talmon, "Esther," 446.

M/H	*Susanna*
Introduction:	Introduction:
1a) king Ahasuerus's rule	1a) Jews gather at Joakim's house
1b) Mordecai's virtue:	1b) Susanna's virtue:
uncovers plot	righteous
1c) Haman promoted	1c) elders appointed
Conflict:	Conflict:
2a) Mordecai refuses to bow	2a) Susanna spurns advances
2b) Haman prepares Mordecai's	2b) elders prepare Susanna's
execution on gallows	execution according to law
Resolution:	Resolution:
3a) (high) court test:	3a) (low) court test:
Mordecai vindicated	Daniel vindicates Susanna
through records	through cross-examination
3c) Mordecai elevated	
3b) Haman executed	3b) elders executed
on own gallows	according to law
	3c) Susanna praised
3d) "Mordecai great among people"	3d) "Daniel great among people"

Several similarities show up through such a comparison, as well as several differences from Dan 3, 6, and Bel. First, M/H and Susanna begin, like the conflicts above, with the protagonists and antagonists at about the same level of authority, but these stories portray the ascendancy of the antagonists over the protagonists. The ascendancy of the antagonists is then contrasted with the protagonists' fall at the antagonists' hands. From the point of conflict on, then, the antagonists are propelled upward and the protagonists downward, until the court test reverses this quickly.

These summary diagrams indicate that it is reasonable to define a central group of court conflicts as a separate subgenre of the court legend, and that certain themes are found expressed there. Throughout this volume, I have maintained that there is no one structural pattern of the wisdom court legend, but that the broader genre designation, "wisdom court legend," as well as the narrower subgenre categorizations, are still helpful. I have concluded here with a closer analysis of the court conflict, but many of the same themes are found in the contests and other related subgenres as well, although usually in a less obvious way. The significance of the court legends for the Jewish audience can perhaps be seen on several levels. First, court legends offer a response to ethnic competition and a rather benign response to inequities and restrictions on social mobility. Second, they promulgate a wisdom teaching to the effect that the person marked by wisdom receives the just reward, even in pagan society. Third, they affirm a theology of weakness, and also a "psychology" of weakness, that is, they provide a wish fulfilment of a scribal ideal of wisdom and righteousness.

One might assume that wisdom and wise heroes and heroines are the focus of stories in every age and in every place, but wisdom as moral uprightness, as opposed to cleverness, is not especially common in imaginative literature. From a literary perspective, sin is usually more interesting than righteousness, and foolishness is usually more entertaining than wisdom. One has only to compare Hamlet's Polonius to Lear's Fool to see to what sort of character a great mind is naturally attracted. Thus, a concentration of stories about wisdom in one time and place presents a remarkable historical datum, to which this study pays tribute.